Writing a Novel and Getting Published

FOR DUMMIES®

A Wiley Brand

2nd Edition

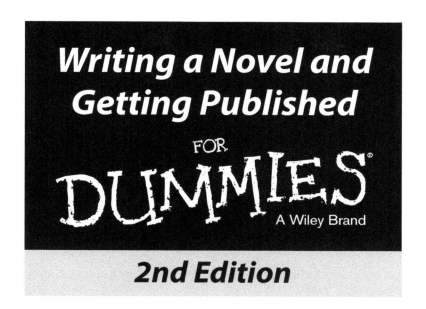

Writing a Novel and Getting Published

FOR DUMMIES®
A Wiley Brand

2nd Edition

by George Green and Lizzy Kremer

Writing a Novel and Getting Published For Dummies,® 2nd Edition

Published by: **John Wiley & Sons, Ltd.,** The Atrium, Southern Gate, Chichester, www.wiley.com

This edition first published 2014. First edition published 2007.

© 2014 George Green and Lizzy Kremer.

Registered office

John Wiley & Sons Ltd, The Atrium, Southern Gate, Chichester, West Sussex, PO19 8SQ, United Kingdom

For details of our global editorial offices, for customer services and for information about how to apply for permission to reuse the copyright material in this book please see our website at www.wiley.com.

The right of the author to be identified as the author of this work has been asserted in accordance with the Copyright, Designs and Patents Act 1988.

All rights reserved. No part of this publication may be reproduced, stored in a retrieval system, or transmitted, in any form or by any means, electronic, mechanical, photocopying, recording or otherwise, except as permitted by the UK Copyright, Designs and Patents Act 1988, without the prior permission of the publisher.

Wiley publishes in a variety of print and electronic formats and by print-on-demand. Some material included with standard print versions of this book may not be included in e-books or in print-on-demand. If this book refers to media such as a CD or DVD that is not included in the version you purchased, you may download this material at http://booksupport.wiley.com. For more information about Wiley products, visit www.wiley.com.

Designations used by companies to distinguish their products are often claimed as trademarks. All brand names and product names used in this book are trade names, service marks, trademarks or registered trademarks of their respective owners. The publisher is not associated with any product or vendor mentioned in this book.

LIMIT OF LIABILITY/DISCLAIMER OF WARRANTY: WHILE THE PUBLISHER AND AUTHOR HAVE USED THEIR BEST EFFORTS IN PREPARING THIS BOOK, THEY MAKE NO REPRESENTATIONS OR WARRANTIES WITH THE RESPECT TO THE ACCURACY OR COMPLETENESS OF THE CONTENTS OF THIS BOOK AND SPECIFICALLY DISCLAIM ANY IMPLIED WARRANTIES OF MERCHANTABILITY OR FITNESS FOR A PARTICULAR PURPOSE. IT IS SOLD ON THE UNDERSTANDING THAT THE PUBLISHER IS NOT ENGAGED IN RENDERING PROFESSIONAL SERVICES AND NEITHER THE PUBLISHER NOR THE AUTHOR SHALL BE LIABLE FOR DAMAGES ARISING HEREFROM. IF PROFESSIONAL ADVICE OR OTHER EXPERT ASSISTANCE IS REQUIRED, THE SERVICES OF A COMPETENT PROFESSIONAL SHOULD BE SOUGHT.

For general information on our other products and services, please contact our Customer Care Department within the U.S. at 877-762-2974, outside the U.S. at (001) 317-572-3993, or fax 317-572-4002. For technical support, please visit www.wiley.com/techsupport.

For technical support, please visit www.wiley.com/techsupport.

A catalogue record for this book is available from the British Library.

ISBN 978-1-118-91040-5 (pbk), ISBN 978-1-118-91041-2 (ebk), ISBN 978-1-118-91044-3 (ebk)

Printed and bound by CPI Group (UK) Ltd, Croydon, CR0 4YY

C9781118910405_060224

Contents at a Glance

Table of Contents

Introduction

 ·

*P*eople who tell you that writing a novel is easy don't know what they're talking about. From experience, we can tell you that writing a novel is hard work. However, the thousands of books published every year, and the hundreds of thousands still in print, prove that hard work can pay off.

The other good news is that this book provides inspiration and support for your efforts. You're creating something new, but you don't have to do it from scratch; every problem you face has been encountered and solved already by other authors. If you want to know how to do something, this book offers advice and examples on everything from refining your writing to finding a publisher. Welcome and good luck!

About This Book

This book gathers together everything that you need to know about writing and publishing a novel. It saves you time and effort by distilling our insights from 40 years of novel-writing, teaching creative writing, and working in publishing into one place. If you were to plough through all the books that we've read, and have all the experiences and training that we've had, you wouldn't need most of this book but you would need to expand your home to accommodate your library and be 40 years older. This book prevents you having to re-invent the wheel. Often writers write something and think, 'Hmm, that's good, I wonder if anyone's thought of doing something like that before?' This book gives you the answers to such questions.

This book also helps you to avoid repeating other people's mistakes. We've made mistakes ourselves and gathered mistakes from other people so that you don't have to mess up. This saves you time, stress, and embarrassment.

So, would you rather read 20 books that each tells you a bit of what you need, or one book that has just about everything? It's really no contest.

We use a lot of different novels as examples to illustrate what we're talking about. You don't need to have read them to understand the points we're making (although, of course, we think that these are books worth reading). You'll notice that we use Jane Austen's *Pride and Prejudice* quite often as an example. If you read just one book in tandem with this one, that's the book we suggest. It's a great story, beautifully structured, and you'll find lots to talk and think about. But you don't have to read it – we've arranged this book so that you have everything you need right here.

Foolish Assumptions

All authors must make a few assumptions about their audience. The good news is that we're certain you'll fit one or more of the following groups:

- ✔ If you're a complete beginner considering the possibility that you may one day write a novel, this book gives you the grounding you need. You can start at the beginning and work your way through.

- ✔ If you have a great idea and some experience of writing but don't know how to take it forward, this book points you in the right direction. You can select the areas in which you feel you need guidance and move on from there.

- ✔ If you've written some of, or even completed, a novel and it doesn't seem to be working, this book can help you ask the right questions about what you've written and find the right answers. You can use the book as a problem-solver.

- ✔ If you've finished your novel and are wondering what to do next, this book has the information and tips you need. You can use the book both as a checklist and a guide to the world of publishing.

Writing a Novel and Getting Published For Dummies, 2nd Edition, can help you succeed, however far into writing your novel you are.

Icons Used in This Book

The little drawings in the margins, called *icons*, highlight information that's especially interesting, important, or both. Here are the icons we use in this book.

Especially good advice is highlighted with this on-the-target icon.

This icon indicates information to keep in mind while you're reading a single chapter or for the rest of your writing life.

Ideas to shy away from and concepts that can get you in trouble merit this alert.

This icon marks illustrations of points we explain in the text. Sometimes an example is more useful than an explanation, but we never provide just an example – we have more to say than that!

The unexpected bit of advice and the 'try this, it's odd but may work for you' technique both get this icon.

Beyond the Book

As you explore this book, be sure to check out the free bonus content available at www.dummies.com/extras/writinganovelgettingpublisheduk. You can find articles about using visual aids to get you past that tricky 'getting started' stage, how to write a lot in a short space of time, how to make sure that your story has something in it for everyone, and why finishing your novel is like cleaning your house. We also give you a free bonus Part of Tens chapter, 'Ten Novels You Need to Read and Why'.

You can find the book's e-cheat sheet at www.dummies.com/cheatsheet/writinganovelgettingpublisheduk. We include a couple of great checklists, including one to review before you submit your novel to an agent or publisher and one that serves as a reference while constructing your novel.

Where to Go from Here

You have several options at this point:

- ✔ You can flick through the chapters and read something that interests you or that covers an aspect of something that you're working on. That's fine.

- ✔ You can start at the beginning and go through the book, choosing the things that are most useful to you. That's fine, too.

- ✔ You can start at the beginning and read the whole thing. That's what we suggest. Of course, you're going to pay greater attention to some bits than others, that's only to be expected. And when you've worked through it, you can use it as a reference book, checking on things that you need to refresh your mind about.

- ✔ You can use the book in any weird and wonderful way you choose, because you're just so darn creative and you never do what people expect. And that's fine, too.

Part I

Getting Started with Writing a Novel and Getting Published

In this part . . .

- ✔ Get the right work space and tools to start the job — whether that's your expensive new laptop, or a simple notebook and biro.

- ✔ Consider your readership and the length of your novel.

- ✔ Be realistic about approaching publishers with your work.

- ✔ Get to grips with grammar basics.

- ✔ Start thinking like a writer.

Chapter 1

Entering the Writer's World

*W*riting a novel isn't like assembling a flat-pack wardrobe. It'd be much easier if it were. You'd be able to lay out all your words and ideas on the floor, check the instructions, and make sure you had everything you needed. Then you'd just follow the steps, and at the end of it you'd have built a novel. Easy.

But writing a novel isn't like that. The process is different for every writer, although that isn't the same as saying that everyone's experience is completely different. Much of the process is common to many writers. But the most important part of your writing experience is unique to you.

The problem is that, unlike assembling a wardrobe, when you write a novel you don't have a blueprint. There's no set of instructions you can look at and say, 'Ah, I see what it's going to look like when it's finished, here's a box of all the things I need, and I see clearly how I'm going to put the pieces together.' There are guide books, like this one, which can help by showing you how other people have met the same challenges you face. But the bottom line is that no one else can write your novel for you.

The key concepts to keep in mind as you write your novel and think about getting it published are:

✔ Never give up – never stop writing.

✔ Never stop reading and finding out about your craft.

✔ Have faith in what you're trying to do, but always be prepared to consider the possibility that you may be on the wrong track.

✔ Trust the process.

Knowing Yourself

Knowing yourself means being honest about yourself and your situation. When you know yourself, you know what your avoidance strategies are likely to be, and so you can prepare for them.

You have to know yourself to know whether you're capable of doing the things you have to do in order to write your novel. Can you, for example, say to your friends, 'I'm not coming out with you just now; I'll meet you later, when I've finished this chapter'? Can you leave phones unanswered, all forms of social media unchecked? Can you say to the people you live with, 'I'm going to shut myself away for a couple of hours now'? Can you do that even though they're settling down to watch a film you want to see? And if they say you're boring and no fun and they're going out without you, can you laugh that off?

Can you make writing one of the good things in your life, instead of a drudge that needs to be avoided except when you really feel like it, which is, let's face it, about once a week? Most importantly, can you arrange your life so that you have time for writing every day or almost every day? Can you treat writing like lunch: you sit down and eat lunch every day, and it wouldn't occur to you not to except in the most unusual circumstances. That's how you need to see your writing. Can you, honestly, see yourself doing that? And if you can't, can you train yourself to do it? Even when you're tired, when you're having a bad day, when you just don't feel like it? Because that's what the authors of the published novels you read and enjoyed did. They didn't wait until the mood overtook them and then dash off a few golden chapters. They sat down and slogged, just like you. That's what successful writing takes.

Knowing Your Reader

Your reader doesn't owe you a living, or even a second glance. The only way you can get readers' interest is by giving them the best possible book you can. How do you do that? Read this book for a start.

Beyond that, you need to make sure that you know who your readers are. A book aimed at party-loving young women working in the media in London isn't going to be the same as one aimed at retired men living in rural Sussex. At least, probably not. (If you can write a book that appeals to both, we know some publishers who want to talk to you!) Know who your readers are, and make sure that you address them.

Who is your reader? The easy answer is, 'Someone quite a lot like me,' and that's not a bad start. If you like reading trashy science fiction, and you write trashy science fiction, your reader's someone like you who likes what you like.

However, presumably you want to attract people who like other things, too, people who are going to read your novel and then say, 'Well, I don't normally read this sort of thing, but this isn't just a trashy science fiction novel, it has a wonderful romantic story, it made all sorts of interesting points about politics, and it made me completely reconsider my attitude to the death penalty. Oh, and it had a great recipe for beetroot soup.' We exaggerate, but you take the point. A book with this sort of wide appeal is called a *crossover novel* and is the publishers' Holy Grail. Write one of these books and everyone gets rich. (A good example of one of these is *The Time Traveller's Wife* by Audrey Niffenegger (Vintage).)

So, who is the crossover reader? Presumably someone open to different experiences. Beyond that, it's hard to say. Who is a Harry Potter reader? You may reply, 'boys and girls aged 8–14 with a taste for adventure', but we all know that the appeal of these books goes way beyond that.

How do you target your reader? You don't, at least not at the writing stage. You write the book that you want to write. Then, when you submit the manuscript, your agent and/or your publisher may well say something like, 'I love it, really love it. Just a couple of suggestions. The romance is really nice, but can it be a bit more intense? And the battle is over a bit too quickly; I'd have liked it to go on a bit longer, with maybe a climactic single combat.' And so on. These people know the publishing market; they make a judgement as to where your book should be aimed and try to push you in that direction, as necessary. (Of course, you don't have to agree with them.)

Keep the picture of your general reader while writing. 'A 14-year-old boy who goes to grammar school and lives in Edinburgh' is too specific. 'Anyone who likes an exciting adventure story and who's interested in boats but isn't too bothered about romance' is the kind of picture to paint at this stage.

You aren't writing for yourself. Of course, you have to like your book, but never forget about your reader. If you ever think, 'Oh, to be honest that's not really as good as I can get it, but I'm not going to worry about making it right,' or 'I'm tired; the heck with that bit, it's a muddle, but I can't be bothered to fix it,' your reader's going to notice and won't forgive you. Your book must always be as good as you can make it. No compromises.

Remembering that Writing Is Editing

Creative writing isn't actually what novelists do. What this book encourages you to do is creative *re*-writing.

Writing a novel – putting about 90,000 words on paper – takes you about three months if you write three pages – about 1,000 words – a day. Writing a *finished* novel can take you anything from three months to thirty years. Fortunately, it doesn't take that long for most people, but it can still easily take a year or so.

That extra nine months is spent re-writing: shaping, changing, re-ordering, re-phrasing, honing, and polishing – over and over again, until your novel's as good as it possibly can be.

The process is no different to creating a sculpture: you can make the vague shape of a javelin-thrower relatively quickly – a lump about six feet tall, a long thin bit at the top, maybe standing on two smaller lumps for feet. Then you start the real work: the chipping, shaping, sanding and so on – the editing and polishing.

Writing is all about getting the details right.

Entering the Market

We aren't going to pretend that getting a publishing deal for your novel is easy. Over 180,000 books were published in 2013 in the UK alone. Of those, very few become sales successes. It's impossible to say for sure what percentage of novels that are written end up getting published, but it's fair to say that, all other things being equal, the odds of you becoming a bestselling author aren't good. Fortunately, all other things don't have to be equal.

So, what can be done to better the odds? Read this book for a start. We've gathered together a lot of advice for you on what to write, how to write it, and how to get what you write noticed by the people who count.

Part V has loads more information about getting published. In Part V, you can also find a thorough introduction to the world of self-publishing. Even if you can't interest a publisher in your novel, you can still find readers online. Nearly as many books were self-published in the UK in 2013 as were published by traditional publishers. You still need to work hard on being discovered, but we have tips for that too.

Steeling yourself

Getting your novel published calls for clear-eyed realism and absolute honesty with yourself. If you think that getting a novel published is easy, you're just plain wrong. You have to deal with the publishing market as it really is, not how you would like it to be. This reality means never being too proud to learn. It means doing research and whatever needs to be done in order to maximise your chances. Above all, getting published means long, hard work.

If this sounds like too much trouble, or if it feels like commercialism and selling out, you have a choice. As a script editor at the BBC once said to one of us when we were much younger, maybe a little pompous, and definitely very naïve, 'Suck it up or move aside.' He was right (if not particularly sensitive or polite).

Doing the maths

You only have to do the maths to realise that publishing a book is not for the faint of heart. According to Nielsen BookData, over 184,000 new books were published in Britain in 2013. *One hundred and eighty-four thousand in a year.* Nearly 40,000 are adult fiction novels, so unless you're writing for the young adult or children's market, you have 40,000 competitors every year. And don't forget every author who's ever been published and is still in print: your DH Lawrences, Graham Greenes, Jane Austens, and so on are taking up a lot of shelf space already, and only so much shelving is available.

That's your competition, and that's what publishers are thinking about when they look at your novel. They ask themselves, 'We've got Greene and Lawrence and Austen already, and the Booker winners and the rest, which have most of the shelves full up before we start. Then there are maybe 40,000 other new novels coming out this year alone. We can only publish a few more this year. Is this book good enough to elbow them aside?' That's why only the best books get through.

And that's the aim of this book: to help you make your novel as good as it can be, and to make sure that it stands the best possible chance of getting noticed and getting through against the competition.

Being polite

Always deal politely and sensibly with fellow writers, agents, publishers, readers, and anyone you come into contact with. Don't whine or complain or insult people. (The old proverb, 'Never kick people out of the way as you climb the ladder, you'll be meeting them again on your way back down' is very relevant here.) You never know who you may need help from in the future, so don't make enemies.

In particular, always be polite to secretaries, receptionists, and so on. Not only is this the right thing to do – these people often do a difficult job for not much money – but they're also the gatekeepers. They can help you, make useful suggestions, and offer to go the extra mile for you. Or they can just put you on hold and leave you there.

Of course, you must look after yourself and not be a doormat, but the best way to deal with someone who doesn't treat you with respect is to walk away with dignity.

Honouring deadlines

Always keep deadlines when you're committed to them.

The trick with deadlines is to make them realistic at the start. Most people underestimate the time it takes to do something, and don't give themselves enough time. Let's face it, most people also don't start straight away, and then try and rush it at the end. Start early and take your holiday when you've finished.

As well as keeping deadlines, find out people's requirements and fulfil them. If a publisher wants your script on pink paper printed in Italic Gothic, don't argue – do it. After all, they get to make the rules of the game. Complaining about this sort of thing's a waste of time and something that amateurs do. Be a professional.

Chapter 2

Meshing Your Talent and Technique

In This Chapter
▶ Blending talent and technique
▶ Tackling technique

So, you've decided to write a novel. You've probably heard the old cliché that everyone has a novel in them. Of course, this saying is true in the same sense that everyone has a symphony in them, or the design of their perfect house in them. Anyone can try to write a novel, compose a symphony, or build a house. The result just isn't necessarily a *good* novel, symphony, or house.

In order to produce the best novel you're capable of writing, you need talent and technique. This chapter tells you what these things are and what you need to do to understand and use them.

Combining Talent and Technique

Writing is comprised of talent and technique:

- ✓ **Talent** is what some people call creativity, although we say it's a bit more than that. Talent is certainly your ideas, but it's also your characters, your situation, your plot ideas, and everything that makes up your story. Most people who want to be writers wonder whether they have the talent to write a novel. But, strangely enough, talent is the easy part. You have the talent you were born with.

- ✓ **Technique** is what a lot of this book is about. Technique allows you to demonstrate your talent. Look on technique as the frame for your picture – the knowledge that helps you tell your story to its best advantage. Also, technique puts everything in its proper place. Technique makes sure that you don't try to put the roof on until the walls are ready to take the weight, and it makes sure that the big feature window is facing towards the sun, not away from it.

Turning to Your Talent to Find a Topic

Talent is something wonderful, and the pleasure in expressing that talent is part of what makes writing so rewarding.

Different writers have different talents. Think about your talent before you choose a topic and start writing a novel. Ask yourself:

- **What sort of writing do I like reading?**

  What you like reading is often the best place to start. If all your life you've read nothing but hard-boiled crime novels, a delicate romance may not be your best choice of book to try to write. Not only are crime novels the genre you know best, but also your talent probably predisposes you to excel at crime writing. This rule isn't set in stone, but it's a good place to start.

- **What subjects do I know a lot about?**

  The cliché is to write about what you know, although you need to be careful about this advice: if you know most about lying in bed and watching TV, this may not necessarily be your best subject for a novel. However, the best books are generally informed by a clear and deep knowledge of the subject. This sort of knowledge allows you to paint a more convincing picture and put in the detail that makes the reader feel that you know what you're talking about.

- **What writing have I done in the past that worked well?**

  Look back on reactions to the things you've written before. Have you ever shown any writing to other people and seen them react enthusiastically? (Remember that they need to be reacting to the writing, not to the fact that you wrote something.) Think about what sort of writing was well received: was it descriptive, snappy, and in the first or third-person, and did it have lots of dialogue? And then ask yourself:

  - Why did this piece of writing work well?
  - What subject can I now write about that's likely to allow me to succeed again?

- **Where do my strengths and weaknesses lie?**

  Are you funny and confident, or shy and self-deprecating? Get to know yourself better, because your personal strengths determine your strengths as a writer. For example, the way you relate to the people around you naturally influences how you create fictional characters.

After you've answered these questions, you can start to think about your technique.

Harnessing Your Technique

According to Chambers dictionary, *technique* is 'a skilled procedure or method'. Technique is all the stuff that you can learn how to do.

Technique allows you to show off your talent to best advantage. You can pick up some technique through experience and by instinct. However, some essential technique is difficult to master, so start thinking about it early.

If you have no idea what technique is, don't worry. You can develop it!

Some writers think that paying attention to technique inhibits them and somehow threatens their creativity. They liken their talent to a magnificent wild horse, galloping freely across the great plains of creativity, lord of all it surveys. Technique, then, is a saddle and bridle on the horse of their talent, curbing its instincts to roam where it will. These writers see technique as restrictive, believing that it renders something spectacular into something domestic, humdrum, and workaday.

We think that's untrue (although, obviously, too much technique can be constraining). To continue the analogy, if you allow the horse to run completely free, it may accidentally run in the right direction anyway, but it isn't going to win any races. Put a bridle and a saddle on a horse, and you can make it travel at great speed in any direction you want; it can carry things, pull things, and chase things.

The best piece of work usually results from the perfect marriage of talent and technique, in which the technique allows talent full expression. Look at it this way: take two equally talented teenage footballers. Get one of them to practise five days a week with a coach who understands the teenager. Let the other one wander the streets alone all day, kicking a ball only if one happens to come close. Five years later, which of the two footballers are you most likely to want on your team?

Technique doesn't get in the way: it allows you to show off your talent to best advantage. The best writing is a mixture of talent and good technique.

Of course, you want to be original – and we want to help you be as original as possible. But originality comes from a deep understanding of the basic workings of whatever you want to do. Picasso revolutionised artistic perspective. To achieve that, he first had to understand how perspective works. If you want to write in a way that blows people away, first you have to understand the nuts and bolts of writing. Writing a novel takes more than just writing words. Throughout this book, we focus on technique. The talent is down to you. A wise man called Joseph Joubert once wrote: 'He who has imagination without learning has wings but no feet.' We go along with that.

Reading Other Authors

One way to improve your own technique is to look at the work of other authors. Writers sometimes say, 'I don't have time to read, I'm far too busy writing.' Well, if that's really true, we're not about to say 'Stop writing!' But actually we don't believe it; even the busiest writer doesn't write all the time.

The following sections set out the three reasons why you need to read other people's novels.

Picking their brains

If you want to become a brain surgeon, the best way to go about it, alongside attending all the lectures and doing all the reading and so on, is as follows:

1. **Watch the best brain surgeon you can find.**
2. **Work out what the brain surgeon does and why.**
3. **Try to copy the brain surgeon.**

We acknowledge the difficulty of this process, particularly the last step. Fortunately, in this respect at least, writing is easier than brain surgery.

Every time someone reads your work and says, 'Oh, this reminds me of so-and-so,' or 'You'd like so-and-so,' or just 'Have you read so-and-so?' write the comment down in the notebook you (of course) carry with you at all times. The person may be talking rubbish, but you'll soon work that out. Reading books that other people refer you to is a lot quicker than reading every book you can lay your hands on.

Find a book by an author who you think may do the same sort of thing you're attempting (whether in terms of subject, style or technique), and read the book. Work out what that author is trying to do and whether it works for you. If it does work for you, adapt the author's methods. If it doesn't work, analysing why it doesn't can help you find alternative approaches. Now go away and practise it yourself.

Other authors are the best teachers you have.

Saving time and effort by not re-inventing the wheel

If you want to, of course, you can work out all your ideas about structure, plot, character, narrative voice, and so on by yourself. But you're going to have to do lots of unsuccessful writing and go through many false starts to get there, and you may still never manage it. Or you can take advantage of the fact that many other authors have already worked on the same problems. Some authors have solved these problems completely; others have been partially successful. Any published author you read is further down the road than you are. So, save some time: read what other authors do, determine whether it works for you, and carry on.

Writing is like learning the guitar. You have to discover how to play the instrument, that's unavoidable. But at least you don't have to invent scales and musical notation before you can even start. That's already been done, so why do it all over again?

Realising that writing's meant to be fun

You can make your life complicated in lots of ways that don't involve writing, so why spend your time writing if it's just another complication? Well, because you have to. Wanting to writing is an itch you have to scratch. Sometimes you forget that, as well as often being difficult, writing is often fun. As Woody Allen said about sex, even when it's bad, it's still good. Reading a good book reminds you of that.

Most of us write because a long time ago we read a book that completely blew us away. We put the book down and said to ourselves, 'I want to do that. I want to tell a story that does to other people what that story did to me.' Thinking about that aim is fun, moving towards it is fun, and achieving it is fun. Reading reminds us of all these things.

Developing Your Style

Defining what constitutes someone's style is tricky. *Style* is a compound of a lot of things, including the words used (short or long? common or unusual? technical? stylised or colloquial?), the way the words are presented (dialogue, description, narrative?), the point of view (first, second, or third person?), the tense, the use and type of humour, and so on.

If you read Jane Austen alongside Tom Clancy, you can't mistake one for the other. Austen's sentences are usually long, stately, and considered. Clancy's are almost always sharp, punchy, and short. Look for patterns as you read other writers' works.

Your style comes from everything you've ever read and everything you've ever written, so you need to read widely and write all you can. Then you need to look at writing (including your own) and see what worked for you and what failed. Think about the language used. What's the writer trying to do, how's the writer doing it, and does it work?

We've all read a bestseller and thought, 'That's dreadful writing, what made people buy this terrible book?' The writing may well be terrible, but the author's doing *something* right because the book's a bestseller. You need to know what that something is; you may want to use it yourself.

Sometimes the reason you enjoy a book is as simple as the fact that the author uses short sentences or lots of unusual descriptive words. If that's a style you enjoy reading, think about how you can do the same.

You may worry that by paying attention to other writers' styles, you're going to end up just copying a style instead of developing your own. This isn't very likely; writing like someone else is very difficult. People who make their living by parodying other writers' styles can tell you that it's hard work. But let's assume that it does happen: you read someone and start writing in the same style. That's only a bad thing if you're reading bad writers. Read good writers and learn from them. Nothing's wrong with that. Getting a bit more Hemingway or Ian McEwan into their style would be a good thing for most people.

Try to find a way of saying things that you feel comfortable with. If someone says something like, 'You should write more like Hemingway,' that doesn't mean you should copy Hemingway, but instead means that you can learn from him. (The person making the suggestion also probably thinks that your writing is a bit too long.)

Don't copy. Read, observe, learn, take what you need, and move on.

Chapter 3

Getting to the Writing

. . . .

. . . .

*W*riting a novel is a complicated process. You have to keep a lot of balls in the air at the same time.

You can help to keep things under control if you think of writing a novel as a project that starts with almost infinite possibilities, proceeds as a gradual system of accepting and rejecting possibilities, and ends up at a single point.

When you start writing, you can go in any direction you want, create any characters you want, and have them do anything you feel like. Then, as you make decisions, you gradually focus in on where you want to be going. You're sure to take some wrong turnings and have to go back, and you'll change your mind many times along the way, but every decision you make brings you closer to the final product.

Deciding Whether to Plan or Dive Right In

When it comes to planning, there are two broad categories of novelist, planners and divers-in:

✔ **Planner:** Some writers have the whole novel planned in their heads before they even start. We know one novelist who covers a wall with cards and notes written on scraps of paper before she even starts writing a novel. She moves the cards and scraps around, and then writes more notes to fill in the gaps until she's clear what happens when and how. Finally, she starts writing.

If you're a planner, you typically make lots of notes and know the characters, basic story, and setting. All the ideas are in place before you really get going. You probably have a pretty good idea of the plot as well – what happens in the story, who does what, and the general shape and structure of the whole thing.

Whatever type of writer you are, having a running summary of the plot is always a good idea – not to tie you down, just to remind you where you thought you were going. The idea is that you update the summary regularly to take account of your latest additions, and it helps you to see whether what you're doing makes sense. This running summary should probably be no more than a page long.

✔ **Diver-in:** Some writers have a glimmer of an idea and start writing just to see where it goes. They have a vague idea of what the story is about, maybe some sense of an outline, a character or two, a plot idea, and they just dive right in, no messing. They prefer to try things out rather than theorise about them – and you may be this type of writer.

Many writers 'write their way into' their books, as if the book doesn't come into focus until they have 10,000 or 20,000 words under their belts.

If you're more of a diver-in than a planner, fair enough. Off you go. Just don't be surprised when you run out of steam at the end of chapter five. (No one knows why it's the end of chapter five, but it always is.) You get to the end of the first big crisis and . . . whatcha gonna do now? So you tinker for a few days, put the manuscript in your bottom drawer with all the others, and start on the next brilliant idea. See you at the end of chapter five of that one too.

So, which approach is better? Well, in terms of time, it doesn't actually make much difference. You can plan beforehand or sort things out as you go along. Table 3-1 shows some of the advantages of each method.

Table 3-1	Advantages of Planning and Diving In
Planning Advantages	*Diving-in Advantages*
You waste less writing time.	You don't have to wait, you can get going, and you strike while the iron's hot.
You're less likely to run out of steam.	By the time you run out of steam, you've covered a lot of paper, and so you have a good sense of whether the idea is worth continuing.
You can have an exciting time moving your characters and events around like chess pieces in your mind.	Your characters and events can excite you by leading you in directions that you wouldn't anticipate.

Whether you plan or not does make a difference to the story. The problem with diving in is that you get committed to your choices. If you've written four chapters and then get a sneaky feeling it isn't working, because of the time and effort you've spent, you're likely to try to make it better through editing, when it may just need throwing away. This is less likely to happen with a planned piece: if you go off course, you haven't spent time and effort on that stray piece, and so changing it is a lot less traumatic.

Divers-in also often have a problem with the *new-character fix*, the tendency to introduce a new character every time they run up against a problem in the story. This can sometimes work well, but it can also lead to a clutter of sketchy characters whose only function is to fix a specific problem.

Conversely, you can over-plan a planned piece. If you've dived in and are writing by the seat of your pants, you're less likely to resist an unusual idea or to let the action arise naturally out of character, whereas if you're planning you're more likely to think 'No, that won't work' without really giving it a try.

To some extent, whether you plan or dive in depends upon how your brain works. Keep in mind your natural inclination. Like most things in this book, what's right for you is what works for you.

If you're like most writers, your attitude to planning is somewhere in the middle: you like to have some idea of what's going on, but you haven't filled in lots of the gaps yet. You write, do some research, write some more, wonder what happens next and do some planning, and then write a bit more. Get started on the novel as soon as you can, but have a bit of a think about where you're going first, and take time out once in a while for more thinking.

Writing and planning aren't equal. You can plan at any time, but you can only write sometimes. So if you have to choose, always write first and plan later.

The *golden mean* is Aristotle's big idea. Put very simply it states that, as a general rule, you do better if you avoid extremes. In this book we use the phrase 'take what you need' a lot, which is another version of the same idea. In just about anything you do – eating, drinking, exercising, or writing – you're better off if you have a bit of everything, but not too much of any one thing. So, be like an Ancient Greek: don't be an obsessive planner or a manic diver-in.

Whichever way you decide to approach it, the important thing is not to let the planning process get in the way of the writing. One day you have to sit down and write the novel! Make a deadline for yourself: choose a day when you're definitely going to sit down and start writing properly. Or at the very least examine your motives: are you *really* planning or are you just avoiding writing?

Anything that gets in the way of your writing is a bad thing.

Planning as avoidance strategy

The idea that some writers use planning as an excuse for avoiding writing is extreme but not unusual. We had a student who was very keen and a good writer. She was planning a historical novel set in the Middle Ages. She absolutely loved the Middle Ages and loved researching and discovering all about the period. When the course was over, we were talking over people's plans and we asked her what her next move was. She smiled and said, 'I have just one more textbook to look at and then I start on the novel.' Six years later we ran into her again. We asked her how the novel was progressing. She smiled and said, 'I'm nearly ready to start, but I just have one more textbook to look at . . .'.

Preparing the Pieces

This section talks about getting your basics right before you start, giving you an idea of the things you need to start thinking about, such as basic plotting, using the classic archetypes, deciding on a setting, and so on. Later chapters go into more detail about these topics.

Doing your research

Presumably you're writing about something you already know quite a lot about, or you're writing about something new to you that's fired your imagination. So research, although important, needs to take second place to the writing. You can paint in the details later.

Finding research materials can be time-consuming, so always ask for help if you need it – don't waste time that can be spent writing! Places to find information include:

- ✔ **Libraries:** Often underestimated sources of information, libraries usually have very knowledgeable people working in them.

- ✔ **News agencies:** Ask whether your local newspaper has a database you can use.

- ✔ **Friends and relatives:** If you know people who were around during the historical time you're writing about, or people with experience of a situation or skill you need to find out about, don't hesitate to ask them. Not only can they be informative, but also they can often give you the sort of idiosyncratic personal details that make something interesting and believable.

✔ **Internet:** A goldmine for finding things out. If you aren't confident online (or even if you are), you can benefit from getting a copy of *Researching Online For Dummies* by Reva Basch and Mary Ellen Bates (Wiley), available at all good bookstores.

Considering plot basics

This section gives you a broad outline of plot basics. Chapter 7 provides a more detailed and fuller discussion of this aspect of writing, but the material here is enough to get you going. We deal with character, which is important in terms of plotting, in Chapter 8.

Finding ideas

Coming up with an idea is in some ways very easy. You're surrounded by ideas: you switch on the TV, open a newspaper, or even just talk to someone, and ideas pour at you from every direction. The hard part is choosing a good idea.

The first thing you need to do is to jot the idea down and let it sit for a little while, maybe a day or two. Then have another look. A lot of ideas that seem good when you first think of them wilt after a short time, which tells you that the idea isn't very good, or perhaps isn't really for you. Letting ideas sit for a while weeds out a fair few of the less good ones, and you don't waste any time on them.

So, what are the criteria for a good plot idea? A good plot needs to be:

✔ **Exciting:** To start with, an idea has to excite you. You're going to be writing about it for a long time, and so if you aren't excited by it at the start, you're going to be in real trouble in six months' time. This may sound obvious, but we know a surprising number of people who start writing novels that they aren't really interested in. They have a horrid time and eventually have to stop because they're bored by the idea. Choose carefully; you're taking on a big commitment.

✔ **Simple:** Start simply. Charlie Chaplin said that to make a story, all he needed was a park bench, a policeman, and a pretty girl. In writers' terms, that's a situation, an antagonist, and something to fight over.

So, to start off, you need a situation (both in the sense of a broad or specific geographical location, and in the sense of a point in time centred on an event, such as a death in the family, a party, a car crash, or whatever). You need a character who wants something, and another character who also wants something, and somehow these two wants need to be mutually exclusive. (For example, Charlie Chaplin and the policeman can both fall in love with the pretty girl, but they can't both marry her. Unless, of course, that's your story!)

> ✔ **Distinctive:** Ask yourself whether your idea's unusual or different in some way. If the story is well known, what makes it different? There's no point in trotting out a thinly disguised retread of a familiar story. What's going to make the reader (and a publisher) think it's a new angle?

Using what you've got

You probably have some pretty fixed ideas about your novel already, although you may not have much of a story to tell someone. At the start, your basic idea may be along the lines of the following example:

> I know that it's set in Florida in the present day, and the main character is about my age, but taller and more athletic, and maybe something bad happened to him when he was a teenager, but I'm not sure about that yet, and I know it's all something to do with a legacy, and there's definitely a murder. The body is hidden under a big pile of leaves; no one finds it for ages. The villain is Russian with a gold front tooth and he drinks too much coffee. The story begins in a forest, and in the first scene there's a small house nearby, with green shutters. The last scene is set on a huge yacht, and I know there's a confrontation scene at a horse race, and that's where the big love scene takes place as well. And there's a chess board, a really ornate one like the one I saw in the British Museum three years ago. The board will eventually be a really big clue to the murderer, although I don't know why yet; maybe it's got a secret compartment. And the main character's mother lives in an old folks' home, and the main character visits her every week, and she's really sharp and puts him right when he's going off in the wrong direction. She's a lot like my grand-mother. And there's a dog, a Dalmatian. I always wanted a Dalmatian. . . .

In other words, your initial concept is quite likely to be a bit of a muddle – a mixture of people and places you know about and want to fit in somewhere. You've seen them, dreamed them, read about them, and imagined them. Some of them are clear; some are hardly there, just a gesture or an item of clothing. You're going to have gaps, some big and some small. It probably isn't going to all fit in the one novel. That's fine. What the example gives you is a sort of map (and a reminder that writing ideas down is important, because you can't see the shape of them until you do).

Trying out archetypes

Before long, any discussion about structuring your writing bumps up against the idea of archetypes. (Our apologies to any psychologists reading this book, because we use the word in a much more general sense than they do.) We use *archetype* to mean the subjects and images that recur over and over again throughout the history of human story-telling. They are the things that writers – seemingly instinctively – reach for when creating a story. You can read up on archetypes if you want, but for now you just need to know that they exist. You're probably aware of them even if you aren't using them consciously. Certainly anyone who reads or writes fantasy novels is acquainted with archetypes (for example, *The Lord of the Rings* is stuffed with them), even if you call them something else.

The same ideas, themes, and motifs keep cropping up in different types and styles of story. (Chapter 5 of this book suggests that a relatively small and finite number of stories actually exist, but you don't need to know about that to understand this chapter.)

Why these archetypes recur isn't always obvious. Why do so many people write about princesses? Why, indeed, are princesses so very important to so many people? Why is blood such a potent symbol? Why do people read about vampires with such a delicious shudder, and why are vampires such a popular subject?

Think about this: the novels *Dracula* by Bram Stoker and *Frankenstein* by Mary Shelley are both hugely popular bestsellers. There are literally thousands of books (and films) about vampires, yet comparatively speaking hardly any about giant dead men made up of spare body parts. (And no, zombies aren't the same thing.) Why is one theme so popular and the other not? We'd argue that a story centred on the idea of blood has a deep archetypical resonance which the Frankenstein story lacks. (As they say in the exam papers, 'discuss'.)

At least part of the reason is that princesses and blood are both archetypes. They both appear in fairy tales the world over. In the story of Sleeping Beauty they appear together!

Here are a few of the most common story-telling archetypes:

- ✔ Family members fighting over something – a farm, a business, a house, a fortune – which symbolises who they are.
- ✔ Fear of contamination of some sort – racial, sexual, physical, social.
- ✔ A huge, impersonal thing such as a mountain, an ocean, a giant lizard, or a gorilla that must be overcome or defeated.
- ✔ A child growing to maturity and encountering difficulty with family relationships along the way.
- ✔ A character with a wound of some kind – physical, emotional, psychological – that prevents them from becoming the person they could be.

Plenty of novels and films contain these archetypes which form the basis of the story, and this is no accident. Everyone knows these themes; many people deal with them in their lives.

Not all stories contain archetypes, at least not in ways that can help you to write about them. However, have a think about the story you're writing. Your story's theme is quite probably recognisable as an archetype. Don't reject it in favour of trying to write something completely original – you'd end up throwing away most stories! Instead, have a think about how the earlier stories begin, progress, and end, and consider whether you want your story to follow the same path. Look at the structure of the original story. The shape of the original gives you a template you can use to tell your own story.

You don't have to follow or copy the traditional archetypical storyline. You can, however, use the storyline to spur your thinking, bounce possibilities off it, and compare and contrast elements. All this helps you arrive at your own version.

The Cain and Abel archetype suggests a story of two brothers with normal sibling rivalry. This rivalry can grow gradually into something that threatens the relationship, or it can be tipped over the edge by the introduction of something new and specific – maybe love or lust, jealousy or greed, and so on. One of the brothers takes irrevocable action and lives with the consequences thereafter. That's the archetype. Now run with it. What if Abel kills Cain? What if the whole thing is a terrible misunderstanding? What if Cain and Abel are sisters? Each change you make has consequences that travel through the story like ripples over water.

When a reader realises which archetype you're using, it gives that person a whole set of psychological reference points to use. Don't be afraid of investigating these ideas.

For an in-depth explanation of why archetypes are important, read Carl Jung's *Memories, Dreams, Reflections* (Fontana). This book gives you the full psychological definition and all the rest. Christopher Vogler's *The Writer's Journey* (Michael Wiese Productions) is useful from a writer's point of view as well.

Setting your location

The first thing to keep in mind is that the location is a character in your story. This may sound a little bit strange, but consider: if you place the main characters of Shakespeare's *Romeo and Juliet* in a comfortable rural cottage in Wiltshire, you have one story; if you set them in the middle of the Sahara desert, you have another – different – story. Your characters interact with the location just as they interact with each other. So you need to choose your setting carefully.

Locations bring things to your story. For example, locations have atmosphere: setting a story in 1930s New York brings one type of atmosphere; setting it in Rome in AD 50 brings another. Locations also have physical features which your characters have to deal with as they move across the landscape. Locations contain things – some dangerous, some helpful, but all potentially part of your story. Locations make certain activities possible and discourage others: you probably wouldn't sunbathe in the Antarctic, you definitely wouldn't play hockey on a minefield, and so on.

Location is one area of writing where 'write what you know' is probably good advice. You may, as many writers do, choose to write about a place similar to where you grew up or live now, purely for convenience; you save having to make it up or research it! That said, you can always research a place and recreate it. And you may choose a location for the exact reason that it's strange and fascinating to you and you want to write about it because of that interest, and that's fine too.

Our advice here is to do one of two things:

- ✔ If you know you want to set the story somewhere specific, wrap the story around the place you've chosen – Venice, Corfu, Newcastle, or wherever.

- ✔ If you don't have a definite place in mind, don't rush to be too specific straight away. Just write the story. As it develops, you'll come to know more and more about what you need to make the story work, and you can make a decision about the exact location later on.

Make a list of the characteristics of the place in which you want to set the story. These words are often – but not always – descriptive of the sort of story you're writing. Words like 'airless', 'dusty', 'chilly', 'foggy', and 'steamy' are the type of thing you're looking for. Keep the list handy and add to it as you go along, or change it if you find the story going in unexpected directions. This list helps to keep you focused on what you're trying to achieve.

Sitting Down and Starting Up

The empty page is your enemy, just as a page full of writing is your friend. Three hundred pages of writing, regardless of quality, are closer to being a finished novel than three hundred blank pages. So anything that helps you to put words on the page is a good thing, and any activity that doesn't result in writing – or worse, prevents you writing when you could be doing some – is a bad thing.

Not getting ahead of yourself

One of the most common questions that published writers at readings and suchlike are asked by new writers is, 'How do I get an agent?' It's a fair question and an important one. But it isn't one that you need to be thinking about at this point. (If you are asking yourself this question, we answer it in Chapter 16.) Thinking about getting an agent when you've written three chapters of your novel is like thinking about becoming a stunt driver after your first driving lesson. That day will come, but you have some work to do first.

Assembling your kit

Finding the tools you need is reasonably straightforward. If you're building a house, you need a hammer, a saw, and a load of other things. If you don't have them, you don't have much chance of success. Substitutes don't work: a rock doesn't make a good hammer, and a feather isn't going to cut your planks for you.

To write a novel you need a space in which to work, preferably one where you don't have to put everything away at the end of a session; you need to be able to pick up quickly where you left off. You need a desk and a chair. You can write in quiet or with music, whichever works for you. But don't get too hung up on the right ambience, or the environment can become a reason for not writing if it isn't perfect. People have scribbled novels on the backs of envelopes while walking around a dingy kitchen trying to comfort a crying baby. Try to make your surroundings pleasant, but don't make it a fetish.

Not all writers are keen on the tools of their trade, but a lot of us are. A nice laptop and a good software package, or, if you prefer, good sharp pencils, nice smooth heavy-gauge paper, a proper fountain pen, an expensive notebook, and a good filing system, are all things that can help when you write and make you feel good about what you're doing. (The advantage of the old-fashioned stuff is that games, the Internet or email can't distract you if things aren't going well. You may want to consider having a laptop without Internet access, solely for your writing.) You probably need a dictionary and a thesaurus within reach, too. Anything that makes the physical process of writing more pleasurable is a good thing. Just don't get so interested in admiring the stationery that you never get around to writing!

And don't forget: writing is work, so remember to reward yourself when you do it.

Beating the distractions

All writers have their distractions – the things they do rather than write. You may play computer games, eat lunch, clean the house, answer emails, or listen to your favourite radio programme; the list goes on.

Fair enough, we're all fallible human beings. But recognise these activities for what they are. If they're punctuation for your periods of writing, if they're valuable thinking time and allow you to recharge your batteries and return to your writing refreshed, fine, no problem. However, if they're substitutes for writing, you need to sit down and have a serious think. Are you writing or are you doing something else? If, as happened to one of us one day, you catch yourself saying, 'I'll just clean the oven, which I've been putting off for six months, and then I'll do some writing,' you're kidding yourself.

No one ever published a novel by not writing a novel.

Writing for writing's sake

If you wait until the muse lands on your shoulder, you can wait a long time. *Start writing*. Write anything at all.

Switch off quality control. Ignore the bad angel, the discouraging voice that says things like, 'That's no good. That word there's wrong. That bit makes no sense at all. You know you'll have to go back and fix that. What a terrible sentence! You can't think of the right word and you aren't about to, so you may as well stop now,' and so on. Whatever your discouraging voice says (and we've all got one, although it comes in different forms), *ignore it*.

Every time you write something, even if you think it makes no sense at all, you're closer to finding out what's really happening. Whatever you write, at the end of the session you're closer to the end of the novel than you were when you started.

Don't make too many firm decisions about your story when you start writing: keep your options open. Concentrate on just moving the story along. Choose a scene that you know, or one you know a bit of, and get it down. It doesn't matter where the scene occurs in the novel. Don't worry about beginnings, middles, and ends. Get whatever you can onto the page. Write scraps of dialogue, bits of description, character sketches, one-liners, or whatever comes to mind. Your novel's a patchwork quilt, and at the moment you're just sticking patches down to see how they look; nothing's decided yet. Just write stuff down and see where it goes and what happens.

Don't worry about writing the first page first. At this point, you're unlikely to even know what your first scene is. You may think you know, but until you're positive you know where the story really begins, you can't really write the first page. And you don't know what the first page needs to say until you've written a fair bit of the story. So don't waste time on the beginning, not now. Start where you know what's happening, and charge on in. (We talk about what makes for a good start in Chapter 7.)

Deal with what you've got in front of you today, and worry about the future another day. Take problems as they appear, and don't try and take on everything at once. If you're building a house, you need to put the walls up before you can put the roof on. Even if you construct the roof separately at the same time as you're erecting the walls, you don't have anywhere to put it until the walls are strong enough to take the weight. So, relax. One day you're going to have to go through your manuscript and check every comma. That day isn't today. Today you're working on the big picture; the small stuff comes later.

Going for doughnuts

One way of covering the page is to set yourself targets, giving yourself a reward every time you achieve a target. We know one writer who has a small fridge beside his desk. Each evening when he sits down to write, he puts two bottles of beer in the fridge. At the end of the evening, after several hours' work, he awards himself both bottles as a prize. (Incidentally, he gets the bottles regardless of the quality of the work he's just done. The reward is for doing the writing.) We know people who write in coffee bars and order themselves a doughnut every time they complete three pages. Some people make a deal with themselves that they can go for a swim when they've spent an hour writing. Some people make a deal with themselves that if they spend an hour writing, they *don't* have to go for a swim. Whatever. Set yourself a target that's realistic and suits you. We're writers, not monks. (Except those of us who are monks.) Writing is hard work. Use what gets you through it. But don't cheat. You have to set yourself a reasonable target, and you get the reward only if you achieve it.

What's a reasonable target? A thousand words – around three pages – seems to be about right for most people. By all means set a target of more than three pages, but not if that's going to mean that you're too tired to work the next day. Pace yourself. And if you've got an unusual week coming up, by all means give yourself an average target – 5,000 words over five days is fine, and it doesn't matter if you do 2,000 words on the first day and then have to miss a day.

Quality isn't the issue. The point is to get the words done; you can think about targets for editing when you've written the novel, but at this stage you just need to write. And then, like the people we mentioned above, if you're the sort of person who responds to rewards, by all means have one.

Making much of practice

> *People call me a lucky golfer. I find the harder I practise the luckier I get.*
>
> Gary Player (champion golfer)

Imagine that one day, having never danced before, you decide to be a ballerina. You go away, put some routines together, and then run them past a ballerina friend of yours. Is she more likely to say, 'Great, keep going just like that and you'll be dancing professionally in no time,' or to offer more realistic advice along the lines of, 'Maybe you need to do some training, learn a bit about the steps, practise the moves, and discover the basics that every dancer uses, before you try for a career in dancing'?

You may be incredibly talented, but look around at other incredibly talented people. Talk to virtuoso musicians, and they'll tell you they play simple scales every day. Talk to world-calibre footballers, and they'll tell you they practise basic ball skills every day.

Imagine that you need a very risky brain operation and you're choosing between two surgeons to perform it. You ask each of them to tell you why you should trust them. One says, 'Well, I've always been good at brain surgery, but I practise all the time to make sure that I'm as good as I can be.' The other says, 'I've always been good at brain surgery, so I don't need to practise.' Which one are you going to ask to drill into your head?

We suggest that you do at least one of the following things each day. Ideally, do them all:

- ✔ Write for ten minutes as soon as you wake up. Write about anything at all, starting with any dreams you remember and going on from there. No rules, just write.

- ✔ Write three pages of your story (about 800 to 1,000 words).

- ✔ Write a 300-word description of someone you met or someone you observed that day.

- ✔ Write 300 words about the writing you've done so far, as a sort of letter to yourself, reflecting on what you're doing and how it's going.

- ✔ Read a chapter of a novel, or a short story, for pleasure!

Enjoying the process

The day that you start a novel you're at the start of a journey. You don't know how long it's going to take or even where you'll end up. So, the first thing to remember is to have fun!

Writing is work, sure, but that's not all it is. Writing a novel is interesting, surprising, revealing, and above all satisfying. If this wasn't true, if it was just work, who'd do it?

Writing a novel is supposed to be fun – at least at the start! A day may come when you get fed up with the whole thing, but that's still some distance away.

Enjoy it while you can. Play with your characters. Have fun creating your situations. Get involved with the ideas and the possibilities that writing gives you. Don't be too eager to box yourself in when you're writing. Every decision you make in the novel means that a whole range of other possibilities are excluded. You need to make these decisions eventually, but be open in the early stages to the possibility that you may be going in the wrong direction. If something looks interesting, investigate it and follow to see where it leads. You can always come back again if it turns out to be a wild goose chase.

Keeping count of your ideas

This may sound odd, but what frightens a lot of people when they start writing is the fast and furious flow of ideas. (It's also one of the things that makes writing exciting.) At first, the stream of ideas is inspiring and exciting, and it makes the whole thing seem possible. These ideas are the reason why most people who write do so.

When you get a good idea, you want to stop writing the bit you're doing and start on the new idea. When you get a new idea, it always seems better than what you're writing – it's bound to. You think, 'I must stop doing this suddenly dull bit of writing and start on this brilliant new idea, or I'll forget it and never get it back.'

Trouble is, after a while, you run out of space in your head to keep track of all your insights and possibilities.

Now the fear comes in. You have all these brilliant ideas, but what if you forget one, particularly the really crucial one? But you don't know which one is crucial yet.

If you stop to go after the new idea, you end up with a lot of very short undeveloped pieces. Keep going long enough, and you may have a novel one day, but it's a slow way of doing it.

What you need is a system. We recommend the following steps for when you get an idea that you can't use immediately:

1. **Put a number at the place in the novel where you think your new idea may be relevant.**

   (We find that starting with number 1 works best!)

2. **Put the same number in a separate computer document or notebook (stationery-purchasing opportunity!) devoted specifically to these ideas, and write down the idea.**

   If you're uncomfortable with moving between computer screens, using a notebook is a good way to start.

   If the idea isn't immediately relevant to the piece you're working on, jot it down on an index card and put it in a box (some sort of filing system is useful to speed up retrieval later) – you can do the same thing with files on your computer.

   Make sure that you have some sort of system for naming the different files. Even something as simple as calling them 'character ideas', 'description', and so on, makes your life a lot less frustrating later.

3. **Then forget about it and keep writing.**

The point is three-fold: make sure that you write the idea down, don't let it derail you from what you're doing, and make sure that you can get to it when you need to later. You no longer have to be terrified that your good ideas may slip away. You just write them down with a cross-reference number so that you can find them again easily.

When you run out of steam on the bit you're writing, go back to your file of ideas. If an earlier idea still seems brilliant, it can become the next piece you write.

Work through each idea to make sure that you give it a fair chance. If it seems to be working, great. If not, fair enough, stick it into a file – call it 'the bin' or anything else you like the sound of. Any time you get to the end of working through an idea and decide that it doesn't work, stick it in 'the bin'. Never throw anything away. Trust us, you'll be surprised how often something that doesn't seem to be working can be recycled later on. And if, later, an idea doesn't seem so wonderful, you've saved yourself from wasting time following up on it.

Maybe the idea is good, maybe it isn't, but you've still got it and you didn't stop writing. You win either way.

Nothing is ever wasted. Keep your notes and your early drafts (no matter how ridiculous they may seem to be); you'll need bits of them one day.

Getting unstuck

Whisper it softly, but you need to face up to the fact that writing a novel isn't always a joyful experience that enriches your life. The day is sure to come when you feel like picking up your laptop and throwing it against the wall – hard. Writing can be infuriating. You've got your story sorted, you know the beginning, middle, and end, the thing is more than half written, and yet the characters just sit there looking static and glum and stubbornly refusing to come to life. This section suggests some ways out for when your characters are stuck in the mud and unable to move.

When you hit a bad patch and can't write anything useful, try these suggestions to jump-start your creativity:

- ✔ **Put your hero in a situation utterly unlike anything they're going to meet in the novel.** James Bond working in a dress shop, Mr Darcy washing up, Bridget Jones conducting a church service. Whatever.

- ✔ **Interview your characters like you're a talk-show host.** The conversation may be dull, but at the very least you can get down the way that the character talks. (Chapter 8 offers some sample questions.)

✔ **Reverse everything.** Take a scene that you're having trouble with and make the male characters female and the female ones male. Make the straight ones gay and the gay ones straight. If it's sunny, make it rainy. If it's day, make it night. If the characters are happy, make them sad. If they're rich, make them poor. If they're young, make them old. And so on. Now, write the same scene. It doesn't matter if some parts don't make sense; other parts may well make more sense than before. Maybe your hero should be a 70-year-old woman after all?

Part II
Building from the Basics

Top Five Hero Types

- **The hero as John Wayne.** Larger-than-life people make good central characters. Readers find them interesting and exciting. However, if you don't want your main character to be heroic, having the character attached in some way to someone who is heroic is often useful, because action tends to surround heroic types.

- **The hero as your mum or dad.** Not all heroes are obviously heroic. A single parent bringing up a disabled child on a low income isn't as obviously heroic as someone who charges a machine gun nest, but both actions involve self-sacrifice and provoke admiration.

- **The hero as Gandhi.** The trick in making a cerebral, altruistic, non-action hero interesting is to show why the person's conduct matters.

- **The unexpected hero.** Some heroes are thrust into situations accidentally. The situations in which you choose to place your characters make readers react differently to them.

- **The hero who isn't.** You can have a hero who does almost nothing at all. However, maintaining interest in such a character is difficult. You need a delicate touch and a fine sense of irony to draw out what matters in the story and keep the reader interested.

Go to www.dummies.com/extras/writinganovelgettingpublisheduk for free online bonus content.

In this part . . .

- ✔ Delve into the intricacies of plot and character.
- ✔ Plot the journey that your main characters will take, and how you'll pace their journey to make your readers keep turning the page to find out what happens next.
- ✔ Discover some helpful techniques for visualising your scenes and characters.
- ✔ Find tips on how to write even when you feel stuck, and then build on those ideas.
- ✔ Feel inspired to make real progress with your novel.

Chapter 4

Following the Hero's Journey

*T*he central idea in this chapter is that all mythic stories follow the same basic pattern. Of course, this doesn't mean that all stories are – or should be – the same, just that they often use a similar fundamental structure, in the same sense that almost all houses have a roof and walls. Yet within that structure lies the potential for vast creativity.

As the chapter title implies, the *hero*, who is the main character, travels – geographically perhaps, but more importantly emotionally, spiritually, from childhood to adulthood, or in all these ways – and in doing so moves away from the position they occupied at the beginning of the story.

If you want to delve deeper into the ideas in this chapter, read *The Writer's Journey* by Christopher Vogler (Michael Wiese Productions), which goes into lots of detail on the ideas we spell out in simpler terms here.

Not all stories involve a hero in the sense that we talk about here. You may, for example, be writing a gentle comedy of manners. However, even if your book is very different to the books and examples in this chapter, there are still some salient points for every author. Most importantly, it's worth thinking of every story as a journey for the main character. The individual starts in one place, and by the end of the story has arrived in another place. So even if you don't think that your story has mythic resonance, this chapter can still be useful.

Setting Your Hero on a Journey

Many of the great stories you know and love conform to the template of the Hero's Journey, moving from a starting point to an ending point, with transformation along the way.

A good example is Frodo's story from *The Lord of the Rings* by JRR Tolkien. Frodo journeys both geographically and personally. He discovers many things about the world and himself, including friendship, courage, and the nature of good and evil. At the end of the story he returns to where he lived at the beginning, but everything has changed irrevocably for him. The stories of Achilles, Beowulf, and Luke Skywalker are also good examples of heroes who journey. Lara Croft and James Bond are examples of heroes who don't journey in this sense, primarily because they aren't significantly changed by their experiences.

From the writing point of view, the important thing is that the hero goes through a number of stages in the journey, which we explore in the next section.

The Hero's Journey is a bit like a tested and reliable recipe that always produces a good cake: you can mess around with the ingredients a lot and still get something pretty good. You can, of course, decide not to use that recipe. You can decide to make a new kind of cake, one that doesn't use sugar, flour, or water. Fair enough, if you can still make it taste like a good cake – and some people can – go for it, and good luck to you. In this book, we encourage you to play around with the proportions, put in extra ingredients, leave other things out, change the shape, and sometimes invent new flavours, but still make something that's recognisable as a cake.

The point is that all readers know and recognise the Hero's Journey type of story. We all respond to it.

If your story is completely unlike the Hero's Journey, that's fair enough. Your main character may spend the entire story dozing in an armchair and thinking about supper, or wandering the streets with a few friends talking about where the next drink is coming from, in which case the Hero's Journey template clearly doesn't apply. But you have to answer a very important question: what are you giving your reader instead? You need to find a way to stir, move, excite, and intrigue your readers – in other words, keep them up half the night because your story is impossible to put down. You need to give your readers a reason to want to read the story. You can certainly find a good solution, but you probably need to spend some time thinking about it.

Patrick Süskind's novel *Perfume* (Penguin Books Ltd) illustrates how to stray out of the strict confines of the Hero's Journey while maintaining reader interest. The protagonist is not heroic in any way, but a characteristic (an extreme sensitivity to smell) makes him unusual. In a way, his journey has already taken place; he's now at a turning point that will dictate the direction of the rest of his life. The reader reads to enjoy the unusual approach and to see what's going to happen. Similarly, Agatha Christie's Poirot doesn't follow a Hero's Journey. The interest for the reader is to watch Poirot deduce who the murderer is.

The Hero's Journey is not the only way to tell a story, but so many stories are variations on this theme that spending a bit of time thinking about it is worthwhile. The point is not that you have to follow the Hero's Journey recipe, but that it's a useful way of approaching the need to make sure that your story intrigues and pulls along the reader.

Surveying the Stages of the Journey

In *The Hero with a Thousand Faces* (Fontana Press), Joseph Campbell suggests that the classic mythic story – what many people, including us, call the Hero's Journey – has 12 stages, which are laid out here:

- **Ordinary World:** The beginning point of the story.
- **Call to Adventure:** Something happens that requires action.
- **Refusal of the Call:** The hero is in some way unwilling.
- **Meeting with the Mentor:** The hero is offered support.
- **Crossing the First Threshold:** The journey begins.
- **Tests, Allies, and Enemies:** The opposition becomes apparent.
- **The Inner Cave:** Getting to the point of the Hero's Journey.
- **Ordeal:** The showdown.
- **Reward (or Seizing the Sword):** After the showdown.
- **The Road Back:** The fallout from the showdown.
- **Resurrection:** The hero's actions are recognised.
- **Return with the Elixir:** The end of the story.

What does all this mean in practice? Table 4-1 shows the stages in terms of two stories you know already and one you may not know. This latter example, *Elizabeth*, refers to the Cate Blanchett film of the same name about the early part of the reign of Elizabeth I. You don't need to have seen the film to make sense of the stages, if you know a bit of history about the queen. It's a great story.

Table 4-1	Examples of the Hero's Journey		
Stages of the Journey	**The Lord of the Rings**	**Star Wars**	**Elizabeth**
Ordinary World	The Shire	Luke's home	Girlhood and romance
Call to Adventure	Frodo discovers that he's the Ring-bearer	Luke escapes and finds out something about who he is	Mary is dying; Elizabeth may become Queen
Refusal of the Call	Frodo is scared witless, doesn't want to do it	Confusion – Luke feels pulled by the two parts of the Force	Elizabeth denies all ambition to save her life
Meeting with the Mentor	Meets Gandalf	Meets Yoda	Walsingham and others advise Elizabeth
Crossing the First Threshold	Sets off to Mordor	Training; discovers the way of the Jedi	Takes first steps as queen
Tests, Allies, and Enemies	Adventures, Sam, Gollum	Adventures, Han Solo, Darth Vader	Wars and conspiracies
The Inner Cave	Final confrontations, the Ring gets stronger	Realises the connection between himself and Darth Vader	Treason discovered
Ordeal	Struggles with himself and Gollum – will he overcome the Ring's power?	Choice between Light and Dark Force	Elizabeth must act against those dearest to her
Reward	Chooses to throw the Ring into the fire	Chooses the Light Force, destroys the Death Star	Her reign is on a sure footing
The Road Back	Gives up hope but is content, and is then rescued	Returns to his friends	She must look to the future
Resurrection	Recovers his strength	Becomes a man	She renounces marriage and the possibility of love
Return with the Elixir	Leaves; life goes on as before, but better	Everyone cheers	She has absolute power and security

Telling the tale of the footloose, good-looking young man in the Australian soap opera

Here we offer an imaginary story called 'The Footloose, Good-Looking Young Man In The Australian Soap Opera'.

A young man, Carl (he's always called Carl), comes to live in the area. He's good-hearted enough but is always getting into trouble — nothing bad, just kids' stuff. He lives a happily aimless existence surfing, hanging out, and chasing girls. (Ordinary World)

Carl really likes a girl called Carla (she's always called Carla), who's way out of his league. One day he tells her how he feels. Carla says that she can't possibly have a serious relationship with an aimless drifter like him. The same day, Carla is rescued from a mugger by a rather hunky policeman. Inspired, Carl thinks, 'That's for me,' and informs his disbelieving slacker mates that he's going to join the police. (Call To Adventure)

Carl applies to join the police. They turn him down, because he hasn't passed his maths exam. Carl doesn't like being made to feel stupid, and he's always had a bit of a chip on his shoulder about his lack of education, and so he tells the police to forget it. He goes off feeling sorry for himself, gets drunk, and falls asleep on the beach. (Refusal of the Call)

Carl is found hung-over on the beach by Mad Bob, who's on his way to do a bit of early-morning surfing. Mad Bob is the only person in town who's never been judgemental about Carl or given him a hard time. Mad Bob, we see now, isn't mad at all, just a man who goes his own way. Mad Bob is also, it turns out, a retired maths teacher. He offers to give Carl maths coaching. If Carl works really hard, he can sit the exam just in time to get into Police Training School. Elated, Carl agrees. (Meeting with the Mentor)

Carl works hard for the first time in his life. Mad Bob gives him a hard time. They earn each other's respect. Carl sits and passes the maths exam and then re-applies to the police. His application is accepted. (Crossing the First Threshold)

Carl's fellow police cadets make his police basic training difficult. His main persecutor is Kyle, who knows about Carl's hooligan past and makes sure that everyone else knows about it too. The other cadets, under Kyle's influence, treat Carl as an outsider. The hard-ass training officer thinks Carl is a slacker and a bad influence, and gives him a really hard time. Several times Carl is about to quit, but he doesn't want to let Mad Bob down, the only person who's ever believed in him. Only one other cadet, Kyle's girlfriend, called Kylie (it's always Kylie), somehow sees into Carl's heart and encourages him to stick at it. (Tests, Allies, and Enemies)

Against all the odds, through sheer bloody-mindedness, Carl sticks it out. The final test (about which the hard-ass training officer has repeatedly said, 'Fail this and you're history') is a practical exercise performed at night, which involves two teams of cadets paddling small canoes to a beach covered with giant spiders and crabs. Buried in the sand are hessian sacks full of jelly-beans. The cadets have to locate the sacks and bring them home before dawn. Carl seems reluctant to go and is accused of cowardice by the hard-ass training officer. Carl confesses to Kylie that he suffers from night blindness, hates crabs, is frightened of spiders, phobic about canoes, allergic to sand and hessian sacking, and hates jelly-beans. This exercise is the ultimate test for him. Carl tells Kylie that he's going to drop out. Kylie's eyes fill with tears of disappointment, and she says that maybe Kyle was right, he'll always be a loser. (The Inner Cave)

(continued)

(continued)

As the cadets prepare to go on the exercise, Carl turns up just in time. He has spent all day committing the map to memory. He paddles successfully to the beach. He forces himself to ignore the crabs and spiders, and is able to pick up the sack without gasping for breath, due to the asthma pills that Kylie has secretly given him. (Ordeal)

Kyle encourages the other cadets to have a jelly-bean party on the beach. They all become ill due to jelly-bean over-consumption. Only Carl and Kylie (who is starting to see Kyle's true character) haven't eaten the beans, and so are unaffected. A sudden storm springs up and sweeps away all their packs, including compasses, maps, and so on. The other cadets are confused and frightened, and belatedly recognising Carl's leadership qualities as demonstrated by his foresight in memorising the map and in not eating all his jelly beans, turn their backs on Kyle and appeal to Carl for help. (Reward)

Carl has the choice of leaving his fellow cadets in danger and returning alone in triumph, or staying to help them. He guides them all home. Kyle lies about what happened and tries to take the credit. The training officer accuses Carl of exposing everyone to danger. The other cadets tell the truth about Kyle, and they acknowledge that they were wrong all along and that Carl saved them. Kyle is expelled in disgrace, and Carl is now one of the gang. (The Road Back)

The now-united best-friends-forever group of cadets graduate together, and, led by Mad Bob with tears running down his cheeks, applaud frantically at the moment when Carl receives his police badge. (Resurrection)

The training officer shakes Carl's hand and confesses that he misjudged him. Carla looks up into Carl's eyes and says, 'I'm so proud of you.' Carl ignores Carla and embraces Kylie, who believed in him and stood by him throughout their training. Everyone except the snobbish Carla cheers wildly. (Return with the Elixir)

Roll credits, and that's the Hero's Journey over.

Of course, not all good stories feature the same 12 stages in the same order. You don't necessarily need all 12 stages in your story, and you certainly don't need to give them equal space. Notice that the stories in the table combine the elements of the Hero's Journey in different ways. The time given to one particular stage in the journey varies in each story. Notice also that the story of Elizabeth is not a triumphal march; she's called upon to make great sacrifices along the way.

You don't have to be writing a fantasy epic to find the Hero's Journey useful. The Hero's Journey can be completed without a knight, sword, small hairy-footed person, ring, or spaceship in sight. It can be David Copperfield's journey in Charles Dickens' novel, and it can be the journey taken by Billy Elliott from the coalfields of Yorkshire to the stage at Sadler's Wells. It can be Johnny Cash's journey from drug-addled egomania to acceptance and redemption (journeys often end in redemption of some sort), and it can equally be Thomas Cromwell's journey from the slums of London to being the most powerful man in the land, to . . . but you should read it for yourself. Each story has a slightly different take on the Hero's Journey, but they all use it to help structure the story.

The Hero's Journey works on all sorts of levels of story-telling, but broadly speaking the Hero's Journey works best with big themes – stories involving strong central characters who are actively engaged in pursuing some form of quest.

Great story-tellers mix things up and use the classic stories as jumping-off points for new departures; that's part of what makes them great. Nevertheless, the Hero's Journey is a useful way of thinking about how to structure your story. Just give a bit of time to thinking about how, if at all, the template applies to your own work. Like everything else in this book, take what you need from it.

Typecasting Your Heroes

Heroes come in many shapes and sizes. The point is not that they're all bulging with muscles or beauty, have incredible intellect, or perform daring exploits. Heroes do things that require unusual qualities – or, more correctly, unusual quantities of familiar qualities. For instance, they may be unusually tenacious or persistent and refuse to give in. Their courage may be physical, or it may be moral. A mother who refuses to accept that her son is guilty of murder when everyone else believes that he did it, and who devotes her life and all her resources to proving his innocence even though the whole town is against her, eventually achieving his release at the cost of her health and her pension, is just as heroic as a soldier who refuses to abandon his post. The point is that the template of the Hero's Journey can help you frame the story, because the journey includes victories and reverses, allows for tragedy as well as triumph, and reminds readers that the night is darkest before the dawn.

The hero as John Wayne

Larger-than-life people make good central characters. Readers like to follow their exploits, and they are (at least superficially) more interesting than characters who aren't as talented, strong, or heroic. Heroes also tend, as the old saying has it, to run towards the sound of cannon fire instead of running as fast as they can in the opposite direction like the rest of us. This tendency means that their lives are often more obviously exciting.

If you don't want your *protagonist* (your main character) to be heroic, fair enough, but having the character attached in some way to someone who is heroic is often useful, because action tends to surround heroic types.

Remember that women are often involved in this sort of heroism, and make just as interesting stories. Joan of Arc is an excellent example (with the added interest of having an unusual mentor in God).

The hero as your mum or dad

Not all heroes are obviously heroic. A single parent bringing up a disabled child on a low income isn't as obviously heroic as someone who charges a machine gun nest, but both actions involve self-sacrifice and provoke admiration.

You can argue that in some ways doing something exciting and dangerous once in the heat of the moment is easier than doing something necessary but difficult and unglamorous for years on end.

The story of a woman who looks after her children because she loves kids and has never wanted to do anything else is less interesting than the woman who could have been a prima ballerina but sacrifices her career to look after her disabled daughter. Neither person is morally superior to the other, but from a writing point of view which character grabs the reader's interest is in little doubt. The more someone has to lose, the more interesting the story is likely to be. Note that what the person has to lose can be material, emotional, or spiritual.

The hero as Gandhi

The trick in making a cerebral, altruistic, non-action hero interesting is to show why the person's conduct matters.

Nelson Mandela was a hero to many people because of his dignity and his refusal to allow nearly 30 years in prison to bend his spirit, not because of his military activities.

If the person imprisoned is a loner who sat and watched TV most of his life and has the imagination of a jellyfish, his wrongful imprisonment is still an outrage but his story is not particularly interesting. (At least, not from the outside. No doubt someone could write it as such.)

However, if the wrongfully imprisoned person is a scientist with a questing mind, vivid imagination, and an interest in finding a cure for cancer, as well as having a loving husband and small children who need her desperately, almost any reader is going to be interested in reading about her (even before she manages to keep her self-respect and not fall apart or sign some dubious confession just to get released). Her imprisonment matters not just because of the injustice it represents, but also because it impacts others and society.

The leader of the Burmese opposition, Aung San Suu Kyi, was held under house arrest for many years. At any time she could have secured her freedom by agreeing to the conditions imposed by the Government. She refused, but was eventually released. This story matters, again partly because of the injustice it represents, but also because of the question it poses: everyone hopes that they're brave, but truthfully, what would you – and your hero – do in Aung San Suu Kyi's situation?

The unexpected hero

Some heroes know why they're in a situation, such as a soldier in a battle. Other heroes are thrust into situations accidentally. Someone who intervenes to prevent someone else being mugged doesn't usually have the luxury of considered preparation, but acts on impulse or instinct. Writing about such heroes prompts readers to ask themselves whether they'd do the same thing. Some people may say that such behaviour's foolhardy, others that it's admirable. Either way, the story is interesting because it speaks to the reader.

You also need to think about the different effect that someone's background, and the context against which they're acting, has upon their action. The story of an elderly woman with cancer, no family, and a week to live, who risks her life leaves a different feeling to the tale of a young, newly married, pregnant woman, about to start her dream job, who takes the same risk. We repeat: one isn't better or worse than the other, but they are different. The situations in which you choose to place your characters make readers react differently to them.

The hero who isn't

You can of course – at least in theory! – have a hero who does almost nothing at all in a story that has almost no action at all. You don't have to have a quest, a mentor, or any of the Hero's Journey stuff. Certainly, in some stories the Hero's Journey just doesn't make sense (although you can still draw on parts of it).

A protagonist can just sit on the sofa for at least some of the story and still be a hero. However, maintaining interest in such a character is difficult. You need a delicate touch and a fine sense of irony to draw out what matters in the story and keep the reader interested.

The story of alcoholics whose conflict is internal and whose struggle is mostly with themselves is one example. They're trying to move themselves from a state of alcoholism to a state of sobriety. The story matters because if they don't they make it, they lose their children. (The children don't have to appear in the story; the reader just needs to be aware of them.) Writing this sort of story as your first novel sets the bar very high.

We suggest that, if you want to write a novel about an alcoholic, you don't entirely internalise the conflicts. Have the character's struggle be at least as much external as internal, write scenes about the effect upon friends, family, and so on. Doing so makes the story easier to manage, and there's no reason why you need to lose the psychological insight.

Chapter 5

Scheming and Plotting: Using Stories

*T*his chapter helps you to use 'story' effectively in your writing. We describe the idea of story, and then talk about how you can use it in your work.

Every novel needs a story. In fact, that's one definition of a novel as opposed to a piece of journalism or a description. Of course, lots of different stories exist (well, about seven anyhow, as we show in this chapter), and lots of different ways of approaching them. Once you understand the basic principles, you can play with them to your heart's content.

Trying to Separate Plot, Story, and Narrative

> *Story is chasing your characters up a tree and then throwing rocks at them.*
>
> Gore Vidal (author)

As a writer, you need to understand the interconnection between your novel's plot, story, and narrative. In the following sections, we offer definitions and ways of looking at these ingredients.

Differentiating plot and story

Plot and story are closely related – in some dictionaries they're almost synonymous – but from a novel writer's point of view they aren't quite the same thing:

- ✔ *Plot* is the plan, or structure, of a novel.
- ✔ *Story* is the events – the things that happen in a novel.

Put another way, plot is the frame and story is the picture: plot includes elements like setting, theme, and so on, which put the story in a context.

Keep in mind that the events in your story don't happen in a vacuum. Think of needing a good skeleton (the plot) to hold up the rest of the body (the story). If the skeleton isn't strong, all the body parts end up in a muddled heap in the floor instead of walking proud.

Many novels feature a fair bit of overlap between plot and story, so that it isn't always clear which is which. But don't worry: you can blend them both and come out all right.

A quick and very unscientific poll among our friends revealed much confusion about the use of the terms story and plot. In this chapter, we keep things simple by using the term story to mean plot as well. Therefore, we take the picture and the frame together.

Telling a story, not a narrative

Ever been trapped by the Dull Guy? He starts talking, and ten minutes later you're wondering whether life is worth living any more. The Dull Guy doesn't understand the difference between narrative and story. An example from EM Forster's *Aspects of the Novel* illustrates the difference:

- ✔ **Narrative:** The king died. A week later, the queen died.
- ✔ **Story:** The king died. A week later, the queen died of grief.

In this book, we use *narrative* to mean a story without motive, or, if you like, narrative gives you the what, whereas story gives you the why as well.

Story also tells you what happened but incorporates certain other important features as well:

- **Motivation:** Story tells you *why* something happened. Narrative isn't interested in why, it only tells you what. Stories are about motive and consequence and things happening for a reason.

- **Relevance:** Story tells you only the things you need to know to fill in useful background and make sense of the events. Narrative often rambles on about people and events completely unrelated to the point of the story. Inform your reader only on a need-to-know basis.

- **Contrast:** Story understands that you need light and shade. Narrative gives everything equal importance, spending as much time on what the weather is like as on the funny thing that happens. Story speeds up, slows down, balances humour and seriousness, and shouts and whispers. Narrative drones.

Take a break. Go find yourself a story.

So Many Stories, So Little Time

Some people say there are just six basic stories. Others say there are seven, ten, thirty-six, or just one. The number of stories varies depending on how you approach it. The various contenders aren't really in conflict, they're just different ways of looking at the idea of story. You pays your money, and you chooses your angle.

We suggest that the most useful approach is that there are seven basic stories.

Sticking with the seven most useful stories

Table 5-1 covers just about every situation you need for a novel. The Requirements column is the classic story, but notice that the entries in the Examples column (including films and folklore as well as books) play around with the basic idea. *Bridget Jones's Diary* isn't everyone's idea of a Cinderella story, but it tells the tale of a woman who thinks of herself as unattractive and unworthy of attention who then finds herself being courted by the handsome prince – or two! – in classic Cinderella fashion.

Table 5-1	The Seven Basic Stories		
Name	**Also Known As**	**Requirements**	**Examples**
Achilles	The Hero with the Fatal Flaw The Tragic Hero	A noble character is brought down by a flaw in character	*Othello*, Tristan in *Legends of the Fall*, Captain Ahab in *Moby Dick*, Sir Lancelot in King Arthur, Achilles
Cinderella	Virtue Ultimately Rewarded	A character eventually triumphs through great virtue or constancy	*Jane Eyre*, *Billy Elliot*, *Cold Mountain*, Sir Galahad in King Arthur most Catherine Cookson novels
The Eternal Triangle	Two's Company, but Three, well . . .	A relationship is harmed through the impossibility of everyone having all that they desire	King Arthur/ Sir Lancelot/ Guinevere, *The English Patient*, *Gone With The Wind*, *The End of the Affair*, *Brief Encounter*, *Martin Guerre*, *Bridget Jones's Diary*
Romeo and Juliet	The Star-crossed Lovers	Two people fall in love, but events conspire to prevent them living happily ever after	*Charlotte Grey*, *Brief Encounter*, *King Kong*, *Harold and Maude*, *Pride and Prejudice*, *The Lord of the Rings*, *Martin Guerre*, *Romeo and Juliet*, *Lancelot and Guinevere*

Name	Also Known As	Requirements	Examples
The Holy Grail	The Quest The Perilous Journey	A character goes on a journey fraught with peril, to find, collect, or deliver something of value	Sir Galahad's story in King Arthur, *The Killing Fields, Rocky, Saving Private Ryan, The Lord of the Rings, Cold Mountain, Moby Dick, The Impossible*
Nemesis	The Past Waiting To Pounce	A secret emerges from the past to haunt the protagonist	*Rebecca, The Human Stain, The Mayor of Casterbridge, King Arthur, Martin Guerre, The Lord of the Rings, Romeo and Juliet*
Triumph of Good Over Evil	'What Fiction Means', according to Oscar Wilde	After the Good Guys undergo many trials and tribulations, the Bad Guys get a kicking	*The Lord of the Rings, Robin Hood, Gladiator, High Noon, Schindler's List, King Arthur, James Bond*

Most stories involve more than one of these seven basic stories, and most can fit comfortably into more than one category. Note that *Brief Encounter* is in two categories in Table 5-1. *The Lord of the Rings* has most of the seven basic stories – unsurprisingly, because it's a very long trilogy. The story of King Arthur has them all as well. *Martin Guerre* is Romeo and Juliet, the Eternal Triangle, and Nemesis. Shakespeare's *Romeo and Juliet*, the template for a story category, is also a Nemesis story. *Cold Mountain* is both Virtue Ultimately Rewarded and a Quest. And so on.

Every story also includes its opposite and everything in between. A Quest, for example, can be very successful (*The Lord of the Rings*), narrowly unsuccessful (*Cold Mountain*), or as in *Moby Dick*, both successful (the whale dies) and unsuccessful (so does just about everyone else). The triumph of good in *Schindler's List* is small when set against the evil that surrounds it, but that's the point.

Most of these examples play with the audience's expectations. For example, a James Bond novel (and film) always ends with Bond victorious, which means that 'Good Triumphs Over Evil', hurrah, but Bond is sometimes a pretty unpleasant character who stoops to more or less any method (boo) to get results. However, the category 'Quite Evil Actually (But Nevertheless On Our Side And So A Good Thing) Triumphs Over Really Very Evil Enemies Indeed' doesn't have quite the same ring. But you get the point.

As you can see from just these few examples, the seven stories come in many forms. The point is finding ways to take these familiar stories and tell them in unexpected ways, mixing familiar ingredients into unfamiliar combinations, and so making new dishes.

Working with the seven basic stories

Writing your own story becomes much clearer after you decide which combination of the seven stories your own novel will contain. Each story has conventions, demands, expectations, and so on: you can decide to go along with the story, go against it, or use some aspects and do something else with the rest of the story. Knowing which of the seven stories your own story resembles gives you a road to travel on, from which you can decide to take side trips or a different route altogether.

You can use the descriptions in the following sections to help you decide what aspects of the seven stories will help your own writing.

Dipping into Achilles

The protagonist in this story needs to have great potential. This may manifest itself as a special talent, academic brilliance, unusual creativity, a great capacity for leadership, or a special knack for inspiring affection. The point is that your protagonist has the capability to achieve something extraordinary, whether discovering a cure for cancer, painting a masterpiece, or making their partner happier than they ever dreamed possible.

Having established that your protagonist has the potential to achieve great things – and has probably already achieved some of them – you must now show the character flaw that may prevent this person from succeeding.

Your book tells the story of how the protagonist struggles to achieve their potential despite the flaw.

Consider the following list of protagonists, each one suggesting different possibilities. For simplicity they're painted in black and white (but remember that the writing process is one of infinite shades of grey!):

✔ A brilliant scientist whose arrogance alienates her co-workers. Your story can consider what effect this may have on:

- Her career

- The project she's engaged in with her colleagues

- The people who may benefit from the success of the project

- Her personal relationships

Any of these scenarios – and lots more – are potential stories.

✔ A champion boxer past his prime whose pride won't let him refuse a challenge or lose a contest, and so he's badly beaten in a fight that he didn't need to take on. Consider the effect on:

- His health

- His pride

- His personal relationships

- His job prospects

✔ A beautiful and gifted film star who can't admit to herself that she's growing older, and so embarks on a disastrous obsessive affair with a much younger man who she knows doesn't love her. Does this action:

- Make her feel young?

- Make her feel old?

- Save her pride?

- Delay the inevitable?

- Bring her happiness?

- Bring her sadness?

✔ A successful general who won't admit defeat even against overwhelming odds, and so loses his army because he refuses to retreat when he has the chance. Does he:

- Admit his mistake?

- Deny his mistake?

- Become honest with himself, his peers, or his family?

- Become a better or worse soldier?

✔ A husband who loves his wife deeply and is everything to her, but who can't remain faithful, and so destroys their relationship:

- Does this bring him happiness or sorrow?

- How does it affect his wife?

- What effect does it have on him?

These protagonists all share certain characteristics:

- ✔ A talent or quality that makes them potentially admirable
- ✔ A capacity to give or achieve greatness
- ✔ A flaw in their own character that may prevent them from achieving their potential

Rewarding virtue in Cinderella

The main character in a Cinderella story possesses something of value or embodies a quality or set of values that other people or circumstances want to take away from them.

The coveted item may be:

- ✔ A possession such as a ring, car, rifle, or painting.
- ✔ A quality such as innocence, goodness, or a free spirit.
- ✔ A physical trait such as a great singing voice, a beautiful face, or enormous strength.

For the protagonist to lose the thing, whatever it is, would be unbearable. Usually the person wanting to take it away has evil intentions, but that isn't essential – in fact, doing it for love can be even more interesting.

The reward for the protagonists here is in the constancy of their position, rather than in a victory. They may win, but that isn't the point. The point is their faith in their own beliefs or position.

Getting caught up in the Eternal Triangle

In this story, usually all three relationships are at least possible, and however briefly, each one should appear to be likely at some point in the story. The attraction is usually reciprocated at some point. That said, stories in which someone is stalked and terrified by a vicious psychopath can also fall under this category – as we keep saying, the conventional story is a jumping-off point not a restriction.

The tension in an Eternal Triangle story comes from the fact that the characters are torn between the possibilities, knowing that they can't have everything they want. This applies to both the conventional story and the stalker one.

A triangle doesn't have to be all about people, of course. A protagonist may be torn between a wonderful job that involves living permanently in Japan, and an adored lover who can't live anywhere but in France.

Enduring romance with Romeo and Juliet

This must be the oldest and most common story of all stories. This story has the most clichés and therefore the greatest number of expectations on the part of your reader.

Use your reader's familiarity. Surprise your reader with who you make fall in love, put unsuspected obstacles in the lovers' way, and drag them through as much complication and upset as you can.

Seeking out the Holy Grail

The Grail can be concrete, something that you can hold in your hand, or it can be a discovery that the main character needs to experience or find out.

The quest doesn't necessarily have to be good, honourable, or worthwhile. Nor does it have to be earth-shattering. (In the film of a real journey in *The Straight Story*, the protagonist wants to mend his relationship with his brother before he dies.)

The important thing is that the grail and the quest matter to the protagonist. (See Chapter 6 for more on the importance of things mattering.) If having a cup of coffee in a particular café is all that your character can think about, that cup of coffee is the Holy Grail.

Facing a Nemesis

Any story in which something or someone from the past comes back to haunt the protagonist is a Nemesis story.

A nemesis can be almost anything at all: a big secret or an event that didn't mean much at the time. It needs to have some connection to at least one of the characters – probably the protagonist. The important thing is that at the point when you're telling the story, the nemesis must affect the lives of the characters in a new way.

Chronicling the Triumph of Good over Evil

All readers think they know what's going to happen in this story. It doesn't matter how deep you bury the hero, how many bullets you fire into her, how high the cliff you throw her over, the reader knows that she isn't really dead and is going to reappear just in time to save the day. The cavalry arrives just before the last bullet is gone, not just after.

Except, of course, good doesn't always triumph – at least not completely. However, be very aware that if you allow evil to win, your reader may feel disappointed, cheated, or even threatened.

A good (and realistic) compromise is for good to win overall, but for enough evil to remain at large that readers know that work is still to be done. ('That good man died so that I could live, and I owe it to his memory to clean up this town, and I swear I'm not going to stop until the whole filthy rat's nest is sent to hell!' Loud cheers from assembled newly courageous citizenry, and close the book.)

Realising Every Story Has Been Told

Immature poets imitate; mature poets steal.

TS Eliot (poet)

Many writers worry. They worry that their story is too influenced by books they've read and that their story isn't original. If you're one of these worrying writers, here's some advice for you: don't.

Of course you're influenced by what you've read. They wouldn't be very good books if they didn't influence you in some way. Shakespeare got most of his best stories from Raphael Holinshed's chronicles.

A writer worrying about whether a story is original is like someone who makes pots worrying whether clay is an original medium to work with. It isn't what you choose, it's what you do with your choices that matters.

Of course your story isn't original. That's the point of this whole chapter.

You can decide to write the corniest, most hackneyed, clichéd, old-fashioned boy-meets-girl, boy-loses-girl, boy-gets-girl story. You then have two options:

- ✔ You can borrow from the novel you read last week and every other clichéd story you know and write something a lot like it.
- ✔ You can do what good writers do and take what you need from everything you've ever seen, heard, or read, and use that as a jumping-off point.

Boy meets girl. Where? In a spaceship – a really big one like in *2001: A Space Odyssey*. Where are they going? They don't know. Boy is a retired pilot, invalided out, rich kid, behaves a bit like . . . who? Mr Darcy from *Pride and Prejudice*? Fine. Looks a bit like your mate Harry, but maybe taller and more serious, like James Stewart. Girl is a munitions expert, no, a sniper, on a special mission. She's Lara Croft, but played by Meg Ryan – kookier, less knowing. No, Lara Croft, Meg Ryan's kookiness, but looking a lot like that girl you had a crush on in the sixth form. With longer hair.

And so on. The point is to plunder everything you need from wherever you find it, and mix it up. Don't be hesitant; don't worry about it. Dive in; it's way more fun.

A brief note on plagiarism

Copying someone's work exactly and presenting it as your own is a very bad idea. Not only is it lazy, illegal, and immoral, it's also stupid and unnecessary (and you're almost certain to get found out). Millions of stories are out there, zillions of possible combinations of events, characters, and places. Why copy someone else when new stories are lying around waiting to be picked up?

How do you tell what's plagiarism and what isn't? Use your common sense. You can't write a book about Hobbits and talking trees set in a place called Middle Earth, but you can write about strange people called the Barti who live in a land called Gwandrig where fish can walk and pigs smoke pipes. (Actually, someone probably already has, but you see what we mean.) The whole point of this book is that you don't need to copy someone else's work.

Chapter 6

Considering the Grand Concept

Discovering what you're trying to say in your novel isn't always easy: sometimes the author's the last to know. This chapter helps you explore your novel's themes and distil its essence, which can be a crucial skill when it comes to selling your book to people.

Finding Your Theme

The theme of your story is, in essence, the answer to the question, 'So, what's your book about?' We don't mean an answer like, 'Well, it's about this bloke who comes down to London to see his girlfriend . . .'. That's the story, not the theme. The theme is what you're examining in telling the story. Most books have more than one theme, but having one main theme and other subsidiary themes is a good idea (and makes the book easier to write). Table 6-1 shows the main and subsidiary themes of some well-known books.

A novel's main theme isn't necessarily the same for every reader. Different people have particular themes that resonate very powerfully with them because of personal experience or strong conviction. So, you can have conversations about a book with people who say something like, 'I thought the book was about slavery,' and you think, 'Well, sure, that's one of the themes, but I thought it was about the importance of families sticking together.' You may both be right.

Table 6-1	Main and Subsidiary Themes	
Novel and Author	*Main Theme*	*A Subsidiary Theme*
Pride and Prejudice by Jane Austen	Nineteenth-century social mores	Love across social boundaries
Wolf Hall by Hilary Mantel	Power	Staying human under pressure
We Need to Talk About Kevin by Lionel Shriver	A mother's struggle to understand her psychotic son	American culture
The Remains of the Day by Kazuo Ishiguro	A man's refusal to admit that he's wrong	Missed opportunities

A novel may also apparently be about one thing while actually being about something else. For example, you can read *Pride and Prejudice* as an amusing satire on upper-class people, until you realise that if the Bennet girls don't marry soon and marry well, they're going to be condemned to becoming governesses (at best) or taking the most menial jobs. Mrs Bennet's concerns therefore move from seeming to be just the social-climbing aspirations of a silly woman to being justified and clear-sighted concerns for her family's welfare. Similarly, *The Remains of the Day* may be read as a tale of one man's blindness to his situation, but it may also be seen as an allegory for society as a whole; the novel functions as both. Themes can operate as different levels within your story.

Having a theme ensures that your novel is about something. If someone asks you what your novel is about and you have to reply, 'Well, not much, really,' that isn't much of an enticement to read it. This doesn't mean that the theme of a book necessarily has to be an earth-shattering event. The theme of Jerome K Jerome's *Three Men in a Boat* is, arguably, 'wasting time', but the book is both interesting and highly amusing. So, ask yourself what your theme is.

A useful approach is to ask yourself, 'What do I care about in this story, and what do I hope the reader is going to care about?' The thing that you care about is your theme.

Testing Your Premise

> *Writing a story without a premise is like rowing a boat without oars.*
>
> James Frey (author)

The *premise* is the reason you're writing the story that you're writing. The premise is, if you like, the novel's purpose. You need a premise because that tells you that you have a story.

Ask yourself what the premise of your book is: what are you trying to show in the story? In what way is the ending related to the events preceding it? Premise is about cause and effect. You have a story in which your characters are involved in conflict and come to a conclusion; things happen as a result of other things happening.

If you can't find a premise in your story, we strongly suggest that you need to get one. A story without a premise is like a car without an engine. An engine-less car still looks like a car, but it doesn't do what cars should do: it doesn't move. A story that doesn't have a premise often *looks* like a story but it isn't one. Really, it just isn't.

In non-fiction, the premise is often easily seen, sometimes just by reading the title. A book called *A History of Julius Caesar's Wars in Gaul* is almost certainly just that. You can safely assume that the purpose of such a book is to tell about the wars Julius Caesar fought in Gaul, as promised in the title, and that the book presents the version of Julius Caesar that the author wants to persuade you is true – that he was a military genius, a charlatan who got lucky, or whatever belief the author holds.

As a reader of a non-fiction book, you consider the premise, test it against what you know of the subject and what others have written and said about it, and then accept or reject the author's view.

The premise or purpose of a novel works differently. A novel doesn't seek to prove what may be called a universal truth. For example, a novel can't persuade you that it's always wrong to kill people. A novel can only tell you that it's wrong to kill people in the situation described in the novel. It can only seek to persuade you that the story is true in its own terms. Fictional universal truths are hard to find.

Suppose you want to write a novel with the premise that 'all men are heartless swine'. You invent a character, Victor, who makes his way through life grabbing everything he wants and trampling anyone who gets in his way. He pursues people ruthlessly and carelessly, casting them off when he doesn't need them. He doesn't have a single redeeming quality. He leaves a trail of bad debts, broken hearts, and failed promises wherever he goes. Is Victor a heartless swine? Undoubtedly. Does the existence of Victor prove that *all* men are heartless swine? Of course not. The novel proves only that your invented character, Victor, is a swine.

Let's take a simple example. If a man dies in a duel fought with another man whose wife he's been having an affair with, the premise is that falling in love with other men's wives can get you killed. The premise is satisfied. If, however, the man falls in love with another man's wife, has an affair with her, and then gets run over by a car while on a business trip, the premise is . . . what? That cars are on earth to punish the adulterous? That doesn't work. You can tell that story, but you need a different premise.

Considering 'About-ness'

A lot of novels written aren't really about anything. They often have some good ideas, may be entertaining and well-written, and have interesting things in them, but they're still somehow lacking. The difference is between real nourishment and junk food: junk food fills you up and tastes great (sometimes), but it isn't like a proper meal.

A novel that's really *about* something can change the way you see the world, change the way you think, and change your life.

Sounds a bit serious? Sure, a lot of novels that are about things are serious, but a lot of them aren't. The point is not that your novel needs to be serious, but that you need to be clear about what – if anything – your intentions are, what you're trying to communicate to the reader, what the whole point of the story is, and what you want the reader to walk away thinking about.

Ask yourself:

- ✔ Why does my novel matter?
- ✔ What's the point?

Thousands of good books are available, and you need to figure out why anyone should read yours.

Novels have to be about something or they are about nothing much at all. They need about-ness.

Making Sure That It Matters

How many times have you put down a book halfway through or left a film saying, 'I don't really much care about these characters'? The rule is simple: things must matter. Whatever your story, if it doesn't matter to the characters, it isn't going to matter to the reader.

There are two main types of what we like to call *mattering*:

- ✔ **External threat:** This type of mattering is when characters are under a very obvious threat. If they are in danger of losing their lives, their homes, their livelihoods, or their best friends, obviously that matters – it would matter to anyone.
- ✔ **Internal importance:** This type of mattering is more subtle, and it is often the reason why stories can work even when nothing much happens.

For example, the idea of a rather domineering aunt visiting you probably isn't a big deal, but to PG Wodehouse's Bertie Wooster, a visit from his Aunt Agatha ('who wears barbed wire next to the skin') is an utter disaster. His aunt matters to him enormously, in a way that makes the reader sympathetic to his situation.

Imagine you're writing a story about an elderly man who's very ill, alone, and house-bound, and all he wants to do is visit the seaside one more time before he dies, even if it kills him, which it probably will. Even if he makes it to the seaside, it would be fair to say that, in the grand scheme of things, very little will happen. However, if getting to the seaside is his obsession, if it means more to him than living for another month, if he has nothing else left, it matters to the readers and they're sure to cheer him on.

Whatever the situation – no matter how trivial – as long as it matters to the character, the reader is going to care.

Think about the opposite, too. If a man is about to lose a house, that sounds important. But what if he has seven houses? Then it doesn't matter. But maybe this house was where he was born and brought up? Well, that matters. But he hasn't been there for over 20 years, he's been corrupted by money and success, and he's forgotten the things that used to be important to him. So it doesn't matter then? Ah, but his childhood sweetheart lives there now, and she represents what he was before success made a monster of him, so maybe it matters after all.

Explaining Your Concept

Would-be screenwriters trying to finish their scripts are often given the following scenario:

> You've written a screenplay. You know with every fibre of your being that it's wonderful. It's funny, sad, exciting, and it's got a part that Brad Pitt would kill for, but no matter how hard you try, you just can't seem to get anyone with any clout to actually read it. You know that if you were able to get someone to just read it they'd love it, but you can't get anyone to do that. You've spent yet another long day touting the screenplay around agencies in Hollywood with absolutely no success at all. You're very, very fed up.
>
> You decide to treat yourself to a restorative drink in the revolving restaurant on the 15th floor of a very famous hotel. You get into the lift. Only one other person is in it. You realise that the other person standing beside you is a Very Famous Film Director (VFFD), a man who you know from your obsessive reading of the movie trade papers is looking for a new project. The VFFD looks at you, smiles the smile of a man who's having a good day, and presses the button for the revolving restaurant.

You realise that you now have the VFFD's undivided attention for the time it takes the lift to get to the restaurant. The building is high and the lift is slow.

You have around 30 seconds to persuade the VFFD that the screenplay in your hand is the very thing he's looking for.

What do you say?

Now, put yourself in that position. You've 30 seconds to persuade a publisher to read your book. You say, 'Please, read my novel.' The publisher looks at you with the expression of someone who's heard that sentence a thousand times, the expression of a woman who's read novels all her life and is weary – weary to her bones of reading and being disappointed. But still, as you look deep into her eyes, you can just see a faintly flickering hope that the next novel she reads will be the one she's been waiting for all these years, the one that changes the way people think and buys her an island in the Seychelles. 'Okay,' she says, 'I'm very busy and I have dozens of other people asking me to read their novels, but I'll consider yours. What's your novel about?'

'Um. Loads of things.'

The publisher sits back, disappointed already. 'Right,' she says. 'Everyone says that. I'm sure that if I read all 400 pages I'd enjoy it. Just like all the other novels I'll be offered today. Unfortunately I don't have time to read any of them. It needs to be something special to lift it above all the others. So, what's so special about yours?'

'But . . .'.

'Unfortunately I only have 20 seconds left to listen to you.'

'But . . .'.

'Ten, now. So, go on, persuade me. Why should I read your novel instead of any of the others?'

Think like a Boy Scout. Be prepared. Find a way to say within 30 seconds why the average reader or the all-powerful publisher should spend good money to buy your novel and then spend a chunk of their short time on this earth reading it.

This exercise is one of the most useful that any fiction writer can do (whether you're a screenwriter, novelist, radio playwright – it doesn't matter). It's important not because you may get stuck in a lift with a publisher one day. It's important because if you can't answer the question, you aren't writing to the best of your ability.

Making your pitch

One way of explaining your novel within 30 seconds is to give what film folk call the *high-concept pitch*, which involves giving a list of reference points that don't need further explanation. The screenwriter may say something like, 'Imagine the story of *King Lear* set in a Texas oil company, but the chairman and his sidekicks are space aliens.' Or, 'It's *Jaws* meets *Invasion of the Body-Snatchers*, and only a bunch of nerdy red-haired step-children with glasses stand between the alien sharks and world domination.' Or, 'It's *Macbeth* set in a school for delinquent teenagers.'

You get the picture. This sort of thing can be useful for novelists too:

- ✔ Imagine Martin Amis writing *War and Peace* set 1,000 years in the future.

- ✔ It's as if JK Rowling wrote *Lord of the Flies* and set it in London in 1977. With jokes.

This exercise is useful (and quite fun). Try it for your own work. It gives you an idea of what's important.

Digging down to the bones

If you don't know why your novel is unusual, special, and worth reading, you need to sit down, look out of a window for a while, and have a good think.

Start by asking a key question: what's the centre of the novel? Your novel is crammed with all sorts of interesting characters, events, and themes. They're all related and all important, which is just as it should be.

But dig deeper and compare the relationship between the elements in your novel to the relationship between the bones in a skeleton. The pieces of your story need to be related to each other like your spine is related to your ribs – they're similar in content and they're all necessary. The difference is that you can take a rib away and the body can carry on. Take the spine away and the whole thing is just a heap of bones.

So, which bit of your novel is the bit that holds everything up, the bit without which everything else is just a heap of disconnected stuff?

If you know the answer, great. If you've looked out of the window for a long time and still don't know, don't worry: you're only planning and starting at this stage. But eventually you're going to need to know what your novel is really *about*, and there's no harm in thinking about it now.

Chapter 7

Structuring the Story

*T*elling a story isn't just a matter of starting at the beginning and carrying on until it's finished. Telling a story properly means giving it *pace* (making sure that it moves along fairly smartly) and *contrast* (making sure that it isn't all on one note, by mixing tragedy with humour, speeding up the action and intensity and then slowing it down, and so on). A useful way of thinking about these requirements is to imagine the story as an arc. At points on the arc you need to make sure that certain things are happening. For example, you need an arresting beginning, you need to set things up well, and you need to get to certain points in the story quickly. This chapter helps you do all these things.

The story-teller and the reader are engaged in a dance that's full of expectations and games. Make sure that you play the games well.

Beginning Well is Just the Start

> *We want a story that starts out with an earthquake and works its way up to a climax.*
>
> Samuel Goldwyn (film producer)

From a writer's point of view, Goldwyn's maxim is both the best and the worst sort of advice. The good part is that it reminds you to get the reader's attention from the first line of the story. The bad news is that it means that the bar is set incredibly high: if you begin with an earthquake, how do you prevent everything after it from being an anticlimax? Most stories containing an earthquake end with the earthquake; it's easier.

Assuming that you decide to have an earthquake, we suggest that you begin with the *idea* of an earthquake rather than the reality. If you begin the story with the earthquake in full spate, with screaming victims and collapsing buildings, you're making life hard for yourself. Instead, begin with the earthquake in the sense that the clues start to pile up that an earthquake is imminent: early, very small tremors; geologists' reports; and the mad psychic who says the sky is falling. (If you've read Robert Harris's novel *Pompeii*, you'll recognise this story.) If your story is about a relationship falling apart, let your readers know early on that, even though the relationship seems strong, something is not quite right. Of course, not every ending needs to be foreshadowed, but think of it as a long journey upward to your climax.

If you do decide to have an earthquake at the beginning of your novel, we suggest that you now have a choice. You can, of course, finish with a much bigger earthquake. That's tricky, because you risk selling one or other of the earthquakes short. However, it's a fair enough idea. Alternatively, you can use the earthquake as the motor of the story in a completely different way: society has been devastated by the earthquake, now what happens? An example of this sort of thing is Nevil Shute's *On The Beach*. This novel doesn't begin with an earthquake, it's even worse: it begins with a nuclear war. The world is coming to an end, what shall we do now? The book isn't about nuclear war as such, it's about the *consequences* of the war. The climax of the book is emotional rather than physical. If you're interested in this sort of story, read *On The Beach* to see how it can be done.

Your first sentence must make the reader want to read your second sentence, your first paragraph must make your reader want to read the next paragraph, your first page must make the reader want to turn it over, and so on. Keep the chain strong.

Supplying the needs of your first paragraph

The first paragraph needs to be wonderful, exciting, and perfect, of course, but realistically it needs four things:

- ✔ To grab the reader's attention
- ✔ To set the tone for the story
- ✔ To give information
- ✔ To make the reader want to turn the page

The first paragraph *doesn't* need:

- ✔ A big lump of description with nothing happening
- ✔ A trick or surprise that doesn't work
- ✔ A sense of confusion

Your first paragraph is very important, and so spending time on it is worthwhile. Your opening paragraph is the book's calling card, and can either persuade or dissuade the reader. It has to be every bit as good as you can make it.

The crucial point is to offer a world that the reader wants to experience. Of course, not all experiences and worlds are to every reader's taste. Not everyone enjoys the same things. However, focus on establishing that something interesting is going on and the reader is well advised to pursue it further.

Knowing what readers look for

Consider a potential buyer for your novel. He's standing in an airport, embarking on a transatlantic journey, when he suddenly realises that he has a ten-hour flight in front of him and nothing to read. He rushes to the newsagent, but doesn't see any books that his friends have recommended, and he isn't interested in the latest bestseller that's advertised all over the place. He wants to buy something new, to discover a fresh reading pleasure. So, what does he do? He does exactly what everybody does in any bookshop, except perhaps he does it slightly more quickly. Confronted with shelves full of books, typical book buyers follow these steps:

1. **They pick up the nearest book with an interesting title or a nice cover.**

   This sounds shallow, but think about it: when did you last pick up a book with a boring cover and a dull title?

2. **They flip it over and glance at the back blurb.**

   They may glance at the endorsements as well if they recognise the person supplying them.

3. **They open the front cover and read the first paragraph.**

   Then, more often than not, they put the book back and pick up another one. The whole process takes around 30 seconds. Not much of an audition for a piece of writing that probably took a couple of years of effort.

Most people buy a book because something in the first paragraph makes them want to read it. This something is called the *hook*. The hook can be any number of things – a killer first sentence, a weird situation, something funny – but the point is that, like a hook catching on your clothing, it snags your attention. It stops you putting the book down again and picking up the next one. It makes you think, 'Ah, this book's for me, I'll enjoy this.' The hook is why people buy a book: after all, it's why *you* buy a book.

So have a look at what's on the first page of your novel. Never mind the beautifully written 300 pages that follow it. Yes, you need them, but they aren't important at this stage. No one is ever going to read those beautifully written pages if the first paragraph – and indeed, the second and third – doesn't make them want to buy the book. Your beginning may be well written, it may be true, but does it hook someone who looks at it for just 30 seconds?

Choosing your hook: Covering who, what, when, where, and why – or not

Aspiring journalists are often told that the first paragraph of a newspaper story needs to contain the information who, what, when, where, and why. This advice is probably true and useful for a journalist, but as a novel writer you need to approach things differently. You can reveal all the information about your story to the reader, you can hide most of it until the end, you can dole it out in small chunks throughout the story, or you can take any combination of these approaches. The point is that, for the novelist, information is power. Think about detective novels (for example, those of Agatha Christie). If you give away the murderer's name on the third page, this defeats the purpose of a whodunnit. Equally, if you give away too little information, the reader doesn't have a chance of working out the identity of the murderer and will lose interest in the plot. You need to create a balance, and if you do it right, the giving and withholding of information creates hooks to pull the reader into and through the story.

The following sections explain how you can use and manipulate the details of who, what, when, where, and why to make compelling hooks.

Omitting information

Providing enough information to tantalise your readers while leaving out key bits makes readers want to uncover the whole picture. Of course, the information you include has to be interesting enough to make readers want to pursue the story.

Don't play the withholding game for too long; readers quickly get the feeling that they're being played with. But a first paragraph that makes promises before launching into the story is a first paragraph that works.

Take a very simple beginning such as, 'The man lay still on the beach, left behind by the receding tide. He had been dead for over an hour.' This opening tells you some of what (an un-named man), some of where (on a beach somewhere), and a bit of when (you assume it's the present, and you're told he's been there an hour). It doesn't tell you who he is (someone important?) or, crucially, why he's there (murdered? drowned? sick?). The reader, you hope, wants to find out what's going on.

The following sentences need to build on this hook. 'The autopsy determined that his lungs were dry. He was dead before he went into the water. A small pearl-handled penknife protruded between his sixth and seventh ribs, and a livid bruise covered his right cheek and temple. Neither of these injuries was the cause of his death.' Detail sucks readers in. Who stabs someone with a penknife? Not a professional killer for sure. And who's been hitting him? And why? And what did kill him?

Some stories concentrate on one of the five possibilities (who? what? why? and so on). Take the beginning of Carlos Fuentes' *The Old Gringo*: 'Now she sits alone and remembers. She sees, over and over, the spectres of Tomas Arroyo and the moon-faced woman and the old gringo cross her window. But they are not ghosts. They have simply mobilised their old pasts, hoping that she would do the same and join them.' You immediately wonder who 'she' is. You're hooked by the suggestion of the supernatural, expressed in terms that suggest it's normal, and the what and why questions are both invoked.

The aim of this sort of first paragraph is to get readers to wonder 'What on earth is going on here?' so that they buy the book to find out. You need to put in information that the reader finds provoking, interesting, or mysterious, and/or leave out information that makes the reader think, 'Oh, I see', or 'yes, I knew that,' and move on to the next book on the shelf.

Kicking off with quirky

The first couple of sentences of Steven Sherrill's *The Minotaur Takes a Cigarette Break* combine deadpan prose with strangeness of subject: 'The Minotaur sits on an empty pickle bucket blowing smoke through bullish nostrils. He sits near the dumpster on the dock of the kitchen at Grub's Rib smoking and watching JoeJoe, the dishwasher, dance on the thin strip of crumbling asphalt that begins three steps down . . . .'.

Readers are apparently told who straight away, but in a way that just makes them ask the what question even more loudly. 'Hang on a minute! The Minotaur? The bull-man thing that Theseus killed? Smoking while sitting on a pickle bucket? What's going on here?'

Singling out one detail

You don't need to be wilfully strange; you can create a very ordinary situation and disrupt it with a single incongruous detail.

James Meek's *The People's Act of Love* begins as follows: 'When Kyrill Ivanovich Samarin was twelve, years before he would catch, among the scent of textbooks and cologne in a girl's satchel, the distinct odour of dynamite, he demanded that his uncle let him change his second name. He didn't want to be 'Ivanovich' any more.'

A seemingly ordinary boy who wants to change his name (which is already a bit unusual, though hardly unique) is suddenly someone who recognises the scent of dynamite – and in a girl's school satchel of all the unlikely places. Bang! The reader is hooked.

Giving most but not all

David Lodge's *Author, Author* begins like this: 'London. December 1915. In the master bedroom (never was the estate agent's epithet more appropriate) of Flat 21, Carlyle Mansions, Cheyne Walk, Chelsea, the distinguished author is dying – slowly, but surely. In Flanders, less than two hundred miles away, other men are dying more quickly, more painfully, more pitifully – young men, mostly, with their lives still before them, blank pages that will never be filled.'

Here you're given the who (Henry James, the 'distinguished author'), the what (two of them: a dying man and a battlefield), the when (December 1915), and the where (London and Flanders). What you don't know is the why. Why is the author telling us about this death, and why is he drawing a parallel with the deaths in Flanders?

The prose echoes that of Henry James, who is the dying author. The reference to blank pages is deliberate. This paragraph is quietly interesting, and the hook is subtle. Death is usually interesting. The parallel with the war is interesting. Writing about writing is interesting. All these things are suggested in the first paragraph, which gives a lot of information in a short space. But the reader still hasn't got the why, wonders 'What's going on here then?', and reads on.

Placing your hook

Your first paragraph needs to have a hook. You can try to catch the reader immediately by placing the hook in the very first sentence, or you can develop it throughout the first paragraph. The following sections discuss each location.

Going for the quick catch

The mistake a lot of writers make is to push too hard, particularly in writing first sentences. Anthony Burgess parodies this in *Earthly Powers* when he writes: 'It was the afternoon of my eighty-first birthday, and I was in bed with my catamite when Ali announced that the archbishop had come to see me.' Faced with a first sentence like this, the reader may well think, 'Uh-oh, trying too hard,' and move on. (A few lines later, Burgess reveals that the narrator is a writer, and that this is his idea of a joke. Read it; see whether you think it works.)

Here are a couple of really good first sentences:

- ✓ 'It is a truth universally acknowledged that a single man in possession of a fortune must be in want of a wife.' The beginning of Jane Austen's *Pride and Prejudice* immediately displays a note of satire that many readers are going to enjoy, and has the advantage of setting out one of the book's themes straight away. It also provokes the reader into a response: 'I don't agree', 'Yes, quite right', or 'That's an interesting thought.' All these reactions are likely to keep the reader reading.

- ✓ 'It was a bright cold day in April, and the clocks were striking thirteen.' George Orwell wrote what must be close to a perfect hook in the first line of *Nineteen Eighty-Four*. The effectiveness of the line lies in its ordinariness: the reader has almost moved on to the next line and then thinks, 'Hang on just a minute, *thirteen* o'clock?'

Writing a first sentence with a really effective hook is hard. If you can do it, great. If not, focus instead on the lines that follow it.

Baiting a larger hook in the first paragraph

Most effective first-paragraph hooks involve combining an ordinary situation with something unusual: a clock strikes an impossible number; a cigarette is smoked outside a diner by a mythological beast. In both cases, the domestic and the strange collide. As shown in the earlier section 'Choosing your hook: Covering who, what, when, where, and why – or not', you can choose from a number of approaches to create a first paragraph that hooks the reader.

Check your first paragraph for something that may strike the reader as odd, off-kilter, or interesting. If there isn't anything, you may need to re-think it.

Along with most other so-called experts, we advise against long introductions about the novel's geographical situation, unless the situation itself is in some way interesting. If the character is on an ice floe, in a sinking boat, or on the back of a 50-foot-long dragon, you may well want to use that fact as the hook in your first paragraph. However, three pages of detailed description of the flowers on a hillside, no matter how beautiful, tax the patience of most readers. Elmore Leonard said, 'Don't set the scene,' and he's generally worth listening to.

Following on from that, try to make your first paragraph active. The simple way to do this is to make sure that your opening paragraph is populated: have a character present straight away, and avoid straight descriptions of scenery with no people. If you're describing a dam that's about to burst, fair enough, but make sure that the reader knows immediately that people are in front of it, or you just have description.

Building a Three-Act Structure

As a very general rule, a novel's beginning (usually called the *exposition*), in which everything is introduced to the reader, makes up the first 25 per cent of the book's length. The middle (the *building* part), in which everything gets more complicated and the climax is set up, comprises around 50 per cent. The end (the *climax* and the *denouement*), where the culmination of the story is played out, is the last 25 per cent.

You may be aware of something called 'the rule of three'. Even if you haven't heard of it, you've heard it. Jokes often have three people in them: there was an Englishman, an Irishman, and a Scotsman . . . People say that things often come in threes. If you listen to politicians giving prepared speeches, they often use groups of three. Julius Caesar's 'I came, I saw, I conquered' is an example. Once you're aware of it, you hear it everywhere.

The rule of three also applies to writing. Most theatre plays have three acts, and this structure is a useful one to apply to your novel.

The acts in a play are very roughly equal in length, although the second act is often the longest, and each serves a specific purpose. Broadly speaking, the first act sets things up, the second act develops them, and the third act winds them up. This may seem obvious, but it's the most sensible way to do things. (You can't develop things until you've introduced them!) This structure helps with pace as well. If each act is an hour long, and you spend the first two acts introducing things, you're going to have to move very quickly to get everything developed and wound up in the remaining hour.

This applies to novel writing as well. So, by the end of the first act of the novel, you need to have introduced the major themes and preoccupations of the story as well as all the main characters. (We mean introduce in the sense of making readers aware of them. A major character can be off-stage but should be a presence in the book, even if only through the effect that their absence has.)

By the end of the second act, you should have everything all lined up and ready to go for the gallop to the end of the book. If you're still spending a lot of time explaining to the reader what's going on, the novel is probably off balance.

The third act brings everything to a climax and (sometimes) follows it with a brief denouement, which can be so brief you almost miss it!

You may also want to have a sort of pause at the end of each act, rather like an interval in a play. Not that the story stops, but it reaches a point where the characters pause and take a breath before carrying on.

Casting Light and Shade

Light and shade is about contrast and variety, making sure that your story isn't all on one note. Varying the presentation of your story is extremely important. Put simply, people like variety.

Listen to the way a story-teller relays a ghost story to children. The story-teller's voice starts out normally and then as the story starts to warm up, it slows and deepens, and as the ghost appears, it speeds up and gets louder. Film-makers do the same thing, and as a novel-writer, you need to follow the same principle.

Ghost stories are useful for studying the way that contrast and variety help tell the story. Just before the ghost appears, someone gets a shock as a candlestick falls over, and then exhales with relief as a cat runs past. 'Phew, that's a relief,' the person says, and so do the audience, and everyone relaxes. *Then* the ghost appears. A relaxed, relieved, and unsuspecting audience jump twice as high and scream twice as loudly because they let their defences down.

Allowing the audience to relax just before the shock arrives makes the shock bigger. Similarly, every actor knows that the way to make tragedy hit the hardest is to get the audience laughing just before it happens. Altering the pace and the tone of your writing, speeding up and slowing down, lightening and darkening the mood, is a crucial part of telling a story.

So, how do you do that? Altering pace in the most literal sense is easy: people have been rushing about or shouting at each other, and they stop. They take a breath and talk quietly. More generally, scenes can become longer, and characters can use longer sentences and take longer to do things. You can take longer to reveal new things to the reader. All this indicates to the reader that things are going more slowly.

Altering the tone is also fairly simple. If your book has been full of jokes, bring in something serious. If it's been light-hearted, darken it a bit. (Have something unpleasant happen to someone, or give the character some bad news that can't be shrugged off in the normal way. Make life intrude.) If the hero has been shooting people for most of the story, let them have a love scene, if they've been chased, let them take a breather in a situation completely different from that of the chase scenes, and so on. (Yes, well spotted: pace and tone are fairly closely related!)

You're after contrast, and so to make something stand out, surround it with a background of a different type.

If you're reading about a man hit by a car because he's wandering around drunk on a motorway, you may feel shock and surprise, but not the surprise of the unexpected. If on the other hand, you're reading about a man sitting in his garden laughing at his children in a paddling pool, and suddenly a car comes flying through the hedge and hits him, your shock is hugely increased. Partly, of course, because this is literally unexpected – you don't expect cars to crash into people's gardens – but more crucially you're lulled into a sense of security that is then rudely exploded. Watch the first few minutes of the film *Sexy Beast* to see this done well.

Providing light and shade in your novel is a purely practical necessity. You don't want your story, or even a scene, to be all on one note. You want variety. If everything is a scream or everything is a whisper, your reader soon finds it dull. You need to mix things up: make the scene lively, bring the volume up and take it down again, make the subject matter serious and then lighten it again, or bring in different people. Give the reader something new to look at every so often.

Regulating the Pace

Put simply, *pacing* is speeding up and slowing down. Pacing applies to individual scenes, characters, relationships, the prevailing tone of the story, and just about everything.

To manage pace, think of yourself as a reader of your own novel, and considering three questions:

- What's happening at the moment? (Has the dinner-table conversation gone about as far as it can?)
- Has what's happening gone on for long enough? (Have you had enough of the relationship between the teenagers for the moment?)
- What's the best thing to replace what's happening? As you've picked up by now, you usually want to put something in its place that's different in some crucial way. If the story's been noisy for a long time, you may want a quieter scene with just one or two characters.

Remember, you begin your novel with something to snag your reader's interest. Then you keep the reader's interest through a series of 'two steps forward, one step back' movements. The point is to play the reader as a fisherman plays a salmon. If you keep the story wound up too tightly, the line breaks and you lose the reader. Similarly, if you let the line go too loose, the reader slips away. You need to vary the pace without letting it slacken off.

You need scenes in which people sit still and talk, and you need scenes in which people run around. In some scenes important things need to be decided, and in other domestic scenes the characters can be relaxed and off guard. You need some scenes in which things are revealed, and others in which things are hidden.

Think about contrasts. If you're about to speed things up, consider having a slower scene beforehand. If the story is about to get exciting, do you want to precede this with a peaceful scene, to increase the contrast? If you're piling on the tension, should you give some relief as well, to prevent it all being a bit too much?

Keeping a Finger on the Pulse of Your Novel

Just as you consult a map to help you navigate unfamiliar territory, it makes sense to check in on your novel periodically to see that it's progressing as it should and to make any course corrections. The next sections offer tools to evaluate your novel's progress in the light of the elements we talk about in this chapter.

Following your story's progress

Broadly speaking, a story should get deeper and wider, become more complicated, and sink its hooks into the reader more firmly as it goes along. If your first chapter has an earthquake, and the characters lie in bed all day for the rest of the story, you've got a job on your hands to keep the reader interested in the characters.

In general, ensure that your story goes through the following process as it progresses:

- ✔ Begin with a brief spurt of action to get the reader's attention.

- ✔ Calm down slightly to allow time to set the scene. (James Bond is a good example. A James Bond story always has a frantic beginning, and then Bond goes back to London to be told his next mission. This gives time for background, humour, and information.) You can use this time to fill in back-story, show the reader the important relationships in the story, and so on.

  Be careful, though: don't just dump information on the reader. Show – don't tell – wherever possible, and don't spell things out. Once you show the reader the start of a relationship, you can develop it while things are happening later in the book.

✔ Gradually increase intensity as the story progresses.

✔ Maintain momentum through a series of rushes forward and slippings back, although it never slips back as far as the beginning point.

✔ End the final chapter(s) as a culmination and climax of what's gone before. The final chapter is a *culmination* in that it brings together everything that has gone before, and a *climax* in that the emotions and actions are at their peak.

To put it another way: get the readers' attention, tell them what's going on, keep their attention by maintaining rising tension, and then give them an ending that wraps up what's gone before.

This very simple and basic template works for any story.

Plotting your graphs

At the beginning of this chapter, we talk about the story being the shape of an arc. A useful way to use this idea is to get some graph paper and draw the arc. (No, there's no maths here, don't worry!) This section talks about what to graph and how to graph it.

Composing a *graph of action* for your novel is useful at the start and the end of the writing process:

✔ At the start of the writing, a graph of action is a statement of intent – 'This is what I plan to do, represented in graphic form' – which can be useful and can help you plan.

✔ At the end of the writing, re-plotting the action is a way of checking that you've done what you set out to do.

Say you have 20 chapters. You divide the graph page into 20 sections, and for each chapter you make a mark representing the relative action level of the story: the higher the mark, the more action is in the chapter. The resulting graph needs to suggest variety, so that the story isn't all on one note, and it should have an overall upward tendency – not, for example, beginning with an earthquake and then subsiding into nothing much.

You plot a *graph of complication* in the same way, except that you represent the twists and tangles of the story. One complication is new characters, another is new relationships, and so on.

A *graph of difficulty* is what it sounds like: the number and degree of obstacles put in the way of the protagonist.

Drawing graphs like this is useful because it helps you to get to know your novel better, which has to be good, and it gives you the big picture. You can even map them all onto one graph and compare them.

As a general rule, the graphs of action, complication, and difficulty need to be swinging upward as the novel progresses.

So get some graph paper and draw your own graphs. Put down how you intend to get the reader's attention, and carry on from there. Once you've done it, pin the graphs up somewhere so you can see them. If necessary, update them.

Rating scenes

This exercise helps you work out how your novel is faring in terms of contrast, tone, pace, and so on, by making sure that your scenes do what they need to do.

Put out the journal for your novel or start a new notebook, and then dive in (see Chapter 14 for more about keeping a writer's journal).

1. **Write a list of all the scenes in your story, in order, and number them for easy reference.**

   A good method is to number chapter 1, scene 1 as 1/1; chapter 1, scene 2 as 1/2; chapter 2, scene 1 as 2/1; and so on.

2. **Rate each scene on a scale of 1 to 10 on two measures: *speed*, or how fast the events in the story are moving, and *light*, which means both the degree of complication and the degree of tension and intensity. Add the two ratings together.**

   A scene with a lot of action and tension may score 9 for speed and 9 for light, for a total 18. A scene with less action but the same amount of tension may rate a 4 for speed, and a 9 for light, making a total of 13.

   This rating is obviously both subjective and rough and ready, but be as honest with yourself as possible.

3. **Use your rankings to help you see where you need to speed things up or slow them down.**

   The higher the total, the more important the scene is in terms of the pace of the book.

   Your ratings show where you need to let the action take a break and where you need to wind up the tension again. The ratings also show you whether the story arc is on a generally upward trend, which is what you're aiming for.

Obviously, the numbers vary depending on the sort of novel you're writing, and prescribing absolute rules is impossible. However, some useful general points can be made. If the total is less than 10, have a really close look at it. If a scene isn't moving the story along and isn't involving the reader, it needs to be very short (if it's needed at all). Any scene that doesn't get into double figures is, by definition, a slow and fairly uninvolving scene. Can you make it faster, shorter, or more interesting? (Ideally all three!)

It's worth repeating that we're not just talking about thrillers here. Jane Austen's stories move fairly slowly – they're meant to – but plenty of events are always happening, and there's always tension. The speed of the novel doesn't earn high marks (although in terms of the story, it does speed up), but the tension starts early on. In *Pride and Prejudice*, readers discover that Mr Bennet has only daughters and that when he dies they're going to have no income and no easy way of getting one. That tension never goes away, and throughout the book it always seems more likely that the Bennet daughters may become destitute than live happily ever after. In human terms, romantic terms, and financial terms, their existence is precarious. So the tension, although understated, is in fact quite high throughout.

If your scene-rating numbers aren't creeping up throughout, you need a very good reason not to do something about it. In fact you'd need a reason no one's thought of yet!

Part III
Examining the Elements

Top Five Tips for Writing Realistic Speech

- ✔ **Don't** try to keep very close to the way people talk normally (pauses, changes of subject, going nowhere), even if your book is about normal everyday people.

- ✔ **Do** remember that normal everyday speech can be funny and informative, and can reveal character. People tend to speak in terms of the things they know about; their everyday lives and pursuits.

- ✔ **Do** cut out any parts of dialogue that get in the way such as endless repetition and dull subject matter.

- ✔ **Don't** allow dialogue to go nowhere. Unless it has a purpose in the story, it shouldn't be there. Every piece of dialogue you write has importance for your story.

- ✔ **Don't** worry about a reader thinking, 'This person talks in logical sentences; it isn't like real life at all.' You're telling a story, and unless someone sounds like a pompous Jane Austen character, your readers aren't going to notice that the dialogue isn't true to life.

Go to www.dummies.com/extras/writinganovelgettingpublisheduk for free online bonus content.

In this part . . .

✔ Expand on the basics and add meat to the bones of your story.

✔ Create convincing characters, and interesting relationships between those characters.

✔ Ensure that the dialogue is convincing.

✔ Check that sub-plots are relevant and add depth to your book.

Chapter 8

Creating Characters

*A*n average-length novel takes around ten hours to read; more if you don't read particularly quickly. That's a long time to spend with people you've only just met, so you need to think about your characters and how to keep them interesting to your readers throughout the course of your novel.

Characters need to be believable, which isn't the same thing as realistic. In fact, story-tellers often try to convince you to believe in someone highly unrealistic. Characters also need to be interesting, which isn't the same thing as good or worthy. The popularity of crime novels suggests that the most interesting characters are often flawed and even criminal. Most importantly, characters need to interest you, the writer. If you aren't interested in your characters, the reader is just as unlikely to care.

If your characters badger and lecture the reader, or are annoying, tedious, disgusting, boring, or boorish, your reader isn't going to want to continue reading about them unless you provide a very good reason.

Figure out your characters' characteristics: what do they do, and what is it about them, that makes a reader want to follow them to the end of the novel?

Your challenge is to create characters interesting enough to make the time pass in such a way that when the story ends, the reader feels a pang of regret. If you write only to amuse yourself, and don't think about your reader, you can bet that your readers won't enjoy themselves. Give your reader a reason to stay with your characters.

Contrasting the Main Types

Here are some useful terms commonly used to describe the various types of character:

- **Protagonist:** This is the main character, the character with whom the reader is most likely to identify. The protagonist is the person who the story is about.

  The protagonist is probably what most people regard as the hero of the novel, although that term can be misleading – a protagonist may not be particularly heroic!

  A book can have several main characters who have a substantial impact on the story, but usually only one protagonist. You can write a novel in which a group of four characters are equally represented and equally important, and argue that the protagonist is the group rather than an individual, but this is very rare. Almost inevitably one character dominates in some way.

- **Antagonist:** This character is the main obstacle to the protagonist's aims and desires, and stands in the protagonist's way.

  As with protagonists, you can have more than one antagonist, although one of them is likely to be more important than the others.

  The antagonist doesn't have to be 'bad' any more than the protagonist has to be 'good'. The antagonist can be very attractive and sympathetic, perhaps more so than the protagonist. In *1066 & All That* by WC Sellar and RJ Yeatman (Methuen Publishing Ltd), the authors suggest that the difference between the two sides in the English Civil War is that the Cavaliers were 'wrong but wromantic' and the Roundheads were 'right but repulsive'. (Yes, 'wromantic' is spelt like that as a joke!)

Your protagonist can be a bit dull, perhaps not a particularly nice person, whereas an antagonist can be glamorous, witty, sexy, attractive, good company, and so on. Or you may present your protagonist as a saint and your antagonist as a black-hearted fiend. Or, like most characters, they can both be somewhere in the middle. You can even make your protagonist 'good' but flawed and your antagonist 'bad' but attractive and capable of kindness: it's your choice.

When you're writing a story, a villain isn't necessarily the opposite of a hero, although this can be the case if you so choose. But if you talk about protagonists and antagonists, it indicates that you're thinking about your characters in terms of their position in, and relationship to, the story, not as relative moral positions – although, of course, they may be that too.

Have a look at Chapters 9 and 11 on relationships and conflict, respectively, to see how you can use these characters.

Building Your Characters

When you start writing your novel, you probably have a clear idea of some of your characters, a slight idea about some of the others, and know almost nothing about the rest – you don't even know they need to exist yet! So now you need to think about what type of characters you need to populate your novel.

To some extent, the subject and setting of your story dictate some of your characters. If you're writing a story set in a school, you need teachers, juniors and seniors, perhaps parents, and, depending on the type of school and the story, bullies, prefects, locals, domestic staff, and so on. If your setting is an advertising agency, you may need creative types, administrators, accountants, designers, a boss, juniors, new arrivals, experienced old-stagers, secretaries, customers, and so on. Now these are just broad types, but they are obviously necessary and they point you in the right direction.

Now you need to think about the type and tone of your story. If you're writing a light-hearted comedy, you need people who make you and the reader smile, so most of the characters need to be cheerful, sympathetic, and basically good-hearted. Alternatively, if you're writing a Gothic crime mystery, your characters are largely gloomy, frightening, and disposed to mayhem and murder.

Starting with yourself

A useful place to start is with the character of your protagonist. And for most writers, the protagonist at least starts out as a version of themselves. If you don't have a better idea, then that's a good place to start. (You can always change the character as you go along.)

Using yourself as a model means that you have a good degree of insight into your novel's protagonist – you know their likes and dislikes, the sort of person they are attracted to, the sort of person who drives them crazy, and so on.

Then, unless you have a better idea, make the antagonist someone who's opposite to the protagonist in some important respects.

As the story develops, you can always change your characters. You may find that your protagonist on page 200 is rather different to the same character as described on page 5 – that's fine, and probably inevitable.

Mixing in your friends

The easy way to create interesting characters is to mix up the abilities and personalities of people you know, and splice them together. Say, for example, you need an antagonist. You want the antagonist to be female, blonde, about 25, athletic, and fluent in five languages. Even if you don't know anyone who fits that description, you can assemble your antagonist from people you do know. Your friend Jenny is 27 and blonde, and so you can start with her. Imagine that Jenny has the physical abilities of an athletic friend and the language skills of a linguist friend. Now, your antagonist looks like Jenny, but is athletic like your athletic friend, and uses language like the linguist. Maybe your athletic friend is a martial arts expert and your linguist friend is a bit arrogant. Now you have a composite antagonist who is a bit like Jenny but whose behaviour is totally different. You can build up all your characters in this way if you need to.

Putting your friends together makes you think of unusual combinations. You end up creating characters like this: 'She's as tall as my friend Anne, but thinner, with bone structure like my Aunt Mary. She has our goalkeeper John's sense of humour and my sister Jane's intelligence. She's got a hairstyle like Celia at work, only darker, and my father's vanity about it, and my little sister Abigail's dress sense. And she drives very well but way too fast, like Jeremy from the pub but luckier than him.' And so on. Not only does this give you an interesting mixture, but it also helps you keep tabs on characters.

Some writers worry about using their friends, in fear that the friends may recognise themselves. (See the 'Who's George?' sidebar.) You certainly shouldn't use your novel as an opportunity to vent at your loved ones, but if you use your friends and family as inspiration rather than as a template, you should be okay. Your family and friends probably aren't going to recognise themselves, because they see themselves through their own eyes, not yours. Change them physically, avoid describing their exact actions in a situation that actually happened, and you needn't be concerned.

Who's George?

George is talking to Richard, a friend of his who's published seven novels. They get onto the subject of using their friends in a story.

George says, 'You've never used me as a character in a story.'

'Yes I have,' says Richard.

'Which one?' asks George, surprised.

'The third one,' says Richard.

'I've read that twice,' George says, 'I'm not in it.'

'Yes you are', says Richard.

'What's the name of the character?' asks George.

'George,' Richard replies.

And the punchline? George goes back and reads the book again, and he *still* doesn't recognise himself. Which proves that the poet Robert Burns was right when he asked, 'O wad some Pow'r the giftie gie us/To see oursels as others see us.' (Rough translation: 'I wish someone would give me the power to see myself as others do.') And if we had the power, we'd be surprised every day.

The point is that if you get every one of your friends to describe you, they'll all come up with something different, and if you describe every one of your friends to them, they'll all think you're describing someone else. So don't worry.

Of course, use common sense. If you describe a male, red-headed, seven-foot tall, one-legged friend called Mordred with great accuracy, he may well recognise himself. But even then, he probably isn't going to object much if the character is attractive, witty, and generous. Would you? So long as you don't describe the character in such a way that it can only be a specific person that you know, you've really nothing to worry about.

You can certainly sometimes create characters entirely out of your imagination, but that's hard work. When you have to, fair enough, but why re-invent the wheel when you have characters to hand? Use the people you know, and if you mix them up you're never going to run out of characters.

Keep a list of your characters' characteristics in your writer's notebook so that you don't get them mixed up. Sorting them out as you go is much easier, whereas doing it at the end is a huge pain.

Interrogating your characters

We know several authors who keep notebooks full of information about their characters which doesn't make it directly onto the page. These authors argue that they, like method actors, need to know as much as possible about characters before they can accurately portray them.

The rationale is obvious enough on one level. If you write about a brilliant brain surgeon, everything you say that has a bearing on brain surgery needs to be correct, or else any reader who knows anything about brain surgery is sure to disbelieve your story straight away.

On another level, all writers have their own depth of need for knowledge about their characters. Some authors can write convincing characters on what may seem to others a very shallow acquaintance. Others never tire of getting to know their characters better, and constantly ask them questions.

Whatever works for you is fine, but definitely try asking a few questions of your characters. You can discover all sorts of things you never even suspected about the people you created. Try the following questions and, of course, make up your own. There are no wrong answers, just go with what feels right.

Basic information that most writers generally want to have about their characters includes:

- Name
- Age
- Gender
- What they're very good at and what they're very bad at
- Who/what they hate
- Who/what they'd die for

You can then delve a bit more deeply to discover your character's loves, fears, and personal preferences, and ask them questions like the following:

- What's your favourite colour?
- What's the most frightening dream you've ever had?
- If you had to give up meat or vegetables, which would it be?
- Ferrari or SUV? Champagne or single malt? Guitar or piano? Sugar or salt?
- Describe your pets.
- What magazines and papers do you read? Why? Is that the real reason?
- Leather or plastic? Venice or Rome? Sea or space? Chinese or Indian meal?
- Of all the people who've died who you haven't known personally, whose death upset you most?

- ✔ Who would you like to play you in a film of your life?
- ✔ What do you like to do on a perfect holiday?
- ✔ What's your favourite item of clothing?

You can explore your characters' history. Fill in their back-stories by answering questions such as:

- ✔ What was their first big disappointment?
- ✔ What was their first day at school like?
- ✔ Did they love their father or mother more?
- ✔ What phobias do they have?
- ✔ What is the first thing they ever stole?
- ✔ Who or what was their first love?
- ✔ What unusual thing attracted them to their first lover?

Then you can go for the really detailed, even quirky, information:

- ✔ If they got a tattoo, what would it be and where?
- ✔ What word or phrase do they over-use?
- ✔ What do they regard as the worst possible sin?
- ✔ What do they usually carry in their pockets?

You can flesh out your characters, as well as practise your writing skills, by taking time to describe various aspects of their personality and behaviour, including:

- ✔ What's their voice like when normal, angry, and sad?
- ✔ Do they smoke, and if so how?
- ✔ How do they walk?

The point is not necessarily to get a definite list of conclusive character points. This sort of list places the characters in unexpected situations, and you have to think about how they'd react. You may not actually know the answer, but thinking about it should bring you closer to a real knowledge of your characters.

Not knowing the answer to some of the questions in the list would scandalise some authors. To them, the answers are as important as knowledge about brain surgery when writing about a brain surgeon. But you may need to know just the basics – and not even all of them – which is just fine.

You may want to think about the friends you cut up and spliced (not literally!; see the preceding section 'Mixing in your friends'). If you use your friend Colin in a character, you can ask yourself, 'How would Colin act in this situation?' You may not have direct knowledge of Colin's preferences for most of the questions, but because you know the type of person he is, you can work out the answers.

Naming Names

What's in a name? Well, often quite a lot.

Whether it's Montague, Capulet, or Corleone, you need a good name – and a good name is one that fits your character. If the Godfather had been called Don Piccolo, would he be as impressive? Maybe, but maybe not.

A character's name does one of three things:

- ✔ Reinforces the character
- ✔ Is neutral
- ✔ Contradicts the character

Most names of characters are neutral, because most names are neutral in real life.

Names that reinforce the character are fine as long as they aren't too obvious. Calling a very successful businessman Mr Rich obviously won't do, except in the broadest of comic writing. However, a name that hints at a quality can be effective.

A friend of ours has written a novel with a hero called Dirk Thunderflash (yes, it's a comedy). 'Thunderflash' is a good example of how not to do it in most novels, but names like 'Dirk' do perhaps suggest certain rugged qualities. Similarly, a name such as 'Angela' suggests angels. There can be little doubt that people make associations when they hear someone with a name that means something or reminds them of something.

These associations also work for less pleasant characters. A character in the film *The Dirty Dozen* is called Maggott, and yes, he's a nasty piece of work. (One wonders whether Rhett Butler would have been quite so glamorous if he'd been called Rhett Maggott.) Calling a character by a name that makes readers think of an insect is a shortcut to what the character is like, although it's easy to see how it can also be heavy handed.

Of course, a name that works against a character can be useful. What if the man called Maggott had been the hero and a fine upstanding young man? What if the really rather nasty serial killer is called Damien Featherlight-Hopscotch? (Okay, a name like that would make anyone touchy, but you take the point.) You can use names that act in counterpoint to the character. A woman called Angela can also be a monster – after all, there are fallen angels as well. But in general we suggest that you stick with neutral names unless you have a good reason not to.

It may seem useful to call someone who is a bit devious Ms Slye, or someone who's a bit overweight Mr Lard, but actually it isn't funny and it patronises the reader. Worst of all, it's downright lazy. The Victorians thought that this sort of thing was funny, which is why Dickens called a bad teacher M'Choakumchild and a small ugly person Squod. Ian Fleming got away (just about) with calling his female characters names like Honeychile Rider and Pussy Galore, because that was in keeping with the unrealistic and rather camp world he'd created. Unless you're very sure it will work, we advise against it.

Telling them apart

You don't want to write a novel that features Jane and Jeff Jackson, and their kids Jody and Jerry, in which the antagonist is called Jack Jefferson, a minor character is named Jane, her sister is called June, they live in Johnstown in James County, the dog is called Johnny, and the neighbour is called Jimmy-Joe Jones but everyone calls him Jonesy . . .

An extreme example, but you take the point. Names should be clearly differentiated unless you have a good reason for similarities. One possible reason for choosing similar names is for comic effect, although that effect is likely to be laboured in any case.

People's names aren't really a subject for humour unless you're very good at it. (Memo to an ex-student: calling the dog Cat and the cat Dog isn't big or clever.)

Meaning something

Names certainly carry a form of meaning. Some names suggest physical attractiveness, others don't. Some names suggest intelligence, others a shortage of social skills. Some names imply dullness, others liveliness. When Margaret Mitchell wrote *Gone With The Wind*, she originally intended to call Scarlett O'Hara by the first name Pansy, but she decided to change it. Somehow, we feel, it wouldn't have been the same book otherwise.

Placing names in time

Some names are identified with historical epochs. The popularity of names is often related to the accession or birth of royalty. The accession of King George produced a rash of boys of that name, and plenty of young men are named William and Harry just now. (We suspect that George is about to stage a come-back.) Quite a few young women are called Kylie, too, a name unheard of in England 30 years ago.

The Victorians called their daughters by the names of the graces (Modesty, Chastity, Grace) and flowers (Rose, Hyacinth) in order to associate them with the qualities suggested by those words.

If you want to place your characters in a particular time or age, one way is to give them names that were once common and are now almost unknown. Agnes, Agatha, and Evelyn are names that are common among the older generation, but you don't see many younger people with those names.

Naming only when you need to

You don't need to give everyone a name. 'The waitress', 'the policewoman', or 'the boy's father' are perfectly fine to identify walk-on characters who the reader isn't going to see again and doesn't need to remember. In fact, the more attention you give to a character in terms of naming and close description, the more a reader is going to think, 'Aha, I'm going to need to remember all this stuff, because my attention is being drawn to this person.' So don't elaborate on characters unless you mean to follow up with them later on.

Creating the Back-Story

Back-story is one of two things, depending on the situation:

✔ Information that readers (and the characters in the story) need to make sense of a character's actions, but that isn't directly relevant to the story.

It can be a character's history – often told to someone through a device such as a letter, a newspaper article, or an elderly relative. Often, the reader doesn't read about it as an experience the character has within the framework of the novel.

✔ More general information that you, the writer, need to make sense of the character that you're writing about.

A lot of writers feel that their characters need back-story. (See the 'Interrogating your characters' section for more about creating back-stories.) Whether or not the back-story is necessary to your story, taking the time to find out about your characters generally pays off. Your characters are like your friends: the more you know about them, the easier it is to predict what they may do or say in a given situation.

Just how much back-story you need to put in the novel varies from story to story. We suggest using it on a need-to-know basis. Determine whether the reader needs to have the information, and if not, ask yourself why it's there. And remember, one crucial detail is always worth a dozen vaguely relevant ones.

Showing the reader something about your characters is more powerful than *telling* them about it. So if your protagonist's fear of being let down by men has its roots in the way her father always let her down, illustrate this with an anecdote about how he never sent her a birthday card rather than dishing up the back-story ready-analysed on a plate. Readers like to draw their own conclusions about characters; your job is to offer them all the evidence they need to do so.

Motivating Your Characters

The reader must be able to understand what motivates a character. This doesn't mean that the reader must necessarily sympathise with the character's reasons, or even be able to imagine them. It's enough that the motivation is clear.

A character who doesn't care about the consequences of his actions can be interesting for a short while, but psychologically he has little staying power because there's no temptation for him to do much else. A character who has good reasons not to do something, but still does it, particularly when it's to his disadvantage, is someone who can keep a story going for a long while. (And yes, you may well have both characters in the same story, each acting as a reflection to the other. In fact, it's a good idea.)

Of course, working out the character's motivation may be part of the point of the story. That's fine, it just means that the reader discovers motivation backwards. The point still stands.

The mistake that a lot of writers make is to forget that, in a story, *everything happens for a reason*. Write those five words down and put them somewhere you can see them.

Think about it. People almost never do things at random. They always have their reasons. You may think their reasons are idiotic, but obviously they don't. People never say to themselves, 'My reasons for doing this thing are stupid and nonsensical, so I'll go for it.' Remember, however, that sometimes people do say, 'My reasons for doing this thing may be childish, personal, and illogical, but I'm going to do it anyway, because it'll make me feel better, if only briefly.' The point is that their reasons are good enough justification for them.

People very rarely act without thinking. They sometimes act on seemingly random impulses, but there's always a reason, such as kindness, boredom, excitement, love, or curiosity.

Normally, the reader asks whether the character's motivation is convincing in terms of their personality, but it's fine to have the reader ask whether the person's character is convincing in terms of their motivation.

Of course, character is highly dependent upon situation. Most people don't steal food and would be surprised if you suggested that they would, but if they were penniless and watching their children starve, they might see things differently. Most people would say they couldn't kill someone, but if they saw a person they loved being threatened, things might well change.

Another crucial point is that characters shouldn't act out of character, by which we mean they need to be consistent within themselves. This doesn't mean they behave the same all the time, but they need to be true to the character you build for them. If they are gentle most of the time and then explode into violence, you need a reason. At the same time, people sometimes do things that don't fit their usual pattern of behaviour. So even if characters do something purely because they feel like it – feeling like it is a reason in itself.

Plant clues throughout the story to make sure that the reader thinks at the end, 'Yes, I can see that he would do that.' Of course, you don't necessarily want the reader to recognise the clues you provide as clues at the time.

When the character's motivation is revealed, the reader needs to say, 'Ah, I see, the money is missing and it looks like John took it. That makes sense, because John always had a problem with his brother, because of the fact that he stayed behind to run the farm and look after their sick father while Ted went out and made a fortune. His resentment shows in lots of small ways, so I can see that it might drive John to steal from Ted.' What doesn't work so well is when the character's motivation is revealed like the punchline of a joke: 'And he stole from his brother because – taa-daa! – he was jealous of his success!' If the reader thinks 'But there was never the slightest hint that John was jealous, and Ted's always been really good to him. I just don't believe it,' the story is in trouble. Even if John is a skunk who is actually accepting Ted's generosity and still hating him, your readers need some clues.

Actions are always motivated – there's no such thing as a motiveless act (unless the person is psychopathic). Aristotle once said that a character in tragedy is defined by his actions. We would go further to say that motivation is the key to character in all dramatic situations.

Writing Characters to Care About

The best thing any reader can say to you is, 'I really cared about what happened to your characters.' (Well, the *very* best thing any reader can say to you is, 'I'm an eccentric millionaire and I loved your book so much that I'd like to offer you an independent income for life so you can write more,' but let's stay real here.) If readers cared about your characters, they loved your story and loved your people. They felt as though they knew the characters, as though they inhabited the book alongside them. They laughed when the characters laughed, cried when they cried, and cheered when they won through.

Fighting fair versus Bambi Meets Godzilla

One way to make your readers care about your characters is to make sure that, whatever happens at the end, up to that point it's a fair fight.

The US humour magazine *National Lampoon* produced a short film called *Bambi Meets Godzilla*. Viewers see around 28 seconds of the cutest little deer imaginable gambolling about on the forest floor. Then, WHAM! A huge green reptile's foot comes down and flattens the baby deer. Roll credits; the end. A lot of novels can get like Godzilla taking on Bambi.

Taking a cue from history

Check the history-book shelves. (Don't worry, you don't need to know any history to follow this bit. And you don't need to go to a library. Use a search engine if you prefer.) Try to find a book on the US invasion of Grenada. You'll have trouble. It was only 30 years ago, and no one cares. Why is no one interested? Because the US is easily the most powerful nation in the world, and its army invaded an island that was defended by about 20 unprepared old men and children armed with short sticks. There was never even the slightest iota of doubt that the US would win. It was over in a few days. The invasion of Grenada just isn't interesting as a story, because the odds were too heavily stacked against one side. The defenders didn't have a chance.

Now go back to the bookshelf or the search engine. Try to find a book on the Battle of Thermopylae. No problem doing that: you can find dozens of historical accounts and novels about it. This battle was over 2,000 years ago, and it still fascinates people. Why? Because the most powerful empire in the world – at that time the Persian Empire had an army of millions of men – was taken on by just 300 Greeks, and until the Greeks were betrayed they were winning. The story of Thermopylae is interesting, because the odds were stacked against the Greeks, and they proved the odds wrong.

Thermopylae takes the expectations of the Bambi versus Godzilla story and turns it on its head. The Persian army is a million men strong, the Greeks have no chance at all . . . hang on, did Bambi just grab hold of Godzilla's foot and sink his teeth into it?

Everyone loves to see the underdog win and the old sportsman come out of retirement to beat the cocky and apparently unbeatable young challenger.

Boosting the bad guy's chances

You may be tempted to make the bad guys just too clueless to stand any chance. Whatever dastardly scheme the bad guys come up with, your hero triumphs with just one athletic bound and a winning smile. This sort of thing is great fun to write, but it doesn't work over the long haul.

If the antagonists are so over-matched, useless, and out-gunned that you can't imagine how your hero can lose, what's the point? We know the ending on the first page. Even Superman, who is invulnerable to bullets, tanks, falling buildings, and anything else the opposition can throw at him, becomes weak as a kitten at the first sight of a hunk of green rock. Every Superman needs his Kryptonite, or you don't have a story.

The antagonist must be in with a chance. The best stories go further than this and make the antagonist far stronger, better prepared, better armed, and at least as smart as the hero. The hero frantically rushes around narrowly avoiding destruction while he finds out what's going on and tries to gather what he needs to defeat his more powerful enemy. Brain may eventually beat brawn (or vice versa), and good beat bad, but you can make it a close-run thing.

Endowing your hero with just enough

The characters you create are like your friends and family, and falling in love with your dashing, gallant hero can be all too easy. You want your protagonist to win, and so you make this character too clever, brave, and resourceful by half.

If you load the dice in favour of your protagonist, you have to work very hard to make your readers interested in their problems – and only then if those problems are real ones.

The best thriller stories are ones in which the hero is constantly in peril, often because of their excessive sense of honour, and you can't see how they can possibly escape, when suddenly at the last moment they find an unexpected but convincing escape route.

Don't make your protagonist too strong, and give the character a flaw. Make the antagonist a fearsome and worthy opponent. Games between evenly matched teams are always more interesting than one-sided ones. If all that happens during every conflict is that the bad guys get a pounding, the reader doesn't really care about the outcome. You can insist that Bambi is a threat to Godzilla all you like, but the reader knows differently. As we suggest elsewhere, every Superman needs Kryptonite; every Iron Man needs his dodgy heart.

Creating a real person

You don't want a main character who's too obviously smart or who has something (drop-dead good looks or unlimited cash) that means that no one else can possibly hope to beat them or prevent them getting what they want.

Yes, your protagonist should be clever and have talents, but maybe it shouldn't be immediately obvious how those skills are going to help in every situation.

Creating real problems

Readers need to care about your protagonist's problem. If your hero's hanging by a piece of string suspended upside down over an acid bath, you have the reader's attention. However, if your hero's someone who already has almost everything and wants the rest, readers probably find it hard to care.

Mustering sympathy for a gorgeous and rich woman who can't get the exact kind of sushi she wants at 3 a.m., or for the rich man who hasn't any olives for his Martini is hard. (You can, though, if you want, get readers to feel sorry for the domestic servant who brings the news about the olives and gets shouted at for not doing their job properly, because we care about their predicament. If you want us to care about the rich man, it probably needs to be over something that his wealth can't sort out for him.)

Of course, if the point of your story is that, *despite* apparent advantages, your character's blessed life is in fact hollow and empty without the true love and earthy perspective that only an attractive personal assistant can provide, the story is actually one of self-realisation and redemption, and that's fine.

The best way to get a reader to take an interest in reading about someone who has everything is either to satirise the character or put them in peril. Anything else is difficult. Generally, it's more interesting to read about someone trying to make it than read about someone who already has it made.

Brandishing a sonic screwdriver

Those of you who watch the *Doctor Who* television series may be familiar with the Sonic Screwdriver, a very useful piece of kit. The Sonic Screwdriver can do anything. It doesn't matter where the Doctor and his sidekick are or what's happening to them – hanging upside-down in tanks of acid, pegged out in the sun with ants all around them, pinned down by annoyed dinosaurs – the Sonic Screwdriver always has the solution.

If your hero has something like a Sonic Screwdriver, whatever problem they face, your reader just says, 'Well, that's silly, why don't they just pull out their sonic screwdriver and turn the acid to champagne, the ropes to liquorice, and the dinosaurs to puppies – end of problem?'

Better by far if the antagonist has the infallible secret weapon. Now the hero has problems, now the reader is paying attention; let's see the hero get out of that!

Take your time. Leave the hero to dangle for a while; let the situation seem hopeless for a bit before they escape.

In every James Bond movie, Q gives Bond a gadget at the beginning of the film, and you know that this gadget's going to come in pretty darn useful by the end of the film. You know this, and you're in on the joke.

Problems arise when the reader suspects that the gadget was only introduced to get the writer out of a hole that they dug themselves.

Writing Characters Big and Small

You don't have to write big characters: small characters have stories too, real and interesting ones. Not everyone gets to be president. Ordinary people can make good subjects for stories, especially if extraordinary things happen to them and they're forced to act in extraordinary ways. A lot more ordinary people than extraordinary people exist. And remember, most readers are ordinary people too, and you need to make your protagonist someone to whom your readers can relate.

Most stories are about people who are in some way larger than life. They can be ordinary people, but must also be unusual in their actions, in themselves, or in some other way that makes them interesting. In the same sense that you wouldn't stand up in front of an audience and describe how you clean your teeth, you wouldn't say, 'I know this man who's utterly ordinary in every respect' and stop there, because if you do, there's no story. The thing that makes someone unusual is what makes the story.

Think about why your character's story is worth telling. There must be something story-worthy about them.

Big normal characters

Many stories are about people to whom something noteworthy happens. They don't necessarily set out to do anything unusual, noteworthy, or larger than life, they're just in the right place at the right time. They're noteworthy because they've been unusually funny, unlucky, brave, or whatever.

'Look at Tommy: he's drenched!' 'Yes, it's raining.' 'Yes, but he was standing next to the bus stop and this bus came along and went into a puddle about four feet deep and it went over Tommy and he completely *disappeared . . .*'

Tommy getting wet in the rain is not a story. Everyone gets wet in the rain. Tommy getting drenched by a passing bus doesn't happen to everyone, and so it's noteworthy. It's amusing (if you aren't Tommy) and it can happen to anyone. Tommy is normal, but an abnormal thing happened to him. For a while, his story is larger than life, and so readers relate to it. The same thing, or something like it, may have happened to us, and yet it's unusual.

The point is that, although the people can be ordinary and the thing that happens in their life may be, in the grand scheme of things, relatively humdrum, nevertheless for them it is in some way life-changing. And that change, and its consequences, is the story.

A more complex form of larger-than-life situation is the story of someone who's larger than life through choice or circumstance. A couple who foster 70 children and still find time to go hang-gliding, run a clothes shop, and stage amateur operatics may be said to be larger than life. A priest in a tiny and remote rural parish who galvanises a whole province to badger the government into building an international airport next to his village may be said to be the same. (This happened near Knock, in Ireland.) These are so-called 'ordinary' people, who are mostly similar to us but who choose to be different in some way, to stand out, exhibit energy and commitment, and touch far more lives than the average person.

Some larger-than-life people aren't as nice as the examples we use here. For example, they can be complicated and they can be bullies. Whether you like them or not depends on whether you consider that they use their talents to help you or not. Similarly, a character in a novel stirs different feelings in the reader depending on the character's relationship to the protagonist. In *Pride and Prejudice*, Lady Catherine de Burgh bullies Lizzie Bennet horribly, and as a reader, you quite rightly dislike her. However, if she were fond of Lizzie and used her influence to help her, although you may think that she went a bit far with her bullying behaviour, you may also conclude that her heart was in the right place. Your attitude towards her behaviour is entirely conditional on the relationship to the protagonist. In the same novel, you rather like Mr Bennet because Lizzie loves him. However, if you saw him from another point of view, you might conclude that he's actually rather cruel and certainly is insensitive to people's predicaments. The relationship to the protagonist tells the reader what to think.

Big abnormal characters

The previous section deals with characters who are relatively similar to most people, but who are unusual in their energy and commitment. But look what happens if you marry that energy to success. Stories about wealth, power, and influence cover the shelves of your local bookstore. Not everyone who's rich and powerful is larger than life – secretiveness can be part of the fascination. But it's easier to write a story in which at least one person is larger than life than to write a story in which everyone is reserved and really rather normal. We're not trying to say that rich and powerful is the only option if you want to create a character who's big and abnormal, but it's one way.

Again, context is all: to run a country, you have to be rich and powerful; to run a small village, you also have to be richer and more powerful than the others in the village; and so it's all relative.

The problem for a writer dealing with larger-than-life characters is that the reader doesn't necessarily feel a connection to them. The lives of the rich and powerful are, to some, akin to the lives of Martians and bear no resemblance to their own. You must make sure that somewhere along the line the reader thinks, 'They're just like me really.'

 The simple way to make a connection between your characters and your readers is through common humanity. It doesn't matter how rich or powerful someone is, how strong and how untouchable, everyone gets tired, everyone gets angry, and everyone has family. When one of F Scott Fitzgerald's characters in *The Great Gatsby* said, 'The very rich are different from you and me,' and Ernest Hemingway commented, 'Yes, they have more money', it was a good joke and also quite profound. Riches, and the things that riches bring, make significant differences, but the weaknesses that human beings are prone to are universal. Set a soap opera in the homes of the mega-wealthy, and put it next to one set in a working class district of a big city, and you can watch almost exactly the same desires and emotions being played out, just in different clothes.

Deepening Your Characters

The trick to giving your characters some depth is to keep it simple and take it one step at a time.

Divining a defining characteristic

Each character in a story needs to have one defining characteristic. This characteristic almost certainly ties up with their motivation, so think of the two together (see 'Motivating Your Characters' earlier in this chapter).

Just so we're clear, we don't mean that in real life people have just one defining characteristic, or that your characters in your novel are one-dimensional. The defining characteristic is a peg to hang the character on. This is the same as making a character red-haired; a way for the reader to be clear on them. If you make a character over-dependent on his mother, for example, that doesn't mean he can't also be kind and gentle, or arrogant and selfish, or fond of basketball and Chinese restaurants and a hundred other things. From the point of view of telling the story, he has this particular characteristic because that's the characteristic most relevant to the story. If you're telling a different story with the exact same character, you may use the same defining characteristic, or you may choose a different one if it suits the story better.

Now, if a character only wants money, that character's defining characteristic may be greed. But it may not be; you may need to dig a bit deeper to be sure. If, for example, the character wants money because someone ruined their parent's business and brought on their early deaths as a result, money is merely a means to an end. The character's motivation is actually revenge, and their urge for revenge on their parents' killer is their defining characteristic. It's what drives the character, and everything they do is related to it. Note that money doesn't have to be what the character pursues; there's more than one way to get revenge: they may choose to dig up dirt and use blackmail instead, or to lead the antagonist's child into a life of crime or debauchery.

A defining characteristic doesn't have to be as dramatic as revenge. You can write a comic novel about a young man whose defining characteristic is an inability to handle money, a failure to commit to a relationship, or a dislike of his stepmother. Or it can be something less negative: he may have an indefatigably sunny disposition, or a refusal to admit defeat.

Every character in your story needs to have a defining characteristic. They can – and should – have dozens of other characteristics as well, but there must be one that, more than anything else, defines them.

Sampling other characteristics

After you've made sure that every character has one defining characteristic, you need to think about their other characteristics.

These other characteristics are likely to be connected in some way to their defining characteristic and to each other. However, people are complicated. Don't make the mistake of giving all your characters similar characteristics and then leaving them alone to get on with it. Your novel is both more interesting and more believable if your characters have the capacity to surprise the reader. Note, however, that it's often helpful if the apparently unusual characteristic actually makes sense. A simple example is the villain who's happy to use violence but reveals a capacity for tenderness, often of a very specific type. People are often surprised that Hitler was kind to animals, but this seemingly contradictory characteristic actually makes perfect sense. Hitler wasn't particularly disposed to kindness, but he was obsessed with betrayal. His pet Alsatian's faithfulness was unconditional, and he was able to count on it absolutely. Someone like Hitler who put such a high price on loyalty is quite likely to like animals more than people, because unlike people, pets don't lie, talk back, or conspire; and they don't try to kill you.

You need to relate all your fictional person's characteristics to the big picture of the character you're writing about. As a general rule, the individual characteristics need to add up to a believable whole. When the reader looks at the character's motivation and characteristics, everything needs to make sense. You can perhaps have a minor character who doesn't really add up, but your major characters need to be better formed than that.

Going on assumptions

Don't be scared of thinking that your character is 'a certain type of person'. Most people fit more or less into a type. At least, that's our common perception of other people, which is what matters.

Familiarity with the sort of generalised groupings people fit into lets you make assumptions about other people. Most of these assumptions are reasonably harmless, although of course you need to avoid stereotyping and dismissiveness. Nevertheless, everyone loves to pigeon-hole people.

You can make use of the tendency to pigeon-hole people. If you make a character red-headed, your readers are likely to assume she has a fiery temper. You can play with the stereotype, subvert it, go with it, and then contradict it: it's up to you.

The assumptions people make about each other have consequences in telling your story. Knowing that your reader assumes things saves you time and effort. You don't need to tell them things that you know they're going to assume. Later, if you want, you can do something with those assumptions.

Be aware of what the reader's likely to think. Everything you tell a reader about a character pushes the reader to make an assumption.

How speed-dating is like writing

The success of speed-dating is based upon two ideas: first, that people can and do make up their minds about someone within three minutes; and second, crucially, that most of the time they get it right.

From a story-telling point of view, you don't need to tell readers much to begin with. Provide a couple of pieces of information and then get on with the story. You can fill in the gaps later, knowing that your readers have made up their minds about the character already. Tell the story and then have fun, if you want to, dismantling and subverting your readers' first impressions.

Chapter 9

Exploring Relationships

*W*riting a novel in which the main character (the protagonist) doesn't relate to anyone else in any way is possible, but it would be difficult. Anyway, why would you want to? Relationships are the most interesting part of any story – they're what keep readers reading.

Romances, friendships, enmities, jealousies, rivalries, family bonds, and tensions are the sort of things that drive any good narrative. This chapter suggests ways for you to use relationships to make your story interesting and believable.

When we speak of relationships in this chapter, we generally mean the relationship between the protagonist and another character. Auxiliary characters, of course, have relationships with each other as well, but we focus on relationships that affect the protagonist.

Determining Helpers, Hinderers, and the Rest

In most stories, characters can be divided into three groups: helpers, hinderers, and the rest.

An important thing to remember is that all the characters – whatever category they fall into – must be in the story for a reason. Don't waste the readers' time helping them get to know someone who's irrelevant to the story. If you want the reader to look in the wrong direction for a reason, that's fine, but don't allow characters to be pointless distractions.

Aiding helpers

Helpers are characters who are on the side of your protagonist. (Chapter 8 explains major characters.) Note that this doesn't necessarily make helpers the good guys, it just means that they're on the side of the character in whom the reader is most interested.

Helpers are allies of the protagonist. They include sidekicks, mentors, partners, friends, and anyone who's allied to the protagonist. Helpers are also those who aren't necessarily known to the protagonist but are naturally on her side (we assume our protagonist is female in this section): for example, they may be people who instinctively help the protagonist because, rightly or wrongly, they perceive her to be the good guy.

Your protagonist needs helpers, even if she's a lone-wolf type apparently going against the world on her own. Apart from anything else, readers can't really believe in your protagonist if literally everyone's against her. It's fine if everyone *seems* to be against her: then you can have fun deciding who's *really* against her.

In practice, people usually have friends who are prepared to believe in them even when the evidence is stacked against them. Of course, too many helpers make the protagonist's life too easy. You need enough helpers to give the protagonist a chance, but not too many.

If in doubt, have too few helpers rather than too many, because readers prefer to see your protagonist having things too hard rather than too easy!

Confounding hinderers

Hinderers are the opposite of helpers, and they include anyone who acts in a way that prevents the protagonist getting what she wants.

At the extreme, hinderers include full-blown enemies and antagonists. However, hinderers are also characters who are just disinclined to help the protagonist for some reason – that's why they're called hinderers rather than enemies. When the protagonist needs something from hinderers, they may be too stupid, greedy, blind, cowardly, prejudiced, busy, selfish, or just plain lazy to help.

Some characters move between being helpers and hinderers, which makes things complicated at times. Sometimes the switch and the reason for it are very obvious. A character may start off as the protagonist's best friend, become jealous (sometimes with justification, sometimes not) and spend a period hindering before their better nature re-asserts itself and they return to being a helper again.

Sometimes the protagonist may alienate potential helpers. Sometimes helpers get the wrong end of the stick and become hinderers for the best of reasons (for example, a policeman who mistakenly believes that the protagonist has committed a crime). Characters who the reader supposes may be helpers can actually be hinderers, because they've been bought or blackmailed, or they may see hindering as the lesser of two evils.

Creating characters is more complicated than black hats and white hats!

Mixing them up

From a plotting point of view, moving helpers and hinderers around is a useful way of keeping the story moving.

For example, friends become enemies, enemies form alliances to pursue common ends, friends turn out to be traitors, and apparent enemies turn out to be sympathetic. Characters can be double and even triple agents. A character can be apparently helping while secretly hindering, and vice versa. Hinderers may not even be aware that they're hindering, but they're a useful way of creating background tension – of keeping a character's stress levels up even when she isn't faced with her actual enemies.

A policewoman trying to solve an extremely difficult and nasty murder case may also be flat broke and going through a divorce, and may risk losing custody of her children, one of whom is in trouble at school and the other pregnant. The policewoman's husband isn't an enemy – he isn't deliberately trying to make her job difficult, and he may not even be aware of what she's going through at work – but he can still be a hinderer if he's part of her problems.

Your novel needs some hinderers. Imagine the same policewoman trying to solve the same murder, but this officer has an independent income, her husband's incredibly supportive and helpful throughout, and her children are entirely delightful creatures who never get into trouble, are always top of the class, and put themselves to bed. You get the point: use hinderers.

You may also want to check out Chapter 11 on conflict, because most conflict in novels comes from hinderers (although not all of it; remember that friends can sometimes cause as much conflict as enemies do!). The important thing is that people, for whatever reason and with whatever degree of justification, try to prevent the protagonist from getting what she wants.

Fitting in the rest

The rest of your characters are everyone else who the protagonist knows, from almost-lovers to bare acquaintances. You need to have these other characters in your story: they can be helpers and hinderers, they can reveal character, and they can act in ways that affect the protagonist. They can also provide light relief and reveal crucial plot points: these characters are part of the palette of colours you use to paint your story.

Subsidiary characters are extremely useful and important, but they often don't appear to be so. They may be people in service industries (taxi drivers, waiters, and so on), guests at parties, parents, fellow customers, or anyone who's in a scene for any reason but not directly connected to the story. These often nameless characters may well have important roles to play, but they generally don't have an ongoing relationship with the protagonist.

Minor characters can help or hinder. And, of course, in some stories, the reader's never sure who's really a friend, who's really an enemy, and who's nothing much at all. . . .

These characters are like pawns in chess: they're as important as you need them to be. A girl walking down the street is apparently unimportant until she walks past the bad guy at the wrong moment. He's about to be captured by the police and sees that she is his opportunity to escape. Suddenly she isn't a passer-by: she's a hostage. Readers don't need to know her name or much about her – the bad guy dumps her and runs off at the first chance he gets, and we never see the girl again – but for the time that she's a hostage, she's an essential part of the plot.

Minor characters are vital background, so keep them in mind. Think of them as protagonists of stories that you're not telling at the moment. They're human and their stories are potentially as rich and fascinating as anyone else's story. For the brief time they're onstage, make them real.

Writing Relationships

Family members, lovers, and enemies all help you to tell your story. The following sections cover the specifics of all three types of relationship.

Families

Family relationships are arguably the most interesting of all. They're often extremely complex and filled with potential paradox. That said, a lot of family stuff is mundane detail about shopping lists and so on.

Make sure that the information you give your reader about the family relationships in your story is useful and relevant. Ask yourself the following questions:

- ✔ Does what I've written about this relationship advance the reader's knowledge about the character, and does it help the reader to make sense of the story, now and/or later?

✔ Does this knowledge advance the plot in some way? And, if not, does the reader really *need* to know it? Family stuff can be amusing and colourful, but there's a limit to how much of it a story can contain before it starts to get in the way. Keep the non-relevant detail to a minimum.

Remember to keep some distance in your story, too. You naturally base your stories on your own family experiences, and that's fine, but remember that something that's interesting to you (because you experienced it) may not be interesting to someone else. So don't forget to ask those questions above.

You choose your lovers, friends, and acquaintances. Family members are the only people you're supposed to love even if you don't want to. Some people are lucky and have a family that they're happy to spend time with out of choice. Some people aren't lucky at all; if their family members weren't family, they'd cross the street to avoid them.

As in life, a character's family can affect the character in ways that non-family members can't. The reason is to do with knowing who you really are. Your family members know your secrets and the embarrassing things you've done; they've seen you at your most defenceless. The persona you put on for people outside the family can be punctured in a moment by a reference to a family joke.

Sometimes it's just a matter of being related to them: it's difficult to remain supermodel-cool when your younger brother turns up at a party and behaves embarrassingly.

Perhaps most interestingly, your family know better than anyone else where your buttons are and how to press them.

Pleasing Mother

We have a friend, Jane, who has excellent taste in clothes. Jane takes a long time to make decisions, but once she's made up her mind to buy something, she goes for it. And she's always right: it looks great on her. Sometimes her friends go shopping with her and comment on the item she's considering. She listens but almost never changes her mind.

One day we met Jane while she was shopping with her mother. She picked up a dress that was indisputably gorgeous and would suit her perfectly. It was a no-brainer. Her mother looked at the dress and shook her head. Jane put the dress down immediately without speaking and walked away to find something else. She deferred completely to her mother's taste, and yet her mother dresses in clothes that don't suit her at all and in colours that make her look bilious.

When we asked Jane about it she said that she doesn't mind what anyone else says about something she wears as long as she herself likes it, even if the other person hates it. But if her mother makes any sort of disparaging comment, Jane can't wear that item again, even though she knows that her mother's taste in clothes is highly dubious.

Only families can do this!

Your story needs to take account of the difference between family relationships and other relationships. Don't make the mistake of thinking that there's no difference between the two. The relationships aren't the same.

The following list contains some other potential differences between family and other relationships that you need to think about:

- ✔ **Families are often extreme.** If the members are comfortable together, they're very comfortable; if the relationship is dysfunctional, then it's really wrong. This tendency makes families potentially more interesting than friendships, which aren't usually as volatile.

  If you want to raise the emotional temperature in your story, doing it with family members is easy and quick. Also remember that emotions between family members are potentially more complicated than those outside the family.

- ✔ **Families use shorthand.** They often don't waste time on preamble, and they can get quickly to the point in a way that other characters can't. Family members often feel that their job is to tell each other painful truths because no one else will. Because of their closeness, they often say things straight out that friends may well hesitate over or say in a more tactful way. From a plot point of view, this can be useful, because you can have a family member blurt something out or cut directly to the chase.

- ✔ **Families seemingly talk in code.** Family members talk to each other in ways that an outsider doesn't really understand. You can use this to set up oppositions between insiders and outsiders in the story. You can also use it to reveal points of conflict or secrecy between relatives, such as how everyone changes the subject when an outsider asks about Aunt Joan, or how the parents flinch and become silent every time their daughter talks about her child.

- ✔ **Families can love and hate each other simultaneously.** This is interesting, because it makes their behaviour less predictable. People outside families tend to be less complicated in their relationships. Use family unpredictability to keep your reader guessing what's going to happen next.

  Also remember that love/hate relationships are usually conducted at a higher temperature than others, so if your story needs a fight, such a relationship's a good place to have it.

- ✔ **Families are tribal.** They pick sides to fight viciously against each other, but often close ranks against an outsider. Again, from a plot point of view, this is potentially interesting.

The crucial point for you as a writer is that the dynamics between family members make for additional layers of interest in your story.

Lovers

Lovers are a form of family. They combine the lack of history that friendships have with the intensity of a family relationship. The two crucial points about lovers are:

- The ties that bind lovers are very strong, but they can be shattered in ways that family bonds generally can't.
- Lovers are chosen, not born.

These two differences are important.

You can use the bonds between lovers as the crux of your story. The story (or part of it) may see those bonds tested up to, and beyond, breaking point. Are they going to break, or perhaps one and not the other? Or can they both continue to love each other? Every reader can recognise these situations, and the potential combinations give a wide variety of possibilities.

Remember also that the opposite of love is hate: a disappointed or betrayed lover may become an enemy.

You can also use the fact in your novel that lovers are in a unique situation: for example, sexual betrayal isn't something that concerns families and friends, but it's a serious issue between lovers. Similarly, the fact that lovers are chosen means that issues of suitability and so on become important. Of course, lovers and families do cross over: most lovers are also members of families. You can use this fact to set up additional conflict.

 You probably already realise that unsuitable relationships generally make better stories than suitable ones. But if you want to write a story about two people who fall in love and are meant for each other, the unsuitability can come from people around them. Think about Romeo and Juliet: their love was strong, and in many ways the two were a good match. Unfortunately, their families weren't. Situation and context can scupper a good relationship just as a wrong relationship can go sour, even with all the support and goodwill in the world.

Enemies

Enemies can come in all shapes and sizes, but you need to consider one crucial point about them: you can't have an enemy in isolation. An enemy's importance to the story lies in their antagonistic relationship to the protagonist.

An enemy must threaten the main character in a way that's important to them. For example, if you want to stay alive, and someone's trying to kill you, you have good grounds for calling that person your enemy. (Their motivation is irrelevant at this point, although obviously it will be a part of the story later.) However, if you quite fancy a doughnut, and someone pushes in front of you in the queue and buys the last doughnut in the shop, even though that person may be extremely annoying, they aren't in a true sense your enemy.

The point here is that in order for your main character to be able to take interesting action, things must matter. If your main character drags the woman who bought the last doughnut out of the shop and beats her to death, that doesn't work for your story, because your protagonist would only beat an enemy to death, and taking the last doughnut isn't grounds for enmity.

Of course, if for some reason the last doughnut is incredibly important to the main character, and the woman who pushed in to buy it knew that and still pushed in, that's different, but it's a matter of disrespect, not of doughnuts.

So, first you need to establish what things are important to your main character, and then you can make sure that the enemy is in some way threatening those things. This threat can be personal and concrete ('I love my home and my family, and you're trying to harm them') or it can be more abstract ('I have a system of morality, and the way you behave threatens it').

Put simply, the enemy needs to be the opposite of your protagonist. Of course, a good story isn't as simplistic as that, but it's essential that, at the core, the main character and the enemy are fundamentally opposed. Otherwise they aren't enemies, and if they aren't enemies, the emotional temperature of your story drops significantly.

Chapter 10

Talking about Dialogue

Dialogue's easy, isn't it? You just listen to what people say, and then write it down, right? Well . . . sort of. And that's the problem. In this chapter we have a look at what dialogue is and the different ways you can approach it. We also discuss some different ways of presenting dialogue on the page and the effect that each approach has on what you're writing.

Discussing What Dialogue Can Do

You can write a chapter entirely without dialogue, but before doing so, you need to be clear about what dialogue can contribute:

- ✔ **Dialogue (usually) speeds things up.** Reading dialogue is almost always a faster process than reading description. At its simplest level, the lines of dialogue tend to be shorter, so you can read more of them in a given time. They also tend to be colloquial, and so the words are shorter, less complex, and easier to read.

- ✔ **Dialogue conveys information extremely efficiently.** 'Where's our ever-loving mother?' asked Jane. 'I just saw her down by the river, frightening the fish,' Jack replied. From these two lines, you glean that Jane and Jack are brother and sister, they have a somewhat ironic and disrespectful view of their mother, and Jack has just come from the river, where he left their mother. To convey this through a narrator takes a good few lines, and can sail perilously close to 'telling' rather than 'showing': as a good writer, you try to show readers instead of telling them every little detail.

✔ **Dialogue reveals character** by what people say, the way they say it, and what they don't say. You need to think carefully about the lines you put into your characters' mouths. The impression that your readers get of your characters is a composite of all the things they do and all the things they say.

Imagine that you're on your first day in a new job. Sandra comes up to you and says, 'Watch out for Jonas, he'll smile in your face as he steals your work and passes it off as his own.' This conveys a number of things, some of them contradictory:

- Jonas is dishonest, or alternatively at least one person dislikes him enough to lie to you about him.

- Your colleague may be looking out for you, or perhaps a war is going on and your colleague is trying to enlist your support.

- A problem definitely exists in your workplace.

You can use dialogue to make characters complex (for example, someone who on first meeting appears to be the office sneak turns out to defend you when no one else does), and to explain some of their complexities (for example, you remind the office tyrant of her little sister who died tragically young). (The 'Conveying Character' section later in this chapter explores this topic in more depth.)

Presenting Dialogue

Some dialogue is self-evidently important in that it provides plot news or functions as a revealing exchange between the speakers. Including this sort of dialogue is relatively straightforward, because it obviously has to be there, and the content is already decided.

Dialogue that isn't so self-evidently necessary is harder to write, but you can try a few different ways of making the apparently inconsequential important and necessary:

✔ Have the listener be struck by the dialogue without knowing why, and thereby direct readers' attention to it.

✔ Have the speaker behave strangely when they speak. For example, have the speaker look the listener directly in the face when they speak, or, conversely, have them fiddle with something.

Any behaviour that's unusual or betrays discomfort gives the listening character (and the reader) a chance to wonder what's going on. It places a hook in the reader's memory that they can return to later. Don't overdo it though; don't have a thunderclap ring out at the crucial point. Just make the crucial dialogue stand out slightly from the surrounding words.

You can accomplish this aim by having a character remember something that someone said earlier. They may think that, although it wasn't strange in itself, it was a strange thing to say at that point.

Dialogue doesn't exist in isolation and needs to be written with the situation in mind.

For example, a woman is told that her mother has died, and her response is to say that she needs to get the car serviced. Her reaction opens up a number of possible interpretations:

- ✔ The daughter misheard or failed to understand in some way.
- ✔ She may be in shock.
- ✔ She doesn't care whether her mother lives or dies.
- ✔ She murdered her mother, and so already knows she's dead.

In one line of dialogue, you set up at least four possible plot directions.

As you write dialogue, always ask yourself what the listening characters – and the reader – know. Whether they know less than, as much as, or more than the speaker has an impact on what the conversation reveals – or doesn't reveal – and on how and what the speaker says.

Read your writing out loud, and listen particularly closely to the way the dialogue sounds. If it doesn't sound right, it probably isn't right.

Listening in at the Bus Stop

Dramatist Alan Bennett once said that many of the best lines in his plays were things he overheard people say while waiting at bus stops. You often hear writers remark, 'People say the most extraordinary things' and 'People speak much better dialogue than I can possibly make up.'

As a writer, you may already often sit in coffee bars (coffee bars are so much warmer than bus stops) and listen to the conversations around you. If you do this for long enough, you're likely to overhear something amusing, interesting, or strange that you can put into a story. If you do ever overhear someone say something wonderful, by all means write it down. It may well come in useful. However, it may also get you threatened for eavesdropping, so be careful.

The idea is very seductive that all you have to do is simply hang around with a pad and pencil waiting for people to say quirky, witty, or wise things, string it all together, and your dialogue is sorted for you. In fact, writing good dialogue involves more than that.

Writers who say that they get their best lines at bus stops may be telling the truth, but they don't say how long they had to stand there before the good lines came along, or how many really bad lines came along beforehand. Always be suspicious of anything to do with writing that looks effortless. The odds are that someone's worked very hard to make it look that easy.

Furthermore, writers like Alan Bennett are very good at polishing the lines they hear to make them better, and they know how to fit them with other lines to make the whole interesting. One good line doesn't give you a good conversation. If you can do what someone like Alan Bennett does, good for you. He's very good at it, and he makes it look deceptively easy. But writing good dialogue isn't easy; in fact, it's very hard.

Another problem with using overheard dialogue is that amusing quotes are frequently only funny in context – as people often say when a supposedly funny story falls flat, 'You had to be there.' Amusing things are often amusing because of who says them, and so to recreate the impact you need to recreate the character for the reader. Comments that seem wise in one situation often seem banal outside that situation, and charmingly quirky can often seem just silly if you don't know the person.

Hearing how people speak to each other

You need to be very aware of how people speak to each other. Listening to plays on the radio can be instructive. Or, if you're in a public place, try listening to conversations without looking at people. See whether you can work out the relationship between people. As soon as you form an impression about someone or a relationship, ask yourself, 'How do I know that?' What did they say and how did they say it? Listen, too, for things that don't sound right, where the words and the way they are said are in conflict. It's possible to say 'I hate you' seductively, just as it's possible to say 'You're just great' in a way that means you're anything but that.

Notice how people communicate approval or displeasure to each other. Listen for sarcasm and affection, especially when they belie someone's outward demeanour.

When you've practised listening to and writing dialogue down, practise swapping the characters around. If you write a piece in which a man tries to pick a fight and a woman tries to keep the peace because the children are with them, once you're satisfied with it, try swapping the roles to have the woman pick the fight and the man mollify her. How does that scene differ from the first, given what you've identified about how the pair talk and relate?

Like, er, it isn't . . . um, like talking, knowarrImean?

A lot of people talk something like this:

> Like, you know, I used to think that, um, I thought, like . . . ah, the thing is that I thought that looking after the baby, like, would be . . . well, easy, but, you know, it's, well, it's like . . . I don't know, it ought to be – I ought to be, well, better at it than I am, but I, am I like being silly? What do you think?

Extreme, of course, but everyone knows someone who talks like that, because everyone does sometimes. Now, this is okay in normal conversation, because the speaker's thinking about what to say next, but do you want to read it? Probably not.

Here's a useful exercise: next time you're talking about something with a friend, record the conversation. Then write it all down, exactly as you hear it. (Don't do more than a few minutes of conversation: transcribing is dull work.) The results depend on all sorts of things, including the age, gender, and background of the communicators, and the topic under discussion, but we bet that you'll see at least some of the following:

- Words and sounds that don't help the listener understand what the talker is saying. Some of these are uttered to give the talker time to think, such as 'um' and 'er', as well as words and phrases such as 'like', 'you know', 'right', and 'okay'.
- Repetition.
- Interruptions.
- Unfinished sentences.
- Sentences in which the speaker changes the subject in the middle.
- Gaps, pauses, and silences.
- Misunderstandings and mistakes.

The fact is that most real conversations are fractured and incomplete. Many are difficult for an outsider to understand. Many are banal and even dull. People repeat themselves, contradict themselves, take ages to get to the point, make jokes that aren't funny, have irritating tics, and so on. Let's face it, very few people talk in complete, well-constructed, grammatically correct sentences. Even fewer people talk in a way that's consistently engaging and witty.

As a writer, you have an interesting job in front of you. You have to write speech that on the one hand appears realistic, insofar as it sounds like the sort of thing that the person speaking may actually say, but that avoids the repetition, confusion, and banality of real speech. (Not many readers want their stories to contain repetition, confusion, and banality!)

To help you accomplish this feat, we offer some do's and don'ts:

- ✔ **Don't** try to keep very close to the way people talk normally (pauses, changes of subject, going nowhere), even if your book is about normal everyday people. Your main characters probably aren't banal or repetitive. Restrict anyone who is these things to short appearances. At the very least, make sure that their contributions are broken up by other people's speech.

- ✔ **Do** remember that normal everyday speech can be funny and informative, and can reveal character.

You can get a lot of humour from contrast – for example, someone who tends to the overblown talking to someone who keeps it excessively simple, or someone who knows a great deal about a subject talking to someone who knows almost nothing.

Character is revealed by the way people speak, because people tend to speak in terms of the things they know about, their everyday lives and pursuits.

We once worked with a woman who was immoderately proud of her grandchildren. It became a game among some members of the office to find a topic of conversation that couldn't be dragged around to the subject of her grandchildren in under a couple of minutes. (We never found one, and trust us, we tried – hard.) This pride in the grandchildren was amusing and rather endearing for a while, but became tedious when we realised that our colleague had no desire to talk about anything else and had no interest, for example, in anyone else's children or grandchildren. Her pride actually sprang from a strong competitive streak, and it was necessary for her grandchildren to be the best in every way.

From the writing point of view, a conversation between one person trying to discuss a serious political issue and someone else relentlessly trying to talk about their grandchildren is potentially humorous and revealing.

A phrase can sum up a whole character for you. A friend of ours has a habit of starting their contribution to any discussion with the words, 'Ah, but you see, the trouble is . . .'. Doesn't that tell you most of what you need to know about them?

✔ **Do** cut out any parts of dialogue that get in the way, unless there's a good reason to keep them (they reveal character, for example), and even then keep them to a minimum. Remember, readers continue to read what they enjoy, and put down anything that bores them. By this we mean things like endless repetition and dull subject matter.

✔ **Don't** allow dialogue to go nowhere. Unless it has a purpose in the story, it shouldn't be there.

For a writer, no such thing as a neutral conversation exists. No words are wasted, every conversation means something, contains something, or reveals something. Every piece of dialogue you write has importance for your story.

✔ **Don't** worry about a reader thinking, 'This person talks in logical sentences; it isn't like real life at all.' You're telling a story, and unless someone sounds like a pompous Jane Austen character, your readers aren't going to notice that the dialogue isn't true to life.

Wroiting loike eet sownds, innit?

Accents and regional speech patterns are tricky. Whatever area of the country you live in, all other accents are foreign to you, just as your accent is foreign to everyone else. So if accents are important in your story, it isn't enough just to represent those accents that you find strange; any accent with strong characteristics needs to be highlighted.

If you're writing a screenplay, you don't have to worry about accents. You write, 'Enter Janet. She's 35, forceful, and has a broad London accent.' The actor does the rest. Novels are more complicated. Suppose you want to set your novel in a place where the inhabitants have a broad accent. To take it a step further, that accent may well not be familiar to most of your audience. It's important to your story that readers appreciate that your dialogue is being spoken in a particular accent. Here are some ways you can achieve this aim:

✔ **Write phonetically:** This just means that you write the words as they sound. In a very strong Cockney accent, that last sentence written phonetically would be something like, 'Vis jast meens vat yous wroi yer verds as vey sarnd.'

Clearly, there are several problems with this system:

- First, not every Cockney sounds exactly – or even remotely! – like this.

- Second, even writing phonetically assumes a common sound system, which isn't always a safe assumption. For example, you may be writing a character from Manchester who pronounces 'grass' to rhyme with 'maths', but your reader from rural Sussex may well pronounce 'grass' to rhyme with 'Mars'.

- Third, some words are almost unrecognisable spelt phonetically, particularly if you're not familiar with the accent and can't even say it out loud to see what it sounds like. An English writer who's never been to the deep South of the USA probably doesn't know the difference between a Georgia accent and a Louisiana accent, and doesn't know how to pronounce the words that best represent the difference between the two, so phonetic writing is wasted.

  At the least, the reader has to step out of the story to work out what you mean, and that's never a good thing. You also have the very real problem that if you present a West Country accent, for example, as being something along the lines of 'Oi bain't bin thur,' a Somerset person may well feel mis-represented and insulted.

✔ **Write certain words phonetically:** This approach avoids some of the problems detailed in the preceding point. You can, for example, represent a character's Cockney accent by spelling any word starting with a 'v' with a 'w' instead. (Dickens uses this in *The Pickwick Papers* for Sam Weller.) This is, of course, not something that all Cockneys do, but it can work. It may even give you some opportunities for humour, such as when your character means 'vest', but the other characters hear 'west'. This may also be a potential cause for confusion on the part of the reader.

All the problems detailed in the previous point still exist in this method, just in a diluted form, but this method is probably less confusing than a full phonetic rendering.

✔ **Use idiom:** This approach is particularly appropriate for accents such as Cockney, where rhyming slang can be used to remind the reader that the character is speaking with an accent. You can also use repeated words and phrases, particularly intensifiers and unusual (and therefore individual) phrases. An American who says 'You betcha', a Scotsman who says 'Och aye', and an Englishman who says 'I say', are all clichéd examples of the much more subtle and clever words that you're going to come up with for your characters.

Beware of stereotyping and lazy phrasing. And watch out for repetition; just because you know someone in real life who says 'like' every second word doesn't mean it's interesting to read.

✔ **Use speech patterns:** This approach is particularly useful and common in people who are speaking a language that's not their first tongue. They may use constructions like 'a football it is' rather than 'it is a football'. They use unexpected words in odd contexts, such as a Danish cousin of ours who uses 'awful' when he means anything from faintly annoying to really irritating, so that a barking dog is 'awful dog'. (We haven't told him.) People may also use occasional words from their first language, because they can't think of the English equivalent or through habit, especially if the English word is similar to the one in their own language. Swedes and Germans both often use 'ja' for 'yes', perhaps because some English people pronounce 'yes' as something like 'yah'.

You can also allow such characters to get a word wrong occasionally, although we suggest you avoid getting too much comedy out of this, because it's often just patronising rather than funny.

You don't have to tell the reader constantly that someone has an accent. Small occasional reminders do the trick. Just give the reader a nudge once in a while, and they remember.

Conveying Character

You find out about people in a number of ways: you can watch what they do or you can ask others about them. However, the most personal way of finding out how people talk is by talking to them. The same goes for the characters in your novel.

Look carefully at your dialogue. Everything a character says helps the reader to get an impression of them.

Hearing what's said and how it's said

In everyday life, you discover people's character from what they say and how they say it. Often people say something that on the surface means little, and yet the way they say it makes it significant. Alternatively, someone may say something in a way that makes it clear that they feel that the information's important.

People also reveal themselves in what they *don't* say. Sometimes, this is easy to see, as in a person who has an opportunity to speak ill of someone else and doesn't do so. Sometimes it's subtler, as in the realisation that someone you've known for a very long time has never mentioned their parents. A mother who never refers to her son's wife by her name speaks volumes without uttering a word. Writing dialogue can be as much about leaving things out as putting them in.

Obviously what someone says is important, but *how* they say it is just as interesting from a writer's perspective. Ask yourself: how is the situation affecting these people? What words do they use? What words don't they use? Do they use characteristic phrases less or more than usual? Are they avoiding something? Are they in tune with the surroundings? Are they more or less excited, involved, or upset than readers may expect? How does what they say and how they say it reflect their surroundings?

When writing a character, you need to establish a basic speech pattern. A character may be verbose, or brisk and direct. But their speech may change when they're placed in a stressful situation. These changes tell the reader that the stress is affecting the character.

A simple example is a character who never uses bad language – and who even objects when others use it – suddenly swearing. Similarly, if a powerful businessman, feared by his employees for the rough edge of his tongue, speaks kindly to someone who's spectacularly messed up a job, at the very least the reader knows that something odd is happening. Then there's a work colleague who's always been friendly suddenly becoming distant, or perhaps worse, icily polite and correct. Instead of cheerful words and phrases, they start to use cold professional language, titles instead of names, and they refuse to talk about anything that isn't directly related to the subject in hand.

Another example is how people use each other's names. Assume that a character is named Josephine Smith. On being introduced, some people call her Miss Smith, some prefer Ms Smith, others call her Josephine, and others, still, call her Jo. Each mode of address tells something about the person speaking. 'Miss Smith' is perhaps a little formal, although it depends on the situation. 'Ms Smith' reflects a certain way of seeing titles. 'Josephine' is familiar, possibly a little too familiar on first meeting. 'Jo' is extremely familiar, and for some people highly inappropriate.

How Josephine Smith responds to these appellations conveys something about her. If she says, 'Please call me Jo,' that's one sort of response. If someone calls her Jo and she says with a smile, 'Actually, it's Josephine,' that's another response. Also, does she say it in a way that suggests that she doesn't like the name Jo, or is she saying to that person, 'I don't know you well enough to let you shorten my name'? More extremely, if she introduces herself as 'Josephine Smith, but most people call me Flopsy,' that's another type of person.

Think about how situations change, and how the words used reflect that change. One simple way is an increase in formality. If someone who has always called someone Jo suddenly calls her Josephine, this is a signal. (Children know that when their parents use the full-length versions of their names, they're in trouble.) Similarly, a change from Josephine to Miss Smith is a signal that something has changed.

Non-responsive responses can be very telling as well. The classic example is when someone says 'I love you' and the other person doesn't reply or says something that doesn't quite ring true, such as 'You're special to me too.' The fact that the other person doesn't reply 'I love you too' may not be significant as a one-off, but at the very least if someone can't say those words, a reader is justified in thinking that they have issues with the speaker or with themselves.

Think also about the words that people use as euphemisms (a relative who 'gets very tired' rather than 'regularly gets stinking drunk') and what that way of talking says about the speaker. Also remember what is called 'the elephant in the room', which is something blindingly obvious that no one talks about. This goes beyond euphemism, such as when people say 'Daddy's getting forgetful,' when it's obvious that the old man is going senile.

Revealing relationships in conversation

You almost certainly have experience of the basic relationships that you need to think about. Here are two examples:

- ✔ **Lovers** often talk in what appears to be some sort of code and focus their attention on each other. They may finish each other's sentences. They often talk in low voices with their heads together. In these ways, they can present a sense of exclusivity, a sense of personal bond. Now, consider how lovers behave who are trying not to reveal their relationship. They often have conversations about 'safe' topics (such as the weather) when in public, for fear of revealing too much. They often exaggerate formality, allow each other to finish talking, don't contradict each other, and so on. Notice how this agreement is often overdone (for example, 'Yes, good point' to something quite mundane).

- ✔ **Enemies** may act in a number of ways: they may loudly insist on their point of view or remain largely silent. Their voices may become shrill with tension (lovers are seldom shrill unless arguing) or low with disgust, fast or choked up with impatience, and so on. They may use patronising, insulting, or dismissive language, with a tone to match. Or they may use another tone to conceal what they're doing. Now think about how people behave when they love each other even though they appear to be enemies. In what ways can voice, tone, words, and behaviour be in and out of synchronisation to produce different results?

Think about someone in the public eye, caught out misbehaving or breaking the law, who goes on television to try to rescue their reputation, and takes their partner (who's usually referred to as 'standing by' them) to prove that all's well. The politician says things like, 'I've been very stupid,' 'I'm getting help,' 'My family is standing beside me,' 'I don't deserve them.' The partner (whose body language is often extremely interesting – watch them slightly nodding as the politician blames themselves) usually studiously avoids blaming the other person for anything directly, while speaking their forgiveness through gritted teeth. Notice how the politician often talks a lot, happy to be confessing, using psycho-speak phrases ('I'm getting help,' 'I have issues,' 'I'm dealing with my demons,' 'It's a long journey,' and 'I'm looking for support'), whereas the partner speaks in shorter clipped sentences with words that are often simple common-sense observations: 'It's obviously going to take time' (notice how words like 'obviously' crop up a lot from someone in this position).

Sampling situations

These three examples illustrate how dialogue can work with particular situations to make it more than just talk:

- In *Pride and Prejudice*, Jane Austen presents the very different characters of Mr and Mrs Bennet. He is witty, urbane, detached, well-read, full of irony, and in every way a delightful companion. She is fussy, hysterical, melodramatic, and has little conversation beyond local gossip and the marriage prospects of her daughters. Their conversation could hardly be more different. For much of the book, Mrs Bennet is the object of humour, particularly through Mr Bennet's ironic jokes at her expense. One of the revelations is that Mrs Bennet's fears that her daughters may end up unmarried are based on a real fear of economic hardship, and that Mr Bennet's irony is a defence that enables him to hide from reality. He is the more entertaining conversationalist, but his detachment puts his daughters in danger of ending up in the poorhouse. Mrs Bennet's apparently melodramatic wailings become more justified in the reader's eyes, while Mr Bennet's irony becomes less appealing.

- The playwright Alan Bennett (not to be confused with the Bennets in the previous example!) often uses dialogue to act as a metaphor for something larger. A vicar's wife talking about the women who compete to arrange the church flowers tells us everything that we need to know about her life, marriage, and state of mind, and yet on the surface she's done little more than make a few wryly amusing observations about the way people compete for her husband's attention. The pain in Bennett is almost always unspoken, held below the surface.

- Quentin Tarantino's film *Pulp Fiction* has a famous scene in which the two main characters discuss the merits of cheeseburgers while driving. The dialogue is mildly amusing, and it gives some insight into their characters. However, the viewer may well wonder about the point of the scene. That point isn't revealed until you realise that the two characters are hit-men on their way to carry out several killings. The banality of their conversation is in counterpoint to the purpose of their journey. For them, killing is their day-to-day existence, and the cheeseburger conversation underlines this situation.

The point is to write dialogue that reflects the relationship between the characters talking. Of course, the most interesting dialogue is when more than one thing is going on, for example when people don't like each other but must work together.

Speech is one of the components with which you can build character, so you may want to have a look at Chapter 8.

Registering Tone

Dialogue doesn't operate in a vacuum. You need to think about how dialogue works in social terms. *Social register*, the relative social positions and relationships between people due to different degrees of wealth, influence, and power, is another extremely important and useful way of conveying information through dialogue.

Social register isn't necessarily about social class, although it can be. Work relationships are often hierarchical, and many groups have a similar structure. In local communities, people assume positions of influence. Within social groups, including small groups of friends of the same age and background, there are lines of influence and power. Leaders come and go. Some groups have different leaders depending on the situation. The fact remains that surprisingly few conversations are between equals. Adults speak to children differently, and men and women talk differently to each other than they do to those of their own gender. Social register and tone are key when writing dialogue, because they can cause and explain people's reactions.

Part of this works through simple differences in modes of address, such as when the landowner calls his gardener by his surname, and the gardener calls him 'Sir'. Also, socially superior people tend to ask more questions, and inferiors do more responding. Inferiors tend to say less of what they are thinking about a subject, unless prompted to do so. Some socially superior people exhibit a degree of patronising behaviour; some inferiors try to flatter their superiors.

Equals don't talk to each other in the same way that they speak to their superiors and their subordinates. Listen to the differences as you interact in your social and work circles.

You need to think about how different relationships are balanced socially, how this balance expresses itself in the dialogue between these people, and what emotions are expressed and repressed during their conversation. Of course, people react to social register very differently: some people value it, some resent it. A character can respond to a social superior in a number of ways – for example, rambling on nervously, rambling in a self-aggrandising way, speaking in confident short sentences, or retreating behind a laconic shield, which may or may not be to the point of rudeness.

Playing with power in relationships

Imagine that a pantomime is being put on at a village hall, and is being directed by a recent arrival to the village. This young woman has some experience of the theatre and is used to working co-operatively with semi-professionals. In this case, however, her cast are all amateurs, with many other commitments. For everything she wants she has to deal with the chairman of the village hall committee (and, it appears, every other committee), an elderly and rather pompous ex-major.

Think about the power relationships here:

✔ She's the new arrival, knows nobody, and doesn't know how things work. He's lived locally all his life, and apparently knows everyone and everything.

✔ She's experienced in theatre. He has no experience.

✔ She's young and female. He is old and male.

The relationship can go at least two ways with each characteristic. Her newness to the district may be a disadvantage, because she has little idea who to approach if she needs something. On the other hand, she isn't tainted by any of the infighting that has gone on down the years, and so she can get things done. The major may patronise her youth or appreciate it. She may treat him as a pompous old bore or a colourful character. And so on. The register and tone in their dialogue reflects all these aspects of their relationship.

Looking at the Mechanics of the Layout

To discover how to lay out your dialogue on the page, get hold of several books published by the company you hope is going to publish your novel, and see how it does so. The publisher may well have a house style, in which case, follow it. If there isn't a house style, you have a few options:

✔ **Going traditional:** The traditional way of laying out dialogue is simple: use quotes for the spoken words, with a punctuation mark placed inside the quotes. Use a new line for each new speaker:

'Do you really think so?' asked John.

'Yes,' replied Mary decisively.

Following this method has the advantages that everyone's used to it and it's easy to remember.

✔ **Dropping the quotes:** You can, of course, decide to drop the quotes:

Do you really think so? asked John.

Yes, replied Mary decisively.

This can work, although it can cause confusion where someone is both speaking and doing something.

✔ **Using dashes:** Some writers put a dash before speech, like this:

—Do you really think so? asked John.

That works all right until the speaker moves around, when you either need to put in another dash or dispense with it.

✔ **Using a new line or not:** You have to decide whether to use a new line for each speaker:

> Do you really think so? asked John. He walked across the room. I wonder if you're correct. He picked up a vase and held it to the light. I'm not sure.

Here the reader has to decide whether 'I wonder if you're correct' is spoken or is description, and, having decided that it's the former, has to decide who's speaking. If you preserve the new line convention, John is obviously speaking. If you decide to dispense with it, confusion results:

> Do you really think so? asked John. He walked across the room. I wonder if you're correct. He picked up a vase and held it to the light. I'm not sure. She moved towards him. I know I am.

This makes it very difficult to know for sure who's talking. You can put 'she said' and 'he said' after each line of dialogue, which helps a bit, but is clumsy.

You can, of course, write your story in such a way that leaving out quotes and not worrying about new lines for new speakers doesn't cause any problems. If this doesn't mean compromising your story, that's fine. It's up to you.

Our advice? If it ain't broke, don't fix it. Everyone knows the quotes and new line system, so we advise using it unless you have a really good reason not to. You have far more important things to be thinking about.

Talking Tags

Tags are the words that follow a line of dialogue to explain who's talking and how. At the simplest level, tags are phrases like 'she said' and 'said Jeannette', as well as phrases such as 'she complained', 'she said crossly', and 'Jeannette fumed'. The main purpose of tags is to make it plain to the reader who's speaking.

A lot of writers seem to run into the problem of finding alternatives to the word 'said'. They use 'said' and then go on to 'whispered', 'mused', 'expostulated', 'hissed', 'ejaculated', and so on. (A thesaurus really is an essential part of any writer's armoury!)

There aren't really any firm rules about this – as ever, what works for you, works; what doesn't, doesn't. Reading any two novels shows you that writers have different ideas about this, but we lay down some general guidelines to make life simple for you:

✔ Tags slow things down, so don't use them unless they're necessary.

✔ You only need a tag when it isn't clear from the context who's talking. If only two characters are talking, you hardly need to use tags at all. Use tags only when one character speaks, does something, and then speaks again; you may confuse readers if you don't use a tag in this instance.

✔ If more than two people are talking, you sometimes need to tell the reader who's talking, especially if someone hasn't spoken for a while, or if a number of people are arguing. However, the speaker is often evident from the context.

Assume that you write something like, 'Sanjay hadn't spoken for some time, but now he put his glass back on the table with unnecessary force and leant forward. His voice was soft but distinct. "I'm really, really tired of this nonsense."' Now, you can add 'he said' onto the end of that, or indeed 'he whispered', but is there any doubt who's talking? If not, you don't need 'he said'. And is there any doubt that he's whispering, given that you've already said his voice is 'soft but distinct'? If not, you don't need the 'he whispered' tag. So always ask yourself whether you need a tag.

Sometimes, writers write a line of dialogue and then put a tag after it along the lines of 'she said viciously' or 'she snapped'. You sometimes need to do this, but less often than you may think. Put it this way: you wouldn't have someone speak about a hundred words and then put at the end 'she snapped', because snapping is by definition a short, sharp retort. On the other hand, if someone's speaking and someone else says 'Don't be stupid!', it already sounds like they're snapping, so you don't need to say it. In practice, you generally only need to say something like 'she snapped' if you want to add impact, or if in some way the tone of the line and its content aren't in tune, such as when someone's being ironic.

Chapter 11

Including Conflict

onflict in stories can come in many forms, but you can't do without at least one conflict in your novel. Conflict gives a story its reason for being, and keeps you up half the night reading. Conflict answers the question, 'Why are you telling me this story?' It's the essence of story and part of every novel you read. You need to be able to recognise conflict and to see when it's missing from your own work. If you've ever read something you've written and thought 'Booooring!', there's a good chance you haven't got the conflict sorted out. This chapter takes you through the whys and hows of including conflict.

Working Out Why You Need Conflict

Conflict *is* story. You can write a story with no conflict, but not a story that anyone wants to read.

Imagine that you're a child again and someone offers to read you a story. They give you a choice between two stories you've not heard before. They briefly describe each story and ask you to choose which one interests you most. Which of the following two stories would you prefer to listen to?

> Once upon a time, there was a kingdom in which everyone was very happy. Everyone agreed what should be done, and the king and queen were very good at making sure that everyone got what they wanted. The princes and princesses all met highly suitable partners and married them, and everyone went on to live happily ever after.

Or:

> Once upon a time, there was a kingdom in which everyone was very happy. Then the good king and queen died, and the new king and queen had lots of new ideas that the people didn't like very much. One of their new ideas, encouraged by their prime minister, was to start a war with the country next door, which no one wanted, but everyone got carried away and before they'd really thought it through there was a huge battle. To stop the war, it was agreed that the respective prince and princess would marry and rule the two countries jointly. This was a good idea, but no one asked the prince and princess what they thought about it. They had never met, and anyway both of them were in love with their own sweethearts, but if they didn't marry then the war would go on, and they didn't want that either. It seemed that their own happiness was doomed.

Most people would rather hear the second story, and not just because it's sadder, but because it has conflict (plenty of happy stories are full of conflict, too).

Some writers prefer to call conflict *struggle*, but whichever term you prefer, use it in your story to ensure that:

✔ **There are things at stake in the story.** Characters want competing things, or two characters want the same thing that only one can have.

   Take a Cup Final football match, for example. The two teams both want to win, and that isn't possible. One of them has to lose, and neither team wants to do that.

✔ **The things at stake matter.** Characters are prepared to fight, cheat, lie, and perhaps even kill for them. If the things at stake were trivial, they wouldn't bother.

   The stakes in the football match aren't trivial. A cup is to be won, glory and honour to be gained, and financial rewards too, as well as the matter of pride, both personal and in the team.

✔ **The reader is required to choose a side.** Partly because of the first two things, the people in the football crowd identify with one or other side. They may decide to support the expensively assembled team of brilliant individuals, or they may prefer the plucky and tenacious underdogs. The point is that very few people at a Cup Final are neutral.

Make sure that you ground your novel on these ideas. People must want different things, they must be prepared to go to some lengths to get them (varying from character to character and situation to situation), and the reader should be involved to the extent that they want someone to win, succeed, or at least not to fail (not all stories are black-and-white fights between evil villains and good guys). In other words, you need struggle and conflict or you've got a friendly novel where everyone supports everyone else in their efforts. Life is a struggle, so make sure that your novel reflects that reality.

Confronting Conflict

This section takes a look at what conflict means in story-telling terms, what it consists of, and what you can build it upon.

Basically, *conflict* is the gap between what people want and what they get. The crucial points in creating conflict are giving your characters something to want and making it difficult for them to get it. If your characters have everything they want, and every time they need something else it appears, you don't have much of a story.

Remember that the word *want* has two meanings: to *desire* something and to *lack* something. So a character may desire money, fame, or another person. They may lack another person's approval or security. (Yes, there's an overlap here: someone may lack money, and therefore desire it. But try to think of it both ways, so that you don't miss anything.)

Wanting with intensity

Wanting is part of being human. People are always looking for new sensations, new ideas, and new ways of doing things; the grass is always greener on the other side of the hill.

The useful thing about wanting things from a writer's perspective is that people usually want things that are in short supply. Not everyone can be a billionaire or possess a genuine Picasso. So the struggle to make money or obtain something is immediately likely to contain conflict. Furthermore, not everyone can be a boss or get to the top of the heap. You have to compete if you want to win, which entails more conflict.

Therefore, stories about people wanting things are a good idea. There are plenty of them, too, as well as lots of different ways to approach them: almost everyone has experience of, and can relate to, a story about wanting something.

So, writing a story can be easy. You just put some wanted item some place and watch your characters fight for it. That is, of course, one way of doing it, and plenty of stories use variations on this idea.

From a story-telling point of view, the important thing isn't the size of the thing that someone wants, it's how badly they want it.

You may suppose that a book about stealing two million pounds is twice as interesting as a book about stealing one million pounds. In fact, the amount has almost nothing to do with it. For a story to be interesting, the characters have to want the prize badly. What the prize is doesn't matter; the situation is made into a good story by the fact that the characters want it badly enough to take action.

A story about someone who, more than anything else in the world, wants to be a movie star and is willing to do absolutely anything – lie, cheat, drive themselves to the limit, or kill – to achieve that ambition is clearly more compelling than a story about someone who'd quite like to be a movie star, but only if it isn't too hard and definitely not if it means having to get up in the morning.

If your protagonist wants something, make them *really* want it. Romeo wants Juliet so badly that he kills himself when he thinks she's died. Some people want a baby so badly that when they discover that they can't have one they steal someone else's. King Edward VIII wanted to be with Wallis Simpson so badly that he gave up being king for her. That's wanting.

If a character wants something badly, the readers stay with them to see if they get it and to see what they're prepared to do if it's denied them.

Strong feelings make action more likely. You also want the reader to say one of two things: 'Hey, yes, I can relate to that, I'd be just as desperate or worried or obsessed as this character in their situation,' or 'I don't feel the same way this character does about this thing that they obviously think is so important, but I can see why it's important to them.' That's crucial.

Aim to make it very clear to the reader that the protagonist wants whatever it is that they want very badly, and that they have their own reasons. Those reasons may be unusual, but they matter to the protagonist. The reader doesn't have to agree that the reasons are good or even sensible, just that the protagonist has them.

Putting up obstacles

The trick is to make your characters want something and then put an obstacle in the way of getting it. The obstacle can be anything, or a combination of things: another person, society, luck or circumstances, family, history, their own self-destructive tendencies, and so on. The obstacle can be an internal problem, such as someone wanting two mutually exclusive things. (For example, a woman may have a strong desire to be famous, but the husband she adores can't bear to live in the spotlight. She can't have both of the things she wants, so she must choose.) The possibilities are endless.

Ask yourself these questions:

- ✔ What does my main character want?
- ✔ What prevents them from getting it?
- ✔ What's going to happen if they don't get it?

If the answers to these questions are, respectively, 'Not much,' 'Nothing really,' and 'Very little,' your story has a problem! Things must *matter*. Your character must want something, there must be some sort of obstacle, and there must be an apparent problem if the obstacle can't be overcome.

Building conflict around buying bread

Imagine that you're talking to a friend, and you're telling them a story.

I went to the shops to buy some bread yesterday, as we'd run out. They had lots of bread, so I bought a loaf and brought it home. Mind you, it wouldn't have mattered if they hadn't had any, because I already had three loaves in the freezer that I bought a while back, and lots of packets of biscuits. We'd have been fine.

You wouldn't tell your friend that story, because it isn't a story, and the reason it isn't a story is because there isn't any conflict.

Now try this:

I went to the shops yesterday to buy some bread, as we'd run out. When I got there the shop was closed, so I had to run like mad to the other shop where I never go on principle because they're a bunch of robbers and my ex-girlfriend who now hates me works there. I had to go in gasping for air and dripping with sweat and buy a loaf of their over-priced bread. She's on the till, glaring at me, and I'm paying over the odds for this bread while she's looking at me suspiciously, and then she asks me why I need the bread so badly. I can't tell her that it's because I need it to make bread-crumbs to cook the meal that she used to make me, and I'm cooking it for my new girlfriend that she doesn't know about, but now I think she guessed what was happening, because when I got the bread home it wasn't the fresh loaf I'd bought. She must have swapped it for a mouldy one, so the evening wasn't a great success, and when I saw my old girlfriend in the street this morning she smiled really sweetly and asked how the evening went.

This is a story because it has tension or conflict between what the teller wants to do (walk quietly down to the shops, buy a loaf of bread, and bring it back to cook a meal to impress his new girlfriend) and what actually happens (circumstances and an ex-girlfriend combine to thwart him).

Considering the Different Sources for Conflict

Conflicts can come from a wide range of sources, but they fall into some useful broad groups.

Disagreeing with other people

Other people are a fertile source of conflict. Generally your protagonist can have disagreements with two groups of people:

✔ An *enemy* is anyone who deliberately tries to harm your protagonist. Enemies are useful because they place the protagonist in situations where they have to decide whether to take action. Of course, enemies have different motivations; they can be justified in their feelings or not, and their enmity can take any form you choose, but the conflict is fairly easy to see.

✔ Your protagonist can also come into conflict with people who are less clear-cut in their motives than enemies, and are therefore sometimes more interesting to read about. These are people (*the rest*) who don't deliberately set out to harm your protagonist, but often end up doing just that. The popularity of stories featuring warring members of the same family is a testament to this area of conflict with other people.

Families can be straightforward enemies, of course, but it's often more interesting to have a mixture of motivations. Relatives often act with what they see as someone's best interests at heart, and yet that person may well not see it that way and resent their actions. Love complicates things too, because relatives can be torn between familial affection and disapproval.

A woman falls in love with someone of whom her family disapproves. Her family send her away for a while, and then intimidate and bribe her lover to leave the area. When she returns, they tell her that her lover has moved away to be with another woman. However, her sister breaks ranks from the family and tells her the truth. The woman blames her sister just as much as the rest of the family. The sister is now ostracised by both sides of the family. Meanwhile, the lover is ashamed of his actions and comes back. The family acted from love and in good faith, but they are still antagonists to your protagonist; she wants one thing and they want to prevent her getting it.

Being in conflict with the circumstances

One of the interesting things about conflict is that it's often situation-specific, by which we mean that a particular combination of circumstances brings about the conflict.

You can write this type of conflict by creating a story and then thinking about the circumstances, or you can think of the circumstances first and then work on the story.

If you start with your circumstances ('It's set in Israel during the Six Day War' or 'It's set on that housing estate just down the road during all that trouble last year'), you need to think about what characters and relationships make an interesting story set against that background. For example, a story about an Israeli diplomat falling in love with an Egyptian soldier has obvious potential for a story, because their respective positions are clearly problematic. If their two countries were not at war, their problems would be fewer. However, a story about two Israeli farmers who are at odds about the ownership of a field can be set at almost any time, and the Six Day War has very little to contribute to the story (at least on the surface).

If you start with your story, you have to decide what circumstances make the story most interesting. A love story between two interesting people can be given conflict by the situation: everything's fine until one of them is injured in a car crash, or made redundant, or war breaks out, or anything that works against the desires of the characters. So, if the characters want more than anything else to be together, conflict arises if circumstances conspire to keep them apart. If the protagonist wants more than anything else to be left alone to work on his farm, circumstances should work towards making it difficult for him to do so.

If your protagonist marries someone from another race, a short list of possible reactions from the family may be shock, horror, concern, amusement, disbelief, indifference, and happiness. The most interesting conflicts are mixtures: a parent is unhappy at his daughter marrying, but his objection has nothing to do with race, but rather with age, culture, or his experiences in the war. You can build conflict by having the concerned father defend himself against the charge of racism, and the family of the intended spouse making assumptions that aren't true, or are only partly true. Or the father may not think that he's racist, but in fact he is. And so on.

A reaction *against* a situation is more likely to provoke conflict than acceptance.

Remember that time, place, and circumstances matter. A story about a pacifist Jewish medical student falling in love with the daughter of an army colonel is one sort of story if you set it in London in 1938. Exactly the same set-up becomes a very different story if set in Berlin in the same year, and different again if you set it in Northern Ireland in 1975, or in Iraq in 2005.

Conflict often grows out of situations containing the wrong person in the wrong place at the wrong time. If the person, place, or time were different, events may be very different.

Struggling with internal conflict

Other people and circumstances are the most obvious causes of conflict, but don't forget a third cause: your characters themselves. Just like people, your characters can be their own worst enemies. Your characters can behave in ways that prevent them getting what they want. Suppose that your protagonist is a talented actor who finds it extremely difficult to work with other people. He may find it hard to get work. Suppose that an athlete is a chronic over-eater, or that an alcoholic gets a job requiring absolute reliability. It's easy to see how behaviour can stand in the way of your characters getting the things they want.

Your characters can also be stymied by their own inner resources – or lack thereof. Suppose your protagonist wants to be an actor, but is cripplingly shy about speaking in public? What if a lack of self-esteem leads your ambitious businessman to be rude to anyone who tries to tell him what to do? Such internal problems can be equally self-destructive. You can have a character who's so compulsive about cleaning the house that they can't leave it in the morning, or someone so mistrustful of others that they're unable to give those who love them the response they deserve.

These tendencies produce conflict. They provoke anger, frustration, and disappointment in others, and all these reactions are likely to result in argument and problems. They also produce reactions within the characters themselves – your made-up people probably aren't proud of themselves for these types of behaviour, and so they have internal conflicts.

Internal and external conflicts both cause and feed off each other. Here are some situations of conflict and struggle which you may be able to use in your novel:

- An obvious source of conflict is war itself. People fight (and kill) each other. The story can lie in the reason why the people decided to fight in the first place, or why they continue to fight (including the idea that they may have forgotten why), or how it can be stopped. A territorial dispute? Fishing rights? An argument that got out of hand? Or maybe they just haven't liked each other for 400 years and aren't about to start now?

Although this type of conflict is obviously important – it's the backdrop for the narrative and has an impact on what people do and why they do it – it may well be the least interesting of the various strands of conflict in the story, because personalising it is quite difficult.

✔ The best stories often centre on a struggle between two people, even if they are representatives of larger organisations (James Bond and Dr No, Lizzie Bennet and Mr Darcy). Personalising a conflict between nations is difficult, although it can be done by taking a small corner of a conflict and reducing it to a struggle between two people or two small groups. A good example is *Enemy at the Gates* (a biography by William Craig, which was made into a film with Ed Harris and Jude Law), in which the siege of Stalingrad in 1942 is boiled down to a struggle between two snipers.

Another way is to pit the main character against war itself, such as in Erich Maria Remarque's *All Quiet on the Western Front*, in which the struggle is to stay alive. You can use war most usefully as a backdrop to your story in order to heighten emotions and make the potential consequences of decisions more serious.

Fighting is a product or symptom of conflict, rather than the conflict itself. It's important to see the difference. Some writers put a fight scene into their story and assume that's enough to supply the conflict.

✔ Another useful source of struggle is between people whose position (social, sexual, personal) requires them to act in ways that they may not want to. Princes and princesses may have to marry people they don't like, or may be unable marry people that they love. People's jobs may require them to live abroad, in places where they don't want to live, away from the people and surroundings that they love. People may have to form relationships to please other people (families may take it for granted that two people who've grown up together are 'just right for each other'). People may have to go into business with people they dislike or even despise. All these situations result in people struggling with their own conflicting desires as well as with the people with whom they're unwillingly in contact, and they quite possibly resent the people and the influences that forced them into the situation. You can use this sort of struggle to force your characters to decide or choose what is most important to them.

✔ Struggle and conflict can also be generated by those around the main characters. Parents, for example, may be in conflict with themselves and each other. They may feel guilty about a number of things, including their parenting and the decisions and sacrifices they made, as well as those that they forced their children to make. Parents may also take the view that duty comes before self, and prompt a struggle between ideas of honour and self-sacrifice on the one hand and love on the other. You can use this sort of conflict to make your characters see how their upbringing influenced them.

✔ The potential for struggle also lies in other centres of authority, such as government, the boardroom, and so on. Individuals can seek their own ends or have a bigger picture in mind. What's good for the individual may not be good for the country: sometimes the interests of the individual must be sacrificed in order for the institution to progress. Don't forget that institutions are often formed of more than one faction, and that factions constantly compete for influence. You can use this sort of conflict to raise wider issues of politics and how it affects the individual.

Hitting people financially or emotionally is just as much an attack – and a form of conflict – as hitting them physically.

Putting Conflict into Your Story

This section helps you clarify in your own mind the type and degree of conflict in your novel.

Try this exercise. Write down:

1. **Your protagonist's name.**

2. **The one thing that they want more than anything.**

3. **What has to happen for them to get it.**

4. **The things that prevent them getting it.**

5. **The effect of not getting what they want.**

6. **The changes that take place as a result of not getting what they want. Do they still want the same thing?**

If you haven't got an answer for one of these steps, you need to think hard. If any of these steps are missing in your novel, your conflict isn't going to come through clearly.

Going through the steps in this section, you may end up with something like this:

✔ Katie's a young teenager who's fallen hopelessly in love with James, her older brother's best friend. More than anything else in the world she wants him to go out with her.

✔ For that to happen, two things must change: James must stop thinking of Katie as just a freckle-faced kid, and his existing girlfriend, Julie, must disappear.

✔ If Katie doesn't get James, she's going to be miserable and feel foolish. Increasingly, as she sees James and Julie together, she feels that the problem isn't her youth, but Julie. Julie's keeping James from being with her. The more she thinks about her options, the more sure she becomes. Katie must let James go, or she must take action.

What's happened here is that, through conflict, the story's moved. It begins with a static situation. Katie loves James, but James loves Julie and thinks that Katie's just a kid. Nothing's likely to happen in this situation, until you ask, 'What's the effect of the fact that Katie doesn't get what she wants?' Either Katie moves forward (she decides that she loves James and is prepared to fight for him), or she moves backwards (she decides that he isn't worth it and drops the idea). Assuming she chooses to fight for him, she must *do* something. Now all you need to decide is whether your story's a comedy or a horror story, and what Katie does to Julie. Or to James.

You can introduce conflict in the same way into a story about two businesses. Company A and Company B share the market 60/40. They're both happy with this position, therefore nothing happens. Then a new CEO takes over Company B. The CEO isn't happy with the situation and starts competing for business in areas that Company A traditionally monopolised. Company A's not happy with this and decides to wipe out Company B altogether. The story's all about what happens and who, if anyone, wins. No story existed until you introduced conflict.

Conflict (and story) is in the space between what someone wants and what they get. Ask yourself what the character wants, what they get, and what the effect of that will be. Your conflict and your story lie in this space.

Part IV
Fine-tuning and Finishing Up

Top Five Tips for Including Minor Characters in Your Novel

- ✔ Writing a story centred on just two people may feel contrived. Most people have other people in their lives. You often need to include minor characters in your story just to make it more convincing; more like real life.

- ✔ Other people make the story more interesting. The actions of minor characters can affect the main characters in large and small ways.

- ✔ Minor characters act as a counterpoint to the main characters. The way the protagonist reacts to minor characters tells the reader something about the protagonist.

- ✔ Minor characters are often necessary to the story as accomplices, confidants, messengers, critics, inconveniences, and so on.

- ✔ Minor characters add complexity and variety to the story, making it less intensely focused on the main characters. They also deepen and add threads to the story.

Go to www.dummies.com/extras/writinganovelgettingpublisheduk for free online bonus content.

In this part . . .

✔ Re-read, correct, and improve upon your novel before you begin sending it to potential publishers.

✔ Check that your characters and settings are consistent. Does Edith accidentally turn into Edie in Chapter 32? Do all the exciting events occur in the second half of the book, and the first half is slower than a tortoise in treacle?

✔ Find initial readers for your book, how to get feedback from them, and what to do with the feedback you receive.

Chapter 12

Adding Depth and Detail

Successful stories need to be about more than one thing and need to involve more than one character. The story needs to build: it needs to flow outwards, involving other aspects. To put it in writing terms: a story needs layering and sub-plots.

This chapter helps you to add complexity to your story without making it confusing.

Stripping Down to the Essentials

The essentials of your novel boil down to three broad areas: plot, main characters, and supporting characters. The following sections address each in turn.

Plotting essentials

You need to decide who and what are the crucial parts of your story. Imagine that a film director's just offered you a lot of money for the film rights to your book, and asked you to do the screenwriting. But the film's going to be a really stripped-down version of your book. You can only use a minimum number of your characters, settings, and events. You have to make some decisions about what is essential and what isn't and then keep the essential in focus throughout the writing process.

However, some of the essential things when you start writing may not be the same things you consider to be essential later on – the book changes as you proceed. Don't worry: that's natural. Check as you go along; see whether your decision's still on track. If not, change it. After you've finished the first draft, take another look. Make that decision again and stick to it, because it's sure to help you focus on what's important.

Focusing on main characters

Decide on your main characters. Their story is the story of your novel. (If it isn't, have another look, because they probably aren't the main characters.) The odds are that the essential characters and situation are the characters and situation you started with, although sometimes characters come in and unexpectedly take a story over.

After you've decided, you can just tell the main characters' story. If you set your novel on a desert island and put only two people on it, that's exactly what you do. Mind you, if they're both married to other people, their spouses are likely to be characters in the story even if they never actually appear. In fact, anyone who plays a substantial part in either of the characters' lives is involved, if only by their absence.

Making the most of minor characters

Most stories aren't about just two people removed from the world. Your main characters have friends, work colleagues, family, and so on. They may well have a large number of people in their lives who are important to them, and these characters often find their way into the book.

Some reasons why most stories have minor characters include:

- ✔ Writing a story centred on just two people may well feel contrived. Most people have other people in their lives. You often need to include minor characters in your story just to make it more convincing; more like real life.

- ✔ Other people make the story more interesting. Your readers like to meet and find out about them. The actions of minor characters can affect the main characters in large and small ways. They can complicate and help simplify.

- ✔ Minor characters act as a counterpoint to the main characters. For example, secondary characters can inspire, shame, sadden, or delight a main character, and prompt the protagonist to behave in ways they may not otherwise have considered. The way the protagonist reacts to minor characters tells the reader something about the protagonist.

✔ Minor characters are often necessary to the story as accomplices, confidants, messengers, critics, inconveniences, and so on.

✔ Minor characters add complexity and variety to the story, making it less intensely focused on the main characters. They also deepen and add threads to the story.

Layering

One of the defining characteristics of a novel is what writers call layering. Short stories can have layering too, but the additional length of a novel demands a greater degree of complexity.

Layering refers to the different stories (sometimes called plot and sub-plot) that run side by side, and to the levels of emotional complexity that your characters can reveal. Layering adds depth and richness to the novel, making it more satisfying for the reader.

Take the following steps to provide layers in your novel:

1. **Establish the central relationship.**

   This relationship is usually between the protagonist and another person. It may be romantic or it may not. Alternatively, it may be between the protagonist and a thing (such as a business or organisation) or a group of people. It can be internal, for example between the protagonist and her emotions or flaws. Devote the majority of your attention – and the reader's – to this relationship, because it's the most important thing in the story.

2. **Establish the subsidiary relationships that each central character brings with them.**

   Every character has relationships – with lovers, family, friends, and enemies – that they bring with them to the story. These relationships may well have an impact on the story. (If they don't, you may want to think about whether they should be in the story at all.) Characters may well have an effect in more than one direction, even if their presence is restricted to a few scenes.

   For example, if the protagonist's cousin appears drunkenly at the protagonist's wedding and is revealed to be an alcoholic, this may have an effect upon relationships within the family and between the protagonist and her heavy-drinking fiancé.

Layering Gerry and Harriet

Harriet and Gerry, the main characters in the story, are lovers. Their parents don't approve and are attempting to break them up. Gerry has two flatmates, who spend all day lying around watching TV and see Harriet as disrupting their comfortable existence. Harriet has a jealous sister who perhaps secretly wants Gerry for herself. The main driver of the story is Gerry and Harriet's romance and how the couple deal with the various pressures. The question that a readers ask themselves is, 'Will they get together by the end or not?'

So far, the story is very focused on Gerry and Harriet. Lot of opportunity exists, even on this small canvas, for additional characters to bring both variety and more stories to the picture. For example, why are the parents so against the marriage? Are both sets of parents equally against it, or one more so than the other? Maybe Gerry's parents married young and regret it, and don't want their son to make the same mistake. Maybe Harriet's parents are wealthy and are worried that Gerry (who comes from a poor background) is a gold-digger. An interesting storyline may centre on Gerry's parents and their own marital problems (which

obviously impact on Gerry himself). Similarly, Harriet's parents may be investigating Gerry and his parents' financial affairs.

If Gerry is poor and Harriet is rich, their friends have good potential for conflict, misunderstanding, and humour. If, for example, an occasion in the book brings all the characters together, the central characters' relationship can be tested against a varied backdrop of other characters. In this example, a meeting between the two sets of parents and the lovers would be a fertile area, as would a party to which both Gerry and Harriet's friends are invited.

Gerry's two flatmates may be interesting characters, too. Assuming that they are sympathetic — as well as lazy — characters, the reader is interested to see how they're going to manage once Gerry stops being there to support them. Their own relationships can be something that Gerry has to contend with while he's trying to keep everything going well with Harriet. If Harriet's a bit straightlaced, and the women that these flatmates are involved with are the opposite, Gerry's in an interesting position.

3. **Make sure that each subsidiary character has a story of their own.**

   These stories don't have to be earth-shattering, long, or complicated. In fact, they mustn't be, or they risk overshadowing the main story. But, like the main characters, the subsidiary characters have wants, desires, and problems, and these need to be evident – if not explicitly discussed in the text. Again, if these characters aren't worth making interesting and rounded, ask yourself why they're in the story.

   The subsidiary stories are like simplified, stripped-down versions of the main story.

 Make sure that each subsidiary story has a direct influence on the main story. It doesn't have to be obvious immediately why a character is in the story, but by the end of the book the reader needs to feel that the character would have been missed if they weren't there.

One difference between the main and the subsidiary stories is that the main story is on stage all the time, whereas the subsidiary stories can be on the back burner for substantial periods of time.

Unless you're very sure of what you're doing, don't have two subsidiary stories going on at the same time. The main story and one subsidiary story fill the page adequately at any given moment; any more is likely to clutter it up. Keep the other stories simmering, but don't let them all be active at the same time. And keep the focus on the main story except for brief climactic moments in the subsidiary stories.

Foreshadowing

Foreshadowing is a technique you use when you want the reader to be aware of something that you plan to introduce later in the book. The later event casts a shadow forward into the book – the reader doesn't know exactly what it is or what's going on, but they know something is afoot.

When whatever was hidden is revealed, the reader should feel as if a veil has dropped away, and think, 'Oh, *now* I see why he did that and why she said that and why things have been a bit strange. I knew something odd was going on.'

Jane Eyre contains a good example of foreshadowing. (If you've not read the novel, skip this paragraph if you don't want the story spoiled!) Towards the end of the book, Jane and the reader discover that Rochester, with whom Jane is in love, not only already has a wife, but also that he keeps her locked in the attic because she's mad. (This book is the origin of the phrase 'the madwoman in the attic'.) Jane and the reader are aware from an early point in the story that something odd is going on. Rochester behaves strangely towards Jane: he's plainly attracted to her, but pulls back at any sign that things are going to turn serious between them. There are howls and mysterious scuffles in the night, and every attempt by Jane to find out what's happening is met with blank denial. The reader doesn't know what's happening, but is in no doubt that the strange situation is at the heart of the story. The eventual discovery of Rochester's secret is thus foreshadowed throughout the book.

Approach foreshadowing with care. Chekhov (the playwright, not the Star Trek helmsman) once said, 'If you hang a pistol on the wall in the first act, make sure someone uses it by the third.' In other words, don't set something up and then not follow through, otherwise you have a shaggy dog story that's all build-up and no punchline. If after all the howling and screaming, the author of *Jane Eyre*, Charlotte Brontë, never revealed what was going on, or worse, passed off the howling as 'just the wind', she'd never have been forgiven, and her novel would never have become a classic.

Sub-Plotting

In the same way that subsidiary characters support the main characters, sub-plots can – and usually do – support the main plot. A *sub-plot* is a story that takes place alongside the main story.

Even the best story can use a bit of diversion, and you can use a sub-plot for several possible reasons:

- ✔ To provide light relief. This can be useful if the main story is very serious.
- ✔ To mirror or give counterpoint to the main story.
- ✔ To add breadth and depth to what may otherwise be a rather thin and spare narrative.
- ✔ To add excitement to the main story.
- ✔ To add complication (or, less often, to simplify) the main plot.

Treat a sub-plot as a story in its own right alongside the main story, as if you're writing two books at once with some shared characters.

A sub-plot has all the elements of a main plot, but is subservient to it.

Jane Austen's *Pride and Prejudice* is a good example of a main plot that's supported in a variety of ways by several sub-plots. The main plot concerns the relationship between Elizabeth Bennet and Mr Darcy. However, each Bennet sister also has her own story. All these sub-plots are important in their own right and have an impact on the main story. The relationship between Jane Bennet and Mr Bingley, for example, is crucial to Elizabeth and Darcy's first falling out, and the elopement between the flighty Lydia and the dastardly Mr Wickham provides the means by which Mr Darcy finally demonstrates his essential decency and generosity. Those two sub-plots are stories in their own right but, although they make essential contributions, they are entirely subservient to the main plot. If this wasn't the case, *Pride and Prejudice* would be a very different book.

Of course, you can have two intertwined or parallel plots of more or less equal importance.

Sub-plots can be quite insignificant, although a point comes when they lack the substance or importance to qualify as sub-plots: they become just stuff, such as padding for scenes, important in their way but not essential.

The relationship between your plots is a matter for you and what serves your story best. A main story supported by sub-plots has clarity and focus, whereas two equal stories may have greater strength. It depends what you need, but approach it with care, and if in any doubt at all, go for just one main plot.

Taking Care with Coincidence

Coincidence is really useful, sometimes too useful. It can get you out of, but also into, all sorts of holes.

You may have read or seen some of the following scenarios:

- ✔ Just as the monster stretches out a claw to slay the trapped and help-less hero . . . wham! The roof of the cave suddenly collapses, killing the monster and freeing the hero.

- ✔ The heroine is tied up. The room is empty; nothing's available to cut the ropes with, and the waters are rising around the heroine. Except . . . can that shining thing really be a tiny sharp edge of glass stuck into the wall? If she rubs the rope against it, will the rope break? We rather suspect it will.

- ✔ A man's wife is killed in an accident. Her heart is used in a transplant. The man meets a young woman and is instantly drawn to her. She is a heart transplant recipient. They fall in love unexpectedly. He thought he'd never love another woman after his wife. Least of all one with his first wife's heart beating in her body. . . .

Coincidences happen in real life, and occasionally they're useful and even crucial. However, in stories they creak, and the more crucial they are, the louder the creaking. Approach them with great caution. Avoid any plot device that makes the reader say, 'Hmmm, that's rather handy.'

If you're relying on a coincidence, at the very least make sure that you set it up beforehand. (In Bond films, the audience always sees Q at the start of the movie giving Bond the gadget he later puts to use at a crucial moment. It's never revealed for the first time as he pulls it out to help rescue himself.) If your heroine snatches a paper knife from the desk to defend herself in a fight, show your readers the paper knife beforehand in its normal context.

A good idea is to have the coincidental item first used by the person it's eventually used against. Perhaps the hero uses the paper knife against someone who opened a letter in front of them earlier.

Prompting Action and Reaction

To start with, your book probably focuses on a small number of people, and often just one: the protagonist. Then, once the protagonist is established, you explore the people's various relationships, and the story becomes more complicated.

One way to add to your reader's knowledge about the characters is through *action*, somebody doing something, and *reaction*, something happening as a result of the thing that's been done.

Looking at films can be helpful when you're writing in this area. You're no doubt familiar with the technique used in cinema of the 'reaction shot'. Imran is telling Alice that he's having an affair. The camera goes into a close-up on Imran as he forces the words out, his head hanging down, unable to meet Alice's tearful gaze. As he says the fatal words, he glances up. The camera goes to a reverse angle to show Alice as she gasps, her hand covering her mouth to stifle it as her face buckles with disbelief. Imagine if that didn't happen and the camera stayed on Imran. He'd carry on talking, trying to explain what happened, and the audience would be screaming, 'Alice is your loyal wife! She donated a kidney to you, and you cheated on her! We want to see how she's taking this!' In fact, the camera does what you'd do if you were standing there watching Imran, aware that he's about to say something important. As Imran drops his bombshell, your immediate reaction is to turn your head to see the effect it's having on Alice. The camera 'looks' for you.

Use the same technique when you're writing. When someone says or does something that's likely to provoke a reaction, show your reader that reaction.

Every action that takes place has a reaction, and then a reaction to the reaction, and so on, creating a linked chain of reactions. Actions have consequences, and those consequences themselves have consequences.

Reaction doesn't have to be active. If someone says something that you expect to provoke a violent reaction (something insulting or unfair) and the other character doesn't react at all, that in itself is a reaction. No response is a response and can often be more interesting, because then the reader thinks, 'Why didn't she reply to that terrible insult? What's going on?'

Ensure that your characters sometimes react as the reader expects, and sometimes not. Unpredictability is one of the tools that you possess to keep your reader guessing. Use it as contrast, not randomly. If a character's been completely passive all through the story and suddenly explodes, or if a volatile character doesn't explode in a situation in which they'd be expected to, that's interesting. If someone's unpredictable all the time, their unpredictability can become predictable! Most of us are fairly predictable most of the time.

Reacting to reactions

If Imran tells Alice that he's having an affair, Alice can react in a number of ways. She can start screaming hysterically and run around the room, or she can look grim, say nothing and hit him with a shovel. These are self-evidently active reactions. However, if she just looks stunned, or sits down as if she's lost the power to stand, or if she says and does absolutely nothing at all, these are also responses. These reactions provoke a response in Imran just as much as screaming and violence do. It depends on Alice's character and how you want Imran to respond in turn.

So, as we say, no response is actually a response!

1. Imran is unfaithful to Alice with Jane.

2. Alice goes to Jane and warns her to leave Imran alone.

3. Jane tells Imran he must choose between her and Alice.

4. Imran is angry with Alice for seeing Jane, and with Jane for making life difficult.

5. Jane has a fight with Imran and writes to Alice telling her the whole story of Imran's infidelity.

6. Alice throws Imran out.

7. Imran realises that he actually loves Alice. He tells Jane it's over.

8. Jane takes it badly and shoots Imran.

Each action provokes a reaction which then leads to further action. Jane wouldn't have written to Alice if she and Imran hadn't had a fight, and they wouldn't have had the fight if Jane hadn't told Imran to choose, and Jane wouldn't have told Imran to choose if Alice hadn't been to see her, and so on.

You can use action and reaction as a way of approaching your plot, just as you use your characters' motivations and their reactions to the obstacles they encounter on their way to achieving their objectives (refer to Chapter 8 for more on motivation). Action and reaction are also useful in approaching dialogue (discussed in Chapter 10) and plot (laid out in Chapter 7).

Chapter 13

Getting Creative

. . . .

. . . .

*N*ew writers are often very concerned about *creativity*, by which they mean generating ideas. This chapter contains some exercises for getting the ideas flowing. Although some writers may be blocked, many others have no problem thinking of ideas: in fact, these writers have lots of ideas – maybe too many! Their problem lies in recognising the useful ideas – the ones that can be turned into a story that they can stick with and people want to read. This chapter offers some suggestions on how to generate useful ideas that you can make into good stories.

Accepting Ideas and Mixing Them Up

Many people find that ideas come to them at the most inappropriate times: in the shower, out walking, and so on. A very common writer's experience that you may have is a writing session that peters out, so you give up and go to bed. Settling down to sleep, your mind is suddenly filled with ideas and answers to all the questions you've been wrestling with.

The point is that ideas tend to come when you don't work for them, whereas if you reach for them, they shrink away. It's as if someone comes up to you and says, 'Go on, say something hysterically funny.' Suddenly you can't think of anything funny to save your life. A writer who sits down and says to themselves, 'Okay brain, off you go, think of something brilliant,' is doomed. Ideas have to be sidled up to, approached obliquely, or even ignored at first. You think hard; nothing happens. You go to bed, relax, try not to think about your story, and the ideas flood in.

Annoying, but that's how it seems to work. So, how do you make this seemingly unhelpful process work for you? The next sections tell you.

Be open

You probably tend to think about ideas for your writing as 'good' or 'bad' – that's just the way the human brain works. If you're working on a scene and have an outline of what's happening, and then an idea appears that doesn't seem to fit your idea of what should happen, you reject it.

Don't judge ideas too early. All your ideas are good ones until proved otherwise. Don't dismiss an idea just because right now you can't see how it fits. You may need it later. Stay open to the possibility that the book you think you're writing may not be the one you end up writing.

You don't know what you need at this stage, so how can you be sure which ideas are good and which are bad? If you're trying to write an out-and-out thriller about a killer dog roaming the countryside, and all your ideas seem to be moving towards a story about a couple in a cottage trying to rebuild their marriage, maybe you should look at writing something more subtle. Maybe the point isn't about a killer dog, but about the fact that the husband is terrified of dogs.

Write down *every* idea you have, no matter how bad you think it is at the time, and no matter how daft, strange, or irrelevant it seems to be. Every so often, go back through your notebook; if nothing else, it reminds you of just how many ideas you've had!

Stop trying too hard

Your mum always told you, 'If at first you don't succeed, try and try again.' If your story's going well – great, carry on. But if it isn't, and you can't seem to see where it's going, you can end up doing what a lot of writers do: keep on banging your head against the wall, hoping that you'll break through.

However, particularly in the early stages, if you hit a wall, don't try to smash it. Instead, look for alternatives: hop over it or go around it. Try altering one of your characters: change their gender, for example. Move the story to another country. Set it in the past. Write something else, unrelated to the part that isn't working for you. The crucial thing is to not stop writing. Your mum was right, but there's more to it. Try and try again, but don't necessarily try exactly the same thing every time: if the hammer doesn't work, try the chisel.

Visualising What You Need

Visualisation may sound a bit New Agey, but if that sort of thing makes you nervous, don't worry. The exercise we offer here is easy, doesn't require any knowledge, and we walk you through it.

The term *visualisation* as we use it involves making sure that you have a clear idea – a clear *vision* of what you're doing before you try to do it. To give you some simple examples: describing someone is much easier if you have a photograph in front of you, and conveying the feeling of a cold day is easier if you've just come in from a winter walk than if you're sitting writing on a beach in the summer. Your impressions are clearer. The advantage of visualisation is that you don't actually have to do the thing you're describing: you just visualise it, in the comfort of your own home! Follow these steps:

1. **Sit back in your chair.**

   Get comfortable, but sit up straight (you don't want to go to sleep).

2. **Start daydreaming about a specific character or scene.**

   You may think you do enough daydreaming already. Don't worry, this is directed daydreaming.

3. **Picture one of your characters – or a scene – in your head.**

   You're an invisible observer in the scene, not an actor. Soak up the situation, assess everything that the character's doing and everything happening in the scene. Stare without embarrassment – no one can see you.

4. **Imagine a number of very different situations for your character, or variations for your scene, and pay attention to what happens.**

   Start with a setting that you're familiar with. Watch what your character does. See whether they're animated, bored, embarrassed, or curious. Look at how they express their emotions. Observe how they stand and what they do with their hands. Look at what they're wearing.

   Compare their behaviour, dress, stance, and so on in all the situations you imagine for them.

   Some of the wide variety of situations for characters include:

   - They're waiting for someone on a first date, and the date is late. How do they react? If it's a blind date, is their behaviour different to what they do if they really like the person they're meeting?

   - They're extremely at ease, perhaps watching a football game.

   - They're in an extremely uncomfortable situation. What are the differences to being relaxed and what doesn't change?

   - They're under real stress – imagine them in a sinking boat or a burning building. How do they behave?

For a scene, explore every aspect. Really absorb everything there is to see and feel. Think about sounds, smells, textures, decorations, lighting, temperature, and so on. Build a really detailed picture in your head.

A scene only comes alive for the reader if it's alive for you. The difference is the same as between relating a story in a monotonous voice or telling it with enthusiasm. If you want the reader to shiver and sit closer to the fire when you describe a cold, damp day, you'd better know in your mind exactly what that cold, damp day feels like. Get used to seeing, hearing, and smelling your scenes in as complete a way as possible.

If the character's walking down the street in the rain, picture what today's particular type of rain looks like on the particular type of pavement you've chosen. Get it clear in your head (or go out and look!). Is it drizzly, misty, spitting with rain, lashing down, frosty, windy, or what?

If someone's following someone else down a street in the rain, you need to know how loud and busy the street is before you can know how easy it is for one of them to follow the other without being noticed. And what sort of sound does their heel make when it hits the ground? What other noises are there? How much light is there?

Be aware. Practise being aware when you walk down the street. It's the opposite of walking around with headphones on. You need to be open to everything going on around you.

5. **Visualise the situation you're working on in your story.**

By now you know your character or the scene pretty well, so you can probably predict how a character will act or what will come next in the scene fairly easily.

If you don't know, go back to visualising more situations.

The better you know someone, the easier it is to predict how they're going to behave. You're likely to find that your characters react in ways you hadn't predicted, and you can use that situation and that reaction in the story.

Now the crucial point: you're visualising, and suddenly you're thinking about the shopping, or a film you saw yesterday, or the thing you said to your partner this morning that you wish you hadn't. Normally when this happens, you think to yourself, 'No! Concentrate! Don't think about anything except the writing!' Commendable dedication, but we all know it doesn't work, does it? The unwanted thought comes charging back into your mind.

Don't fight your stray thoughts. When odd thoughts creep into your visualisation, don't push them away: go with them, pull them into the visualisation and see whether they work.

Here's how it works. In the next paragraph, your imagined thoughts are in italics; the rest is the visualisation.

> Graham's walking down the street. It's raining. He's getting wet . . . *mustn't forget to leave on time tonight, don't want to be late, I'm always late* . . . He's late. He's always late. He walks faster, the sound of his feet clear in the night air . . . *it's night? OK, it's night. Clear, so maybe it's cold, got to turn up the central heating* . . . The frost covers the car windscreens and makes the pavement treacherous . . . *slippery, like when I was six and broke my ankle* . . . His ankle hurts in the cold, as if the old injury remembers when . . . *wish I'd been nicer to John this morning; I didn't mean to be snap-pish, I'm just too stressed this week* . . . Graham hunches his shoulders against the memory of the conversation that morning, determined to be glad to see Alicia tonight and to get through at least one evening without fighting, determined to prevent the shadow between them lengthening into silence or breaking into hissing resentment . . . *bread, bacon, milk* . . . Graham turns into a shop and buys some groceries. On impulse he buys chocolates . . .

Not every mental detour works for your story, but don't worry about that. The point is that if you try not to think about the shopping list, it pushes itself further and further forward. After all, you do need milk. So include the shopping list in the story, let it take its place naturally, and it may well take the story to a place you hadn't thought of.

Don't Think, Write

Okay, you have an idea – not necessarily a complete one; in fact, probably not! – but something you can work with. You've done your visualisation and got it sorted in your head. Now you need to do some writing.

Never let exercises – or reading, research, or vacuuming the stairs – be a substitute for writing. You can vacuum the stairs any time, with the kids screaming and dinner on the go, but you can't write then. So make sure that you write when the opportunity's available.

If you do the following exercises on loose sheets of paper, at the end of the session put the sheets in a box. If you do the exercises in your journal, keep them handy. Go back to them once in a while. You may well find all sorts of ideas you'd forgotten about, as well as reminding yourself of your own creativity. These old ideas can surprise you: *you* can surprise you.

Writing speed pages

Speed pages are timed writings. They generate ideas and get your mind warmed up for work. More importantly, as any writer knows, the blank page (or screen) is incredibly depressing. It can be enough to stop you writing there and then. Speed pages mean that you never have to look at a blank page with dread again.

Prepare by clearing your desk. Put everything on the floor to avoid looking at anything that demands your attention or is part of your normal style of working. All you want on your desk is your journal or, if you prefer (those journals fill up quick and you may want to save it for ideas), a pad of paper and something to write with. The pad should be clean sheets. The pen or pencil should be easy to hold and smooth on the page. Maybe a desk light if you can't see without it. Coffee if you need it. But *no* computer, *no* books. And you need a watch or a clock. Put it in front of you.

Now you're going to write. You're going to write absolutely anything you like. It doesn't matter at all what you write. Any stream-of-consciousness rubbish is just fine. Coherence and sense are fine, but they aren't necessary. Really. If you get stuck and can think only of banal rubbish, don't worry, write down the banal rubbish; that's the idea.

You must follow certain rules:

- You mustn't stop to think.

- You mustn't lift your hand or stop writing, even for a moment. Be strict: no stopping.

- You mustn't cross out a single thing. Spelling and grammar don't matter. In fact, you mustn't even re-read what you've just written. If your eye starts to stray upward, have another piece of paper on top of the one you're writing on, and slide it down as you write so that it covers up the line you just finished.

- You mustn't duck out of writing something, not for any reason. If you hesitate or think 'That's not a good thing to be writing about' for any reason, that means you *must* write it. The less you want to write about it, the more important it is that you dive in. Don't allow no-go areas in your imagination. Attack your writing as hard as you can. No one else is going to see it, no one need ever know.

Easy, huh? (Actually, no, especially not the last part. But you can do it if you decide to.)

Real-life, real-time example!

The nearest book to his computer was Yann Martel's *Life of Pi*. George opened it at random, at page 144. The first line was: 'Nine wax-paper-wrapped rectangular bars tumbled out.' George asked for another line, but Lizzy said no. So that was his line. He put the book down. Five minutes of writing. Countdown: three, two, one, go.

We corrected a couple of spelling mistakes afterwards (*not* during), just for neatness, but apart from that, this is exactly what he wrote.

> 'Nine wax-paper-wrapped rectangular bars tumbled out.' Blimey, what's going on here? Bars of what, for heaven's sake? Chocolate would be nice; gold would be nicer. Why on earth wax paper? Beeswax. Wax flypaper, the old-fashioned kind. Curls from the ceiling. Nasty. Back to chocolate and wax paper. What do they wrap gold in? Chocolate – dark not milk; milk chocolate is for losers – Milk Tray man. Could be wax paper, but someone must have wrapped it specially; the makers would put it into silver paper surely? Tumbled out? Tumbled out of what? A hand? A box? A lorry? A border guard opens the tailgate of a lorry, and a box falls out. Where did the guard come from? Ivan. Checkpoint Charlie, Le Carré, Smiley. Swapping spies. Woollen overcoats. Mist. It's dark. The box breaks open. Bars wrapped in wax paper fall out. Drugs? Chocolate looking like drugs? Drugs looking like chocolate looking like drugs? Gold bars looking like drugs? Chocolate-covered drugs? Can dogs smell drugs through a solid case of chocolate? Check that. Liqueur chocolate? Drunk dogs. Drugged dogs licking chocolate. Chocolate dogs, full of drugs. Chocolate brittle breaks when hits the ground. . . .

Okay, that was about two minutes' writing. It's a stream of consciousness and full of things that may or may not mean anything. If a psychiatrist got hold of it, they'd have a field day we're sure. It isn't a story – it isn't really anything at all. Some of it's just nonsense – word association, thoughts chasing each other around with no real purpose.

Do this exercise for five minutes exactly. Not four, not seven. Five. You write for five minutes flat out without thinking, stopping, or hesitating for as much as a single moment. Which is why it's only for five minutes. It's bound to feel like a lot longer than that, and your hand is probably cramping up by the end.

When you've done five minutes, take a break. Give your hand a rub. Then do it again, with a new start point. Do three if you can. Even better, do two ten-minute sessions.

At the end of 15 minutes (or whatever) writing flat out like this, you have several pages of ideas. These speed pages are an incredibly useful hoard of ideas for the days when the ideas just refuse to come. This exercise is also a very good warm-up before you start writing.

Some people find this exercise easy. If you aren't one of those people, you can give yourself a hand by opening any book at random and taking the first line as your start. One of the best workshops we ever ran was started by someone dipping into a book of poems and reading out the first line they saw. The line was, 'Tonight I was undressed by the wind.' (The poem is by Leonard Cohen.) That line alone kept people writing for ages and gave birth to several stories and half a dozen poems.

At the start of this chapter, we talk about how sitting down and saying, 'Okay, now write something,' is a guaranteed way to wipe your mind clean of every idea you've ever had. That's because thinking too much can sometimes be destructive. Of course, if you're overwhelmed with an idea, go with it. But, and this is more common, if you don't have a particular idea in mind, do speed pages. If you're looking at the page and you don't have anything to write about, this is the way to go. Then look over your pages, pick out the thing that interests you most, and write about that. You've already written two pages and you're up and running.

The point is that already you're not thinking. Not trying to guide your thoughts. Not censoring. That's the crucial point. Never reject something because it seems stupid. If you can't think of anything to write, write 'I can't think of anything to write' and write about that – how annoying it is to not have anything to write, and how that feels. Write about your lamp, your coffee mug, the feel of the pen on the page, your football team, the tiny headache you can feel starting behind your eyes, how much you love your kids, or how much you hate computers. Create a list of people you want to leave money to when you die, describe your route to work, rant about celebrities, write a wish list for Christmas, or describe your boyfriend. Anything. Whatever comes to you. If nothing comes, write about what nothing means to you. Describe the silence. What's the most nothing place you know? There are no wrong answers to this exercise.

Writing 'I remember'

This idea is very similar to the speed pages exercise explained in the earlier section 'Writing speed pages', except that you start your uncensored writing with the words 'I remember'. After those words, you write down anything at all that you remember. Yes, *anything*. Big or small, interesting or banal, generalisation or pinprick, recent or ancient history, event or feeling, yours or anyone else's.

Write until you have nothing more to say about that memory. You may just write one line or a whole paragraph; you may write a couple of lines and then that memory reminds you of something else. If that happens, go with the new memory. You can always go back to the old one. Never push a new memory away. Don't think, don't select, don't censor. Just put down whatever comes into your mind.

However long you write for, eventually you finish writing about that memory. When that happens, write the words 'I remember', and start again. Same rules: anything at all. Whatever comes.

Do this for five minutes, ten if you can. Don't stop, don't lift your hand. As soon as a memory runs out of steam, you write 'I remember' again, and move on.

After you've done a couple of these, look over what you've just written. It's a rare session that doesn't throw up something that you haven't thought about for a while.

Chapter 14

Ending and Editing

So, you've finished the first draft of your novel: you're done. You know the entire story, all the characters, everything that happens. You also know that some bits are better than others and that it still needs a good bit of work, but it all hangs together. Although nowhere near perfect, it works. Congratulations. Take a break, have a big glass of wine, watch a movie, and get some sleep. Then wake up, sit down, and switch on the computer again.

And there it is. Hellooo first draft. Now what do you do? Well, now you have to edit.

Perhaps you're thinking, 'My first draft is often the best. It's fresh and original. Rewriting just makes it stale.'

We're going to be generous for a moment. It's just possible that your first draft is the best that you can create. Just possible. However, given the complexity of creating a 300-page novel, is it likely? Think about anyone's first attempt at anything – baking a cake, writing a history essay, riding a bicycle, speaking French, or playing the piano. It may well be fresh and original, and it's very probably different, but let's face it, it's not likely to be the best it can be.

Sharpening Your Editing Pencil

Editing is the process of rewriting, designed to sharpen, tighten, and clarify your writing. It involves cutting out redundant scenes, writing new ones to make more sense of it all, and moving scenes to new places where they work better. During editing you pick out where you've said the same thing twice, where you've used the wrong word or a lazy phrase, where a character isn't really doing anything, where the dialogue isn't going anywhere, and so on. Don't worry if you seem to be making a lot of changes. That's the process.

Most writers edit at least a bit as they go along. You write something and then get a heap of new ideas that just have to be included as well, and that means changing it all around. Sometimes you edit because you aren't up to doing anything new today, so you tidy up what you've done so far. In this sense, editing refreshes your mind about what you've done. But when you finish all your writing and the on-the-spot and polishing editing that accompanies it, you need to tackle the final editing process.

Editing comes from a slightly different place to the writing that you've been doing. The start of the writing process is all about covering the blank page, and involves starting out with only a partial idea of where you're going, and getting to places you had no idea you were looking for. It's about open doors, investigating unknown possibilities, and looking around for the unexpected. Therefore, the writing process is lateral, organic, and uncritical, rather than linear and analytic. The start of writing a novel is mostly creating, with a bit of editing thrown in.

Now you're going to turn the process upside down. From here on in you're mostly doing editing mixed with a bit of creating. You've been immersed in your story since you started to write it. Now you have to step back and look at it as if you've just picked up your novel for the first time. Of course you still have an intimate knowledge of it – it's still your story – but you're going to have to get some distance, some objectivity. You're going to have to take all the great stuff you've written and hold it up to the light. You want to see whether it really makes sense, whether it's really that great. Let's be realistic, that can be hard.

Numbering the drafts

'How many drafts should I do?' you ask. 'Good question,' we respond. 'How many do you think you need to do?'

It depends how your brain works best. If you like getting into a problem and keeping all the balls in the air at the same time, you can do one marathon editing session. If you like taking a problem and breaking it down into small pieces, you can turn the editing into a series of shorter sprints. Or, like most writers, you can do a bit of both. No problem, whatever gets the job done.

Gearing up for a marathon

Some people do a single huge edit for everything, and that's it. They go through the whole thing once, slowly, checking everything as they go. If they had to do it more than once, it would become a chore. They go steady and they don't jump about. That's the way they like it. They dig deep and they dig wide, and when it's done, it's done. This is hard and will probably still require some tweaking afterwards, but if that's how your mind works . . .

Running sprints

Other people like to do a series of quick edits, each one for a different reason. They go through once for continuity, once for characters, and so on, based on the idea that hopping about stops them being stuck on any one problem long enough to get bored. Individually the edits are much quicker and less thorough, but the idea is that in total they add up to something like the single big edit that the marathon writers use. Digging lots of small holes eventually shifts as much earth as digging one big hole.

In this chapter we put forward a plan that includes elements of both these approaches. As ever, take what you need.

This process requires you to go through the manuscript a number of times. This may seem time-consuming, but it means that you can stay focused. If you try to do everything in one big rewrite, you may just become confused and find it hard to work out what you're meant to be doing. You can't, for example, check how your premise is doing and at the same time make sure that your pace is as it should be. Break it down into small tasks.

Getting your tools together

Any craftsman tells you that the first thing for you to do when you start a job is to make sure that your tools are all present and correct. So you need to:

- **Print your script:** Editing on paper is a lot easier, and it gives you a different perspective than seeing the words on a computer screen (a bit like seeing a film on TV and then at the cinema: the same but different.) Make sure that your script has nice big margins at the top, bottom, and sides. Set the line spacing at one and a half line space minimum, double space if you can. Now print your manuscript off. Yes, it costs you money, and yes, it's a pain, but do it anyway. Do it greyscale or draft quality by all means, which saves your ink cartridge a bit. Now pick the script up, feel the weight, smile to yourself, and put the script carefully to one side. You're going to need it later.

- **Get a pen:** Find a nice pen that you actually enjoy the feel of in your hand and that moves smoothly over the page. Get a pen that suits your handwriting.

- **Get a notebook:** Preferably choose one that lies open flat and doesn't close itself annoyingly as soon as you let go. As big a one as you can find; at least A4 size. You need this for writing notes to yourself.

Diving into the Actual Editing

The editing process involves checking a variety of things in your novel. The precise order doesn't matter as long as everything gets done, although we present the elements in the order in which we suggest you do them.

The key to editing (and if this seems obvious, that doesn't mean it doesn't need repeating) is consistency. If you can keep it simple as well, so much the better.

Not everything matters. When you tell a joke, you tell only the details relevant to the story. A novel's the same. Anything else is self-indulgence, and most readers have a limited tolerance for writers who write just for themselves.

Checking up on your characters

People matter. You probably have quite a few of them in your story, at least we hope so – you can't have a story without people. Check your characters carefully. They may be doing things without your knowledge.

Naming names

A novel is a big thing, and characters come and go. Make sure that each person is called the same thing all the way through the book. If you search for 'Julius', who is your main character, and there's no mention of Julius from page 208 to page 237, he's probably called something else on those pages. It happens more often than you'd think.

Are all the major characters named and their characteristics consistent and plain? Make a list on the front page of your big notebook as each new name appears, and keep cross-checking as you go through. Leave plenty of space by each name. You need it to record the details of each character as you go along.

Check continuity, particularly names. (Computers make this task a lot easier than it used to be.) For example, if a character has an unusual name, you can do a search to make sure that you've spelt it the same way throughout the novel. (Mistakes are surprisingly common!) Put that name into your dictionary, and then any time that name's highlighted you know you've spelt it wrongly.

Addressing the physical details

Beside the names in your notebook, write down any physical details that you've given your characters. Laugh as you realise that your good-looking, six-foot, red-headed hero becomes your squat, dark-skinned hero with a limp and asthma a hundred pages later. Finish laughing, and then fix it.

Savouring personality

Write the traits you give your characters beside each name as they come up in the story, and watch how swiftly a person can undergo a complete personality transplant. A good-hearted, rambunctious hero may transform into a weasel-hearted, cynical anti-hero. Watch, wonder, laugh, and then fix.

Reviewing relationships

Checking that relationships are consistent is important. Draw lines and arrows between the characters in your notebook to represent their relationships. Coloured pens are good for this (stationery-purchasing opportunity!), and make it fun and easy to decipher relationships. Red lines mean love, blue mean family, and green mean antagonism (or whatever code you choose, obviously). Depending on your novel you may need lines for lust, shared secret, previous relationship, and same football team – any relationship that's important in the context of the novel.

Look at the connections. A lot of love lines and no antagonism lines means you're writing a happy book, but is that what you want? Are there some characters with more than one arrow connecting them? If not, are the relationships in your story too simplistic? Are you clear about who's related to who and how? (By which we mean, is it clear to your reader?) Keep checking as you read. Characters can end up with two fathers and a whole bunch of distant relatives with no visible means of support or meaningful attachment to the character or the story.

Unless your story demands it, less is usually more, and keeping the relationships simple is the way to go.

Measuring their importance

Decide whether all the characters are necessary. If any of them disappeared would anyone notice, and if not should you get rid of them? If they're necessary, do they appear sufficiently regularly, and are they part of the story or sort of trotting alongside it? If they aren't earning their keep, amalgamate or dump them.

Setting the scenes

Open your big notebook a few pages in – leaving room for all the useful notes on your characters. Write 'Chapter One' on the left-hand page. Turn the page and write 'Chapter Two' on the next left-hand page. Carry on until you've allotted two pages to each chapter. This way, each chapter is laid out in front of you without you having to turn the page.

For each chapter, write a list of all the scenes that take place in that chapter.

A *scene* is a self-contained unit of action. *Self-contained* means that each scene has a beginning, a middle, and an end. By the end of the scene, something new should have happened to move the action on.

By each scene, write a short sentence summarising why the scene is in the book; something like, 'Stolen gold stolen again,' 'John's infidelity first suspected,' or 'Crucial clue about lost carpet-slippers revealed' is fine.

Every scene needs a good reason to be in the book, and 'I really like it' isn't a good reason. Often, the really good scenes are the ones you have to leave out. It's a hard world, for sure.

Check every scene for conflict – not necessarily people bashing each other, but any sort of struggle. If the characters in the scene aren't struggling in some way – with each other, themselves, or their surroundings – you need something else to keep the reader's interest, or you need to think hard about whether the scene is justified. Chapter 11 talks more about conflict.

Establishing place

You know that most readers like to have a good sense of the physical background to the story, which is a good reason for thinking hard about the place in which you set your novel. Perhaps even more importantly, places matter because places are characters in the novel. They can change things in the same way that a character can. Two lovers in the Sahara desert and the same people doing the same thing in the Arctic isn't the same scene, even if the dialogue's identical. Put simply, snow and sand require different clothes and different moves. Nor can you describe in the same way a gun battle fought between the same two sides in those two different places. The background colours the story and changes it. So it needs to be consistent. Remember: factual accuracy is usually good, but it's more important to be convincing.

Weathering the weather

Write the weather next to each scene you've identified. Make sure that changes are consistent, both inside each scene and between scenes that follow each other. Don't forget to mention any changes that take place. That said, the weather's only a big deal if it's a big deal: no need to describe each change in the weather, unless it matters to the story.

Describing the scenery

The major thing to ask yourself is, 'What's the minimum I need to tell the reader in order for this scene to make sense?' Now look at every other piece of description and ask, 'If I take that line out, how much difference is it going to make?' Unless the answer is 'a lot', maybe you should take it out.

Checking the Outline Chain

Start at the beginning of your manuscript and go through it. Each time a scene starts, make a note of what happens and what the outcome is. A *scene* is a significant event, which may be a number of things such as an exchange of dialogue, a piece of action, and so on.

Make a mark (we suggest you write a number, so it's easy to find again if you need to) on your printed hard copy of the manuscript, and then write a brief description of the scene in your editing notebook. If printing the manuscript off isn't possible, make a note of the page and write the description in the same way.

The scenes you mark and describe are your *outline chain*. (Some people call this a step outline.)

What you're looking for in checking your novel's outline are satisfactory answers to the following three questions:

- ✔ Is the story moving forwards, or does it go around in circles? Clearly, you want a story that gets someplace instead of one that chases its own tail.

- ✔ Are there large gaps between scenes? If so, are your scenes perhaps too slow? Keeping the pace of the novel up is important. Maybe the scene needs tightening. Or perhaps you need to make it faster, using more action. Conversely, a cluster of marks may indicate that your writing has become too brisk, although this is less likely. Consider the possibility anyhow – if the marks are coming very close together, is the writing too fragmented?

- ✔ Does the action move in a generally upward direction towards the climax? It can jerk upwards sometimes, and it can even dip occasionally, but is the overall trend upwards?

Outlining *Regeneration*

Our outline chain of the first chapter of Pat Barker's *Regeneration* (Penguin) shows how to do outlining:

✔ **Scene 1, page 3:** 1917, First World War. Opens with a written refusal to fight any more by Sassoon. Distinction made between those who fight and those who stay at home, who can't possibly understand.

✔ **Scene 2, page 3:** Dr Rivers finishes reading Sassoon's refusal. Bryce informs him that Sassoon is to be sent to him for treatment. Discussion of nature of shell-shock. Political consequences of Sassoon's action, awkwardness of situation for Rivers.

✔ **Scene 3, page 5:** Sassoon on a train. Brief flashback to war.

✔ **Scene 4, page 5:** Flashback to a week previously, to meeting with Robert, who's returning to the war. Discussion of Sassoon's motives for refusal — seeking publicity for the poor conduct of war.

✔ **Scene 5, page 6:** It emerges that Sassoon has agreed to accept 'treatment', in order to prove he's not insane. (If he is insane then the powers that be can ignore his protest.)

✔ **Scene 6, page 8:** Rivers reads the record of Sassoon's war gallantry as Sassoon's taxi arrives.

In six short scenes spread over six pages, Barker gives the reader a great deal of information. She introduces the two main characters, Sassoon and Rivers, and gives insight into both their characters. She shows their respective positions and the problems that those positions have raised for them, and makes clear that a struggle between them is inevitable. Barker also introduces two supporting characters.

Getting all this information and story across in just six short scenes suggests a mastery of economy that bodes well for the rest of Barker's story.

Messing about with the Spelling and Grammar

You cringed on reading this heading, didn't you? Almost everyone does. Grammar sounds like hard work, full of strange words and lots of incomprehensible lists to memorise. If you want to be a teacher of grammar, then yes, you need to know as much about it as possible. Fortunately, if you want to write, you don't have to know it all, just enough.

TIP

While you're running a spell check on your document, don't turn off the grammar check. It isn't always right (don't forget that British and US conventions aren't the same), and sometimes it makes no sense at all, but it can draw important errors to your attention.

Knowing the rules before you break them

Chambers Dictionary defines grammar as 'the science of language from the points of view of pronunciation, inflection, syntax and historic development; the art of the right use of language by grammatical rules'.

From a writer's point of view, it's all about communication. You need to know how sentences work in order to make sure that everything you do helps your readers, and nothing gets in the way of them following the story. If your interpretation of the earlier sentence is 'point of view, writer, communication all about it is', readers may get your meaning eventually, but the trouble is that it takes them a number of goes to understand it. Put yourself in the reader's position. Are you prepared to read each sentence in a story three times to make sure that you've understood it properly? Of course not.

Writing's a game. Spelling and grammar are the rules. You can choose to ignore the rules, but that probably means no one will want to play with you. The good news is that there's lots of help out there. So here are the basics, in crash course format. Skip it if you want to and come back later, but you can benefit from reading this section at some point.

A couple of simple areas cause a lot of confusion. Fix them and you're just about there.

Addressing apostrophes

All your life, people have told you that apostrophes are complicated. We're here to say that they aren't. Take a deep breath while we straighten the whole thing out for you. Here's when you need an apostrophe and when you don't:

- ✔ You *do* need an apostrophe if you add an 's' to a word to indicate that something belongs to someone (also known as the *possessive*). The apostrophe goes before the 's'. Examples are the 'cat's basket' and 'Henry's book'.

  You need an apostrophe but no 's' to show possession for a word that ends in 's', 'Louis' piano', for example.

- ✔ You *don't* need an apostrophe if you add an 's' to a word to indicate that there's more than one of something (this is called the *plural*). Examples are 'two cats' and 'a box of books'.

The only exception (there's always an exception) to these two rules is the word 'its'. With 'its' everything works in reverse. If you add an 's' because something belongs to it, you don't use an apostrophe, as in 'its whiskers' or 'its box'. However, if you want to use 'its' as short for 'it is' or 'it has', you do need an apostrophe (see the next point on contractions). Examples are 'it's a cat' and 'it's been kept in the library'.

✔ You *do* need an apostrophe when you use a word that's actually two words stuck together in a shortened form (called a *contraction*). Examples are 'don't' (do not), 'there's' (there is), 'you're' (you are), and 'we'll' (we will).

Note that the apostrophe goes where the missing letter was, not at the place where the words are joined (unless it's the same place!).

Sorted. That's it. Honest. For practical purposes, that's all you need to know about apostrophes. In a few rare instances these rules let you down, but they're so rare that you really don't need to worry about them and you can easily avoid them. For example, if you want to say that something belongs to Mr and Mrs Wiggins, and you don't know whether you should use Wigginses, Wiggins', or Wiggins's, just say 'the Wiggins family' or 'Joan and Barry'.

Concerning commas

The simplest way to remember how to handle commas is to imagine that you're reading a sentence out loud to an audience. Everywhere you pause in a sentence, that's where a comma goes. The comma doesn't mark the pause but indicates all sorts of other things such as which verb relates to which subject, and how certain information within the clause is non-essential, and a lot of other things besides. But you tend to indicate the same things with pauses when you're reading as you do with commas when you're writing, so one can offer clues about the other.

Anyone who reads manuscripts for a living can tell you that the two guidelines to get you through almost any uncertainties about commas are:

✔ If a sentence has more than one comma, have a really close look at it. Should any of those commas be full stops? (Answer: yes, probably.)

✔ On balance, while you're practising writing, having too many short sentences is always preferable (that is, easier to read) to too many long ones.

That's really all you need for commas.

Punctuating dialogue

The full stop at the end of a spoken sentence goes before the final quotes, as in:

'I want you.' He turned to me.

The same rule applies to exclamation and question marks, for example:

'Do you want me?' he queried.

Use commas to set off dialogue tags:

'I want you,' he said.

Also use commas to introduce dialogue after a tag:

>He whispered, 'I want you.'

Chapter 10 has loads more about dialogue.

Colons and semicolons

Colons and semicolons are a little more complicated than commas. If you aren't sure about them, avoid them until you become comfortable using them. (Avoiding them is usually fairly easy, as in the examples below.) You can always change a comma or a full stop into a colon or a semicolon later.

- ✔ A colon usually precedes a list, an explanation, or a definition. For example, if Smith, Jones, and Brown all score for United in a football match, you can write: 'United won 3–0, with goals scored by Smith, Jones, and Brown.' Or you can write: 'United had thee goal-scorers: Smith, Brown, and Jones.' The first half of the sentence suggests that a list is about to follow, and the colon confirms it.

- ✔ You can use a colon for an explanation. For example: 'Here's what I need: an axe, a saw, and a big bag of nails.'

- ✔ You can also use a colon for a definition. Look in a dictionary and you'll usually see a colon separating the word from the definition of the word.

- ✔ A semicolon is used for two main purposes. It can join two complete sentences that are related to each other, such as 'John has red hair; Jan has black hair.' The semicolon here could be a full stop, but you're using a semicolon to suggest a relationship between the two people.

- ✔ You can also use a semi-colon when you use words suggesting transition in the middle of a sentence (words like 'however', 'otherwise', and 'therefore'). For example: 'Janet worked like a Trojan all day; however, her efforts came to nothing' shows a direct relationship between the two parts of the sentence.

Take a look at *English Grammar For Dummies* by Lesley Ward and Geraldine Woods (Wiley) for a much more in-depth explanation of grammar and punctuation.

Seeing to spelling

Bad spelling is annoying, confusing, and highly unprofessional because it means that someone else has to spend time fixing your mistakes. That takes time and costs money. Fortunately, you now have help through the spell checker on your computer: these programs pick up most problems.

Read through your stuff to find the words that the computer doesn't pick up (such as 'their' when you mean 'there', 'tow' instead of 'two', and a host more). If you're not a good spell checker yourself, ask a friend who is or hire someone to look over your writing before you send it to an agent.

Don't worry too much if your novel has an occasional error. We all make mistakes.

Being professional

If you want to be absolutely perfect in grammar, then yes, it's hard work. The good news is that you don't need to be perfect. You just need to be professional. If your writing is full of basic errors, you look like an amateur. A lot of people out there are competing with you, and they're approaching writing like professionals. When amateurs play professionals, the professionals usually win.

Basic mistakes can obscure your meaning. If you're lucky, your reader tries to puzzle out your intention anyhow, but think about yourself as a reader. If you have the choice of reading a well-presented, easily understood manuscript or a manuscript full of basic mistakes that mean you spend most of the time wondering what the writer means, which do you read?

Your writing doesn't have to be perfect from the beginning (although it obviously saves you some time if you get it right from the start, not halfway through typing your final draft).

Presenting a perfect manuscript

Your manuscript has to be grammatically perfect only on the day you hand it to the publisher – and actually not even then. It doesn't have to be 100 per cent perfect (although that's a good target!), it just has to be professional. You just have to get most things right most of the time. Some mistakes, especially if they're repeated, can be really annoying to a reader. Getting the grammar right is the easiest bit of the whole project. Be reasonable, and your publisher will be too.

If all else fails, you can find plenty of people who make a living copyediting other people's manuscripts. This sort of service is cheap, because word-processing means that copyeditors can correct a draft without having to type it all out again. If you can't rely on yourself, it's a worthwhile investment. Shop around. And don't forget to use friends and family, if they're willing and know what to look for.

Polishing the layout and presentation

Presentation, what your work looks like and how it's laid out, is the last thing you look at. Changes you make when editing affect presentations, so don't even think about the presentation until you've finished editing!

If you're sending work to an agency or a publisher, check its website for guidelines and *follow them religiously*. Check the technical stuff – page numbers, chapters, and so on. It's amazing how many manuscripts have two chapter sevens.

The main rule for presentation is: use your common sense. Unless you have a very good reason for doing otherwise, this rule means:

- ✔ Being kind to readers: Don't wilfully try to confuse them.

- ✔ Doing new and strange things because you need to, not just because they amuse you. Ray Robinson's novel *Electricity* (Picador) has a completely black page to represent the narrator's mind when she has an epileptic episode. In that case, this technique is potentially interesting and thought-provoking, but doing it for no reason is neither of those things. If you print a page in backwards writing or write it in Latin, you'd better have a very good reason. (If you're interested in this sort of thing, Mark Z Danielewski's novel *House of Leaves* (Doubleday) does just about everything you've ever thought of, and probably some things that haven't occurred to you.)

- ✔ Telling the story as best you can. Don't let your personality and preferences get in the way of telling the story. Just because you have a weakness for bad puns doesn't mean that everyone else likes them.

Don't do anything that makes your work hard to read: no strange fonts, mirror writing, weird spelling, and the rest of it. Think very hard before deciding that your story demands you to do something counter to the accepted rules. At the very least, don't make your novel any harder to read and understand than is absolutely necessary. Have pity on your reader.

Have you ever picked up a book, looked at it, and said, 'Oh goody, I'm definitely going to buy this one: it looks incredibly hard to read, and because of the way it's written, I'll have absolutely no idea what's happening most of the time'? Probably not. Neither have your potential readers.

You may feel that you're gaining more than you lose by using strange layouts and techniques on the page, and that's your decision. It's your book. Our advice is, as always: tell the story. Anything that gets in the way of telling the story is a bad thing. So, be very, very sure before you do anything that obscures your story. You may think that being wilfully confusing is a good idea, but your publisher probably won't agree.

The student who succeeded

We once had a student who was writing quite a complicated novel with a lot of dialogue. The action and dialogue were often run together on the page in a way that made it hard to work out what was going on. The manuscript had no quotes, no line breaks, and no clues as to who was speaking the lines. That on its own made the novel hard enough to read, but the really strange thing was that the characters' names kept changing. 'Fred' suddenly became 'John', and then a few pages later went back to being 'Fred' again. 'Richard' became 'Jane' (but stayed male), and there was a dog named 'Cat' and a cat named 'Dog', except that at one point the dog was called 'Dog', and so on. This was very confusing, and meant a lot of stopping to check back to make sure that we hadn't lost track of who was doing what.

We couldn't work out why the student was writing the novel in this way. When we asked him why, he replied, 'I want to really annoy the reader.' To which we replied, 'Mission accomplished.'

You don't have to re-invent the wheel. If you aren't sure how to do something, have a look at several published books to see how other authors handle the issue. (We say 'several', because if you use only one and it turns out to be a radically experimental novel, you may get into trouble!) Look at the same sort of book as the one that you're writing; for example, if you're writing crime fiction, check what other crime writers are doing and see if it suits what you're trying to do.

TIP

One final time: if you want to break the rules for a reason, that's fine, but remember the reader. Break the old rules consistently, so that the reader can at least learn your new rules. The bottom line is that you need to be sure in your own mind that what you gain from not using the traditional methods is greater than what you lose in terms of reader sympathy, and also that breaking the rules doesn't force you to make other changes that you'd rather not make.

Getting Feedback – When and How

Once the first draft is complete, some people want to rush out and show it to everyone they know and ask them what they think. Other people hug it to their chests and refuse to let go.

There isn't really a right or wrong way to react. However, as a general rule, we suggest you avoid both extremes, for reasons explained in the next sections.

Showing it to everyone

Sharing your novel with all and sundry probably gets you lots of reaction and feedback from loads of people. The problem, however, is as follows:

- ✔ Not everyone knows what they're talking about. If you show it to everyone in sight, you get some advice that's not worth bothering with.

- ✔ Even if people do know what they're talking about, they may not tell you the truth. They may like you too much to want to tell you that they don't like your work, or they may (let's hope not, but it's a hard old world out there) be jealous and unable to tell you truthfully what they think. Agendas often get in the way.

- ✔ The people who do know what they're talking about may disagree with each other. You may well receive contradictory advice.

- ✔ Not everyone likes to read the same thing, and so people's advice may be coloured by what you've written about rather than the writing itself.

- ✔ People may look in the wrong place and give you feedback that isn't the type of information you need.

Showing it to no one

Your novel may well be wonderful. It may also, let's face it, be pretty dreadful. It's only a first draft, after all.

You've spent ages with your nose pressed up against it. Can you be sure that you have any sort of perspective on it any more? Every author we've met says that there comes a time when they no longer know if what they're working on is any good or not. You're almost certain to become jaded, over-familiar, and plain fed-up with your work. Be honest with yourself: under these circumstances, are you always the best judge of your own work?

The solution may not be to show the draft to someone, but it's worth thinking about. Most people do, and it works for them.

Compromising

Obvious, really, but the course we recommend steers between the extremes of showing your draft to everyone and showing no one:

- ✔ Show the draft to a limited number of people to start with. You can always expand the circle of readers later if you want to, whereas you can't take it back once you've showed it to someone.

- Show it only to people who are experienced readers whose judgement you respect.
- Show it to people who have no axe to grind, at least to start with.

Tell people what you want feedback on. Obviously you're going to listen to anything they have to say about anything, but make sure that they know the sort of things you're after. For example, you may ask them to concentrate on the structure, or ask whether they stay interested in the main character's problems. If they then come back and tell you how much they dislike the dialogue, well, that's their privilege.

Be careful. Look after yourself and protect the work:

- Show your novel only to people you trust, but try to get feedback from more than one person if you can.
- Always let comments simmer for a day or so. Don't immediately rush off and make the changes your reviewers recommend, no matter who they are or how brilliant their suggestions. Make a note and let it sit for a while. Or, if you're utterly convinced by the suggestion, at least make sure that you don't do the edit on your only copy – if it doesn't work, you may want to go back to your previous version.

  You know that your own ideas that seem brilliant to you today are often less good when you've slept on them. The same applies to other people's ideas. Don't be too hasty.

Making use of the feedback you get

Feedback tends to come in three main types: the so-general-that-it-doesn't-help ('I really liked it'), the very general ('I didn't much like the main character'), and the very specific ('there's a mis-spelling on page 73'). Decide which parts of the feedback you're going to accept and which bits you aren't (although we suggest you check out any mis-spelling!). Do the rewriting that this feedback demands. Don't skimp it. Take your time. Yes, it's hard, but it needs doing. There's no point in spoiling all that work on the very last lap of the race.

Creating Your Final Draft

So, you've got plenty of useful feedback, written an outline chain, checked your grammar, and done a spell check. Now what?

This may surprise you. Put your manuscript somewhere safe, and forget about it. Opinions vary as to how long you should leave it, but about two weeks seems to work quite well for most writers. Go on holiday if you can. If that's not possible, just don't think about the novel. (That's why you need to go away: not thinking about the novel when you're at home and it's nearby is difficult.)

Why should you wait a couple of weeks? Apart from anything else, you need to take a bit of time to be extra nice and grateful to the people who've been taking care of business for you while you've been locked away writing. But mostly you need a break because you've spent the last however-many months with your nose pressed up against the glass of your work. You've been eating, breathing, and sleeping it. You've thought of little else. You've been living in it. You're too close. You need to get some distance.

After this break, your next job is to do a last slow, steady edit which leads to your final draft (the one you send to agents). This edit can't be rushed, so you need to gather yourself, a bit like athletes centring themselves for the final after running the heats. You need a rest to get ready. You also need to step away in order to come back to your novel as if it were fresh to you, so you can take a final polishing run-through.

Part V
Publishing

Top Five Tips for Submitting Your Novel to an Agency

Follow these tips if you can't locate the agency's exact submissions policy:

✔ **Send your submission by post, *not* by email.** Agents don't want to be cornered in their inbox or asked to prioritise your letter over someone else's. They want to put your submission aside and read it when they have a moment.

✔ **Enclose the first three chapters.** Judging whether a novel's of interest from the synopsis alone is very difficult, and many agents simply reject work they're unsure about, as opposed to requesting more material.

✔ **Use double-spaced, single-sided, numbered pages.** You're more likely to get feedback or editorial notes from an agent who can direct you to a page by number or fit comments between the lines of text on the page.

✔ **Send a full plot synopsis.** When read first, a synopsis can help an agent to decide quickly whether a novel's of interest.

✔ **Enclose a self-addressed envelope.** Not offering an SAE is like charging an agent for the privilege of rejecting your work. Don't expect acknowledgement of receipt though.

Go to www.dummies.com/extras/writinganovelgettingpublisheduk for free online bonus content.

In this part . . .

- ✔ Discover practical guidance on finding an agent, including how to write a synopsis, and how to work out which agencies to approach.

- ✔ Understand what advances and royalties are, as well as how to improve your chances of getting them . . .

- ✔ Find information about self-publishing, should you want to make your novel available to readers without delay.

Chapter 15

Publishing Your Novel

*U*p to this point you've focused on creative issues and on polishing and practising your craft. But if you want your novel to be published, you need to start thinking about how to market yourself and your writing to others. This chapter helps you to see yourself as a professional author as well as a writer. With the right strategy, persistence, and a little luck, your novel may start to earn you a living.

In this chapter, we focus on finding a publisher for your novel. Securing a publisher – a route to readers – used to be the necessary hurdle all authors had to leap. With the advent of self-publishing, anyone can publish their work; in Chapter 19 you can find information on how to self-publish an ebook. The challenge now is to be *discovered* – to be noticed, reviewed, and ultimately to be bought. In that sense, the same obstacles face every author, how ever their book is published. The advantage of being represented by an agent and acquired by a publisher is that you don't face those challenges alone.

A publisher can distribute and market your novel on a wide scale and support you with an advance on your royalties while you write. (Chapter 18 covers how book deals are structured and paid.) This chapter offers you an insight into who publishers are and what sort of novels they're looking for. A publisher and an agent are also able to license translations, North American and film or TV rights, which can offer significant income streams.

Publishing is a competitive business and, as with all self-employed careers, it can be risky and lonely. Plenty of talented writers view writing as a hobby rather than a career, mostly because their writing doesn't earn them enough to live on, however much they may want it to. The good news is that opportunities always exist for first-time novelists to find great success.

Becoming an Author

What's the difference between a writer and an author? Well, writers can sit in a room typing on their own for years (perhaps deleting every word from their computer screen at the end of every day) and still call themselves writers. Authors are writers with a product to show for all their efforts. In your case, the product is a novel.

You know the up-side of being an author, but there's a down-side too. For example, once you're an author, you have numerous responsibilities besides just writing every day, buying lots of lovely stationery, and admiring your profile on posters at railway stations. Among a lot of other things that you may have thought were advantages to the author's life, consider the myths and realities shown in Table 15-1.

Table 15-1	Writing Life: Myth versus Reality
Myth	*Reality*
Authors can spend the day writing in coffee bars.	You probably can't actually afford to drink at coffee bars much, so you spend long hours at home with only your laptop for company. Or worse, you're not alone, but with a flatmate who doesn't understand and plays the wrong music at the wrong volume, or else does understand and tries to be helpful and supportive, popping in cheerfully to offer you a cup of tea and ask how it's going, just as you're finally on the verge of solving the intractable problem at the end of chapter seven.

Myth	Reality
Authors work independently.	You have to listen to and take advice from your editor, which means being overruled sometimes and losing the total control you've been used to having over your novel. Self-published authors find themselves part of a vocal online community of reviewers and fellow authors.
Being an author allows you to escape a dull, routine job.	You find yourself reading the manuscript over and over again to check that your editor put the commas in the places where you always suspected, but weren't quite sure, that commas should be.
Authors can keep their own hours.	You have to be a good colleague to your agent and publisher, responding cheerfully to last-minute demands and not minding when they disappear to book fairs for days or weeks, or when they change their mind about every little thing, more than once. If you're self-published, you work more hours than you perhaps anticipated, like any small business owner.
Authors can focus on just being creative.	You have to reconcile yourself to publicising your book by living a second life on social media and being interviewed on very-early-morning shows on local radio stations with DJs who haven't read a book since school, keep forgetting that your novel is 'all made up', and ask you where you get your ideas.
Authors can concentrate on their writing.	You need to help develop your readership through readings and appearances, even though you have a cold and it's dark and chucking it down with rain; as well as blogging and tweeting regularly, even though you're mostly just at home with your laptop drinking too much coffee and haven't really got much to report.
Becoming an author fulfils all your dreams for life.	You have to write another novel, and then another – maybe even one a year.

The path to publication may well be the most exhausting, confidence-shaking (and possibly even the most expensive) one you've ever taken. Here are some other reasons why you may want to consider the option of quietly putting your manuscript in a cupboard and forgetting about the whole thing:

- ✔ Now the novel is finished, you're not sure that it's very good. You need to rewrite the whole thing.

- ✔ Now the novel is finished, you're sure that it's really, really great. Probably the best thing you've read in five years. And the last thing you want is for a bunch of over-privileged, pompous, and unappreciative publishers to tell you that you're wrong.

- ✔ Now the novel is finished, you've got an idea for another one that's really *much* better.

- ✔ You've just realised that you wrote the novel for yourself, not for anyone else. Well, for your Aunt Maud too, who can just have a photocopy.

- ✔ You've just realised that for most people being published is about acclaim or money. You don't need either, because you're a rather rich and celebrated violinist and don't need another string to your bow.

Don't send a publisher or an agent a manuscript you don't have absolute confidence in. If your novel has faults that you're aware of, don't put off correcting them until you're told to do so. The person in charge of reading your manuscript may not offer you detailed criticism. Always work on the assumption that you only get one shot, so make it as good as you can.

Understanding What Publishers Do

Many people assume that editing is the chief function performed by publishers. Editing is a highly skilled but relatively technical role, and the unique power of a successful publishing house lies not just in the skill of its editors but in its ability to choose the best books for publication and to identify, target, and reach the biggest market for your book.

In return for producing and marketing your book, and placing it in physical and online bookstores, publishers hope to make a tidy profit from your work. But they are only licensees. You *license* them – you permit them – to sell your book when you sign your publishing agreement. But *you* remain the copyright owner, and ultimately your novel is always your book, not the publisher's.

Here are some of the jobs that publishers do:

✔ **Editing:** Publishers employ editors to choose the most suitable books for publication and build long-term relationships with the authors they commission and edit.

Another part of the editing process focuses on guiding you to draw out the very best from the story you've written, whether that means developing the characterisation, tweaking the plot, or tightening up your style on a line-by-line basis. If your novel lacks pace in certain sections, or if one character sounds too like another, you can rely on your editor to point this out and to encourage you to fix it.

Your editor also organises for your novel to be typeset and copyedited. They mark up all the missing commas, brief the production and art departments to work out how much the book will cost to produce, and arrange for your book to be designed and printed, as well as published in digital format as an ebook.

✔ **Marketing and distributing:** Publishers' expertise is mostly focused in the areas of marketing and distribution. Although many self-published authors succeed with selling ebooks, publishers are still better placed than most authors to secure sales of books, through publicity, through retail or consumer advertising and promotion, and through the sheer capacity and effectiveness of their distribution business.

Publishers are talking constantly to retailers and to the media about forthcoming books and strategising about how best to find an audience for their authors' work.

✔ **Brokering rights:** Publishers also exploit rights in your books on your behalf, if you sell those rights to them. (Chapter 17 includes information about what rights you can grant to publishers.) These rights include translation rights, US publication rights, audio rights, and newspaper extract rights. But their core business is the production, marketing, and sale of your novel in their home territories.

Meeting the people who work in publishing

Lots of people who work in book publishing studied English literature at university and have read *all* the books on your 'to read before I die' list. But many of the decision makers within the publishing industry aren't the students who best understood Shakespeare's (hilarious!) jokes at school. They may be great communicators, creative rather than intellectual, or understand how to bring products effectively to market. Most of them do love books, and read a lot for pleasure, but they aren't all literature specialists.

Some of your other preconceptions and stereotypes about publishers and agents in the UK are probably correct. They're mostly white middle-class graduates from the South-East of England. Publishers aren't proud of this fact, and a few are taking positive steps to correct it. The good news is that white middle-class graduates from the South-East of England are often more interested in books that expand their frame of reference rather than reflect it. Which means you don't have to be a white middle-class graduate from the South-East of England to succeed as an author, as we hope you've already noticed.

Publishers are often interesting people to meet, because they know a little about a lot of things and are interested in almost anything. They're often clever and inspiring – they have to be, to launch new authors. They're used to meeting and getting on with all different sorts of people, and they're often quite charismatic. They probably aren't in the business for the money (publishing's notoriously badly paid), but because they genuinely love books and are excited by every great new 'find'. You may be the next one! If you become a published author, your relationship with your publisher and agent may not always be rosy, but you can be pretty sure that these people won't have a problem making small talk with you at parties.

Organising into imprints

Most publishing houses organise their publishing lists into mini-publishers, known as *imprints*. Each imprint usually has its own publisher at its head – someone who determines the profile of the overall list and oversees budgets and publication schedules.

Most publishing houses these days carry the scars of multiple buyouts and mergers over the past 30 or so years, and now one publishing house may offer a roof to ten or more different imprints. For example, Arrow, Black Swan, Century, Chatto & Windus, Doubleday, Harvill Secker, Hutchinson, Jonathan Cape, Ebury, and William Heinemann are just a few of the many different imprints at Random House.

Each imprint's publisher and his or her colleagues has a very clear idea of the sort of novel that best suits the imprint's publishing profile. Some imprints specialise in particular areas of the market, such as science fiction. But more usually imprints have a far more vague and idiosyncratic publishing brief, based on how literary or commercial they perceive themselves to be. (For more on how useful – or not – these concepts of 'literary' and 'commercial' are, see Chapter 17.) Publishers may also have an idea of their typical reader: age, gender, where they shop for books, and so on.

Super-size publisher

In 2013, Random House and Penguin Books merged into a mega conglomerate. Commentators say that this conglomeration among publishers is the only logical response to the power wielded by dominant retailers such as Amazon, and that if publishers can resist the pull towards ever lower book pricing, this merger is in every author's long-term interest. However, the reduction in the number of publishing groups competing to publish you is also likely to have a long-term negative impact on authors' income and influence. Conversely, in response to the increasingly corporate climate at the bigger publishing houses and the opportunities presented by the low overheads involved in digital publishing, a number of small personality-driven or niche imprints have emerged, both within those corporates and independently. Publishing today is a complex picture, and indicative of what publishers dub 'an industry in flux'.

Although most imprints don't have any brand value to the consumer (Faber & Faber and Penguin are thought to be the only recognisable imprint brands to the average book buyer), they signify something to book retailers and distributors, book reviewers, and literary award judges.

Agents develop a sophisticated awareness of the reading tastes of the individuals at the different imprints. The simple fact is that the publisher and editors of an imprint are never going to commission a book that doesn't fit their vision of where the imprint fits into the marketplace, and the most frequent rejection letter from editors says 'this novel just isn't for us'. Rejection really can be as much about them, as about you.

Analysing the Kind of Books Publishers Look For

So how do publishers decide on the novels that merit publication? Is it really just about deciding which novels are 'the best'? Well, no, not really.

Of course publishers like to commission novels that they admire, the ones that move them, make them think, or seem to be like nothing they've read before. Some publishers even specialise in publishing books they know have a limited appeal. But even they generally choose to publish the books that they believe are going to sell the most copies rather than the ones they deem to be the best. Sometimes the two things are one and the same – certainly agents, publishers, and writers all hope that this is the case.

Recognising that publishing is for profit

Publishing is a business like every other business: it exists to make money. Table 15-2 compares the publishing process with other businesses and shows that publishing isn't that much different from the baked bean business. (You're the beans in this metaphor.) It's not more high-minded than other profit-driven pursuits, although it can be old-fashioned and a little near-sighted. All other things being equal, most publishers probably prefer to make money by publishing good books rather than bad ones, but realistically, their ultimate concern is the bottom line.

Table 15-2	Publishing Compared with Other Businesses			
Business	*First Step*	*Second Step*	*Third Step*	*Fourth Step*
Publishing	Editing	Manufacturing	Marketing	Selling
Making baked beans	Cooking	Manufacturing	Marketing	Selling
Making floor polish	Inventing	Manufacturing	Marketing	Selling

Looking at what constitutes a novel that sells

Our experience suggests that the following are all ingredients for a commercially successful novel:

- ✔ **A novel with an accessible and intriguing hook.** This novel immediately sounds interesting when you summarise its plot and characters. Usually, the publisher can immediately see how to package it in order to attract customers.

- ✔ **A novel that people recommend and talk about.** This novel offers great story-telling, excitement, or insight. It has an effect on the reader, the sort of effect that makes readers talk about it passionately to friends, buy everyone copies as gifts, or want to review it.

- ✔ **A novel that touches a nerve.** This type of novel speaks eloquently of a particular human experience, or touches on themes of relevance or interest to the world today. You often hear of this sort of novel 'tapping into the zeitgeist'.

✔ **A novel that reminds readers of a book they enjoyed.** This sort of novel is a novel of the moment, or perhaps one that responds to a trend in publishing. The cover may well resemble that of a book it's similar to, assuring readers that they're buying the same sort of thing.

Other sorts of bestselling novels exist, too – for example the ones written by a well-known author or an individual already known to the public in some other way, such as through journalism, politics, or YouTube or Twitter fame. These books are often given a big publicity boost because of their celebrity connections or because the author already has an audience for their work.

When a key tastemaker – whether an individual, prize, or book club such as the Richard and Judy Book Club – has the power to create bestsellers, publishers naturally take their tastes into account when they acquire books. The influence of the Richard and Judy branded retailer and media promotions on the UK publishing scene is immense. The sort of novels selected by R&J (as they're known in publishing circles) are openly emotional, strong, memorable stories positioned perfectly between accessible genre fiction and literary fiction. Even though the R&J lists are diverse, somehow the books all share certain sensibilities.

Publishers look to see whether your novel is very like – or completely unlike – what they already publish. If they already publish a lot of young romance, for example, they may feel that publishing any more is inevitably going to distract them from focusing on building the careers of the authors in whom they've already invested. On the flip side, if they published one young romance last year and it exceeded their sales expectations, they'll be keen to buy another.

Thinking about the Market for Your Novel

Novels that sell have to be good. But they also usually have to feel relevant to the publisher and the customer. Put simply, there has to be a market for them. It's very depressing to be told that there isn't a market for what you've written, but publishers say it a lot when rejecting novels for publication. This section helps you to understand what 'the market' means, and therefore helps you to maximise your chances of getting published.

Now that you have a product – your novel – you have to understand its value. In the case of a novel, this constitutes an estimation of the number of people who may want to read it.

The value of your novel depends entirely on how many people want to *pay* to read your novel. Remembering that you're asking people to pay to read your book can be a very useful discipline.

Immersing yourself in bookshops, bestseller lists, newspapers, magazines, websites, and television schedules helps you cater to public appetites, just like any other form of entertainment does.

Defining what 'market' means

One useful definition of *market* in this context is *appetite*. If a publisher says that there's no market for your type of novel at the moment, what they really mean is that the public has no appetite for it. This doesn't mean that your novel isn't a very good healthy meal, but this summer people are mostly eating salads, not pies. Your pie may well be perfectly delicious, but if no one is buying them this year, you're out of luck. So, being daring or different isn't easy.

Unless the time is right for your novel, it may not find a publisher. If its themes or style are said to be 'unfashionable', 'boring', or 'unpopular', take heart. You may just be ahead of fashion. The phenomenon of not quite fitting into a perceived gap in the market leads many authors to self-publish. Even if publishers can't safely predict a broad audience for your novel, you may find it anyway when you make your book available online.

The public's appetite for a particular kind of novel is determined by many factors, including what novels were successful last year. But as well as cannibalising their previous successes, publishers also draw inspiration from other media, including news reporting and current affairs, popular TV, magazines, newspapers, websites, and cinema.

For example, if a particular style of gory thriller drama enjoys success on television, that style may eventually come to influence the type of thrillers readers want to buy. If a new TV comedy sketch show becomes everyone's favourite topic of conversation while the office kettle is boiling, that type of humour can become the type of humour publishers consciously or unconsciously look for in novels.

Farce and slapstick were enormously successful in theatre, film, and books in the not-too-distant past, but selling a novel with those humorous qualities today, when irony is everything, is impossible.

Be aware of how your novel compares with other authors' books. Don't kid yourself that you're writing like one Trollope when you're actually more like the other one. Nothing wrong with Joanna or Anthony Trollope, but be clear in your own mind which one you are.

Don't fall into the trap of imitating too closely the success of others, or pandering to a recent trend if it doesn't suit your writing style or interests. Agents and editors can easily spot when you're faking.

Sorting out who controls the market

People behave as though the market is mysterious. It isn't. The market is you, us, and everyone else who buys books. Well, you say, that's great because you're certain that you, us, and everyone else would buy your novel! But, hang on, they can only buy your book if they can see it in a bookshop or online. Actually, to be honest, unless your novel's on one of those tables near the door or has made it into an ebook bestseller list, people may not notice it at all. Readers could look for it, of course, but unless they've heard of it, they don't know to do that.

Most of the time, readers walk into a bookshop or browse an online store with no particular plan, and end up buying a book that was displayed in a place where it would catch their eye, at a price they found attractive.

Rounding up the usual suspects

So, who controls the market for your novel? The usual suspects are:

- ✔ **Booksellers:** How do booksellers choose which novels to promote at the front of the bookshop or online? Well, first they sit through regular sales presentations during which publishers pitch their forthcoming titles. Based on the pitch, the jacket, the title, knowledge of their customer base, and information from the publisher about its marketing budget and publicity plans for the novel, booksellers make their choices about which books to promote most enthusiastically to their customers. They know that most customers rely on them to select the most interesting novels.

  So perhaps booksellers control the market?

- ✔ **Publishers:** Publishers pay retailers for the best promotional spots. And they don't make that marketing money available to all the titles on their publishing list. So what they tend to do is select which books they most want booksellers to promote. They do this through specifying which titles each month are their *lead titles* (or 'targeted' or 'superlead' titles, or some other euphemism for 'most important'). Those books are at the top of the list of books presented to booksellers.

  So, perhaps publishers control the market?

✔ **Agents:** Publishers usually buy only the novels that are submitted to them by agents. So agents are the initial tastemakers, sifting through the mass of material submitted every week and choosing only a few books to show to publishers. In truth, however, they usually focus on the sort of books that they can see publishers buying from other agents and getting into those bookseller promotions by the shop door.

So, perhaps agents control the market?

✔ **A combination of all three:** Is it indeed a great conspiracy among agents, publishers, and booksellers? We have to be honest: this is a partly true – if pessimistic – view of the industry. These days you need a consensus before you can promote a new author. And in so far as their interests are mutual (they all want to sell lorry-loads of books), there's undoubtedly a degree of consensus between agents, publishers, and booksellers as to what sort of books are published.

Celebrating the consumer

However, we believe that readers have the most power in the marketplace, despite the tendency for publishers and big retailers to predict and create trends and bestsellers. If you browse any democratic story-telling website, you see the same sort of novels rising to the top again and again. These novels are often a good gauge of the next trend to hit publishing, whether that be erotica (*Fifty Shades of Grey*) or paranormal romance (countless examples, including the *Twilight* books).

Proponents of digital self-publishing say that online bookselling is totally democratic – any book has a chance to catch on via word of mouth and become a bestseller. They dub publishers as gatekeepers whose influence undermines the power of readers to create their own trends. We're sceptical of the 'publishers as gatekeepers' theory, when Amazon enjoys such power, and one of the biggest determinants of ebook bestselling success is price. What's undeniable, however, is that many novels without big marketing campaigns achieve massive sales as a result of word-of-mouth recommendations from ordinary readers. These books just seem to strike a chord. In other words, there's a huge market for them.

Considering the Mechanics of Bookselling

Publishers generally still print a recommended retail price (RRP) on books, although since the abolition of the Net Book Agreement (NBA) years ago, booksellers aren't obliged to charge the customer the RRP. That's why you can buy some novels at half price in supermarkets and online; you've probably already forgotten or aren't aware that this didn't always happen.

Since the abolition of the NBA, consumers have been able to shop around for the best discounts on the most popular books. Retailers such as Amazon and the supermarkets, who can afford to offer steep discounts to customers, now almost dominate the market for bestsellers.

Although ebooks do have an RRP, it isn't listed on Amazon. The only advertised price is the retailer's discounted selling price, which is currently expressed as a discount off the prevailing print price. Authors are paid an ebook royalty which relates to the publisher's receipts from the retailer rather than the RRP (we explain this further in Chapter 18).

Retailers demand ever higher purchasing discounts from publishers. In turn, this puts pressure on the publisher's profit (and on the level of royalties an author can hope to earn, again an issue explored more fully in Chapter 18).

Publishers made an attempt to maintain reasonably high selling prices on ebooks (about 20 per cent lower than the paperback price), quite early on in the big ebook boom, when they insisted on agency model terms in their agreements with online retailers. Under the *agency model,* publishers set the discounted selling price to the customer, rather than letting the retailer set the price. At the time of writing, in 2014, the agency model has been dealt some significant blows and it's unclear whether publishers or retailers will ultimately triumph in the battle to set ebook prices.

Exploring where books are sold

Books used to be sold by specialist retailers, but the market has been transformed by several factors:

- ✔ The growth of Internet retail. Books are one of the top-selling products online. Online retailers carry lower overheads and can afford to charge lower prices to consumers. The popularity of ebooks has drawn customers to buy print books online, too. In 2012, 38 per cent of all book purchases in the UK and 44 per cent in the USA were made online. And remember that customers can download the first few pages of every novel for free. This has had an editorial impact on fiction, which is pacier than ever. Another key factor to consider in online retail is the important role played by the search function. It favours authors whose work is already known to readers over debut authors.

- ✔ The increasing market dominance of multiple retailers. Businesses such as supermarkets are attracted to any market they can undercut. Chart promotions in supermarkets tend to go to authors who've already proved that their books can sell in high numbers. Most retail promotions are price-led rather than, say, theme-driven, and books sold at a lower price rise quickly up the bestseller lists.

✔ Bookselling chains used to dominate our high streets and shopping malls, but they've weakened with the advent of the ebook. With independent bookselling on its knees, we see increasing numbers of discount bookstores and second-hand bookshops in our town centres. Long-established brands with big backlists tend to be most visible in second-hand and discount shops. So you see a growth in sales for established brands as a direct result of retail conditions.

✔ In the UK, WH Smith is still a presence in most town centres. The WH Smith's Travel division runs very successful shops at railway stations at airports. These shops, frequented by commuters and holiday-makers, have often been trendsetting, with an ability to predict the novels that will capture the attention of the captive audience of commuters and holiday-makers.

As for where new voices are sold, the influential Richard and Judy promotion is led by WH Smith. The success of this reading group promotion can lead to sales phenomena – single books that dominate the bestseller lists for months or even years. As every retailer picks up on the successful title and supports it, a lack of diversity creeps into the chains and online, which, in the absence of independent retailers, can't be mitigated easily.

These market factors all help to determine the books being commissioned by publishers. In Chapter 19 we explore in some detail the kinds of books that sell particularly well in ebook format.

By the time you read this chapter, the market will have changed again. Any new bookselling chain, shopping habit, trading law, or technological advance can alter the picture significantly. But the point stands: knowing where a customer will probably buy your book, not only in which shop but in what format and on what device as well, can help you to write a commercially successful book and to market it appropriately.

Pricing it up

Retailers buy books from publishers at a discounted rate. So a £7.99 paperback may be sold to a bookseller at a discount of anywhere between 35 and 75 per cent (or more!). The more copies a bookseller buys, the better the discount the publisher offers. (The more copies the publisher prints, the lower the unit cost per book.) If a bookseller offers to promote a novel in a chart position or front of store, for example, it may ask for a steeper discount by way of payment for that promotion.

Table 15-3 shows how the average costs and profit from a £10 book may typically be divided. The information was sourced from a top corporate publisher.

Table 15-3	Approximate Distribution from a £10 Print Book	
Cost or Profit	*Percentage*	*Amount*
Manufacturing costs	12%	£1.20
Royalties	6%*	£0.60
Distribution/marketing	8%	£0.80
Publisher's overheads	9%	£0.90
Trade discount	60%	£6.00
Publishers net profit	5%	£0.50

* Please note that this is not the typical headline royalty in the publishing contract, but the diminished royalty usually due when high discounts have been offered to retailers.

With so much of the retail price that is paid for each book spent on marketing, selling, and distribution, and with booksellers commanding such high discounts, publishers need to sell quite a few copies of each novel before making any profit. So they can't afford to make mistakes too often.

Although Table 15-3 only relates to print editions, the picture's surprisingly similar for ebooks. Of course the manufacturing cost isn't a feature, but it was always a relatively low component of a book's costing. Publishers point out that, because ebook sales often cannibalise print sales, the start-up costs for a new book need to be spread across the print and electronic editions.

Although consumers continue to buy books – transitioning gradually from print purchases to ebooks – publishers' turnover is flat and margins are squeezed as bookseller promotions narrow and become increasingly expensive in terms of the fees and discounts that retailers demand. As a result, it's harder than ever to convince a publisher that your novel is a sound commercial proposition. Of course, the counter-balance to this is the opportunity offered by self-publishing, which we discuss in Chapter 19.

It's all a bit depressing, isn't it? One thing to cheer you up is that a publisher likes nothing more than something *new*. If you haven't been published before, your publisher can enjoy colourful dreams of just how many people will want to buy your book . . . How does it feel to be *fresh meat*? Now all you need is a butcher. Or, as they're more commonly known, an agent (turn to Chapter 16).

Chapter 16

Finding an Agent

*M*any publishers accept submissions only via an agent, and it's generally acknowledged that if you're looking for a publisher, you need to find an agent first. Even self-published authors tend to have an agent after they've achieved a certain level of success; some self-published authors actually sign with an agent first and then self-publish in collaboration with their agent. (Find out why they might do this in Chapter 19.) Lists of agencies are readily available, but there are hundreds of agencies and it sometimes seems impossible to know where to start. This chapter helps you work out who to write to and how to go about it. Seeking an agent is the first step for many on the bumpy road to publication and may be your first experience of criticism or rejection. It can also be your first experience of praise and flattery – which can be equally disorientating! This chapter offers perspectives on the sort of feedback you can expect to receive.

In order to find the best possible agent for you and your novel, you need to understand how agents work and why they operate in the particular ways they do.

Note: Agents all work for agencies, alone or with other agents, and throughout this chapter we use the words *agent* and *agency* more or less synonymously. For example, an agency may have submission guidelines, but an individual agent probably wrote them.

Understanding What a Literary Agency Does

A *literary agency* is a company whose main business is to promote and defend the interests of its clients, who are all authors. As an author, an individual agent represents you, although other agents at the agency may have responsibility for selling particular rights, such as translation rights, in your work.

Publishing is quite an insular industry, with its own jargon, precedents and business models; good agents have technical expertise and extensive experience that ensures that your publishing contract is as good as it can possibly be. Author–publisher relationships can be fraught with high expectations on both sides, and agents offer authors invaluable advice and guidance at every step of the publishing process.

Agents tend to favour particular types of writing or books but rarely specialise in one genre over another. Most agents are generalists and only avoid subjects whose appeal seems too narrow (technical or niche books, for example – this is less relevant to novelists than authors of non-fiction). As well as the individual agents, agencies also employ assistants and accounts personnel.

The main functions of a literary agency are:

- Protecting and promoting the interests of the agency's clients.

- Finding new authors and signing them up as clients of the agency.

- Offering clients editorial feedback on their work.

- Submitting authors' work to publishers.

- Making publication deals on behalf of its authors, both in the UK and abroad, and negotiating the sale of other rights, such as film rights, audio book rights, and serialisation rights.

- Negotiating the terms of all contracts made by the agency.

- Liaising with and pushing publishers to serve their authors' best interests at every stage of the publication process (for example, through altering the book jacket or paying for retailer promotions).

- Invoicing on its authors' behalf, and processing authors' book income through agency accounts.

- Helping its authors to self-publish ebooks.

- Earning a percentage of its authors' income on deals negotiated by the agency – usually 15 per cent in the UK and 20 per cent on US and foreign rights deals.

Your agent should also review your royalty statements to check that the amounts are correct.

A random list of things that literary agents *don't* do includes:

✔ Ask for a fee to join the agency or to read a submission. A reputable literary agent *never* asks for money before signing you up.

✔ Act as book publicists, securing book reviews, features, or author public relations (PR).

✔ Offer tax, pensions, or legal advice. Good agents have an excellent layperson's understanding of legal and financial matters, but aren't permitted to act as professional advisers in this capacity.

✔ Prepare your VAT return or in any way act as an accountant.

✔ Guarantee that they can make you a publication deal.

✔ Lend you money.

✔ Borrow money from you.

✔ Hold drop-in coffee mornings for groups of unpublished authors.

Of course, we can name several agents who have lent their authors money, helped with VAT returns, placed book reviews, and offered the equivalent of a drop-in service, but then again we can think of agents who helped their authors to move house, suggested names for their babies, offered marriage counselling (this is usually a no-win situation from an agent's point of view), and committed to getting drunk with a particular author every Thursday night. But you can't *expect* these kinds of services . . . or even a Christmas card (Lizzy is particularly bad at those). You *can* expect a certain degree of loyalty, hard work, and passion for your writing.

Any agency's core business is to look after the clients to whom it is already committed. You – the unsigned author – are not the agency's priority, and that's only right and proper. When you do sign up with an agent, the last thing you want them to do is to lose interest in you immediately and spend the whole time looking for new authors, right?

Approaching a smaller agency

Many agencies are very small companies employing fewer than ten people, and a high proportion of those are actually one-man bands. If you're worried that an agent works alone, don't be. The nature of the business suits small groups and individuals, because you don't need fancy offices or regular hours in order to perform the responsibilities of an agent.

Many very small agencies offer an excellent service. Often the agents working solo are very successful agents who left bigger agencies to go it alone, safe in the knowledge that their impressive client list earns enough to support their new business. On the other hand, of course, as with every business, some are chancers who know nothing and nobody.

There are some disadvantages to being a client of a very small agency. If you always want to find someone – anyone – at the end of the phone when you call your agent, you may mind if your time-pressed agent has no personal assistant. But it's just as easy to be ignored at a huge agency, so your choice of agency can be a matter of taste. Many small agencies rely on relationships with third party agencies for sales of film rights or translation rights, so if the sale of these rights is very important to you, find out as much as you can about those third party agencies and external relationships at the outset. Ideally, those agents will be as passionate about your work as your primary agent is.

Surveying a larger agency

At larger agencies, agents often have assistants (who do much more than secretarial work, often forming close relationships with authors themselves). Some of your agent's colleagues (and *their* assistants) may specialise in selling translation rights, serialisation rights, audio rights, and TV and film rights. A larger agency probably has a finance department with bookkeepers and, if you're lucky (make sure that you are by asking at the outset), they also employ people who check royalty statements for accuracy. There may also be reception and admin staff, and interns (the unseen hands keeping the photocopiers churning throughout the publishing industry).

Agents at larger agencies tend to work an unofficial apprenticeship before being awarded the title of agent. An agent who starts as an agent's assistant is given the opportunity to learn the technical aspects of the job, including the ins and outs of contracts, who's who in publishing, how to auction a novel, what constitutes good publicity, and so on, as well as to develop some of the softer skills every good agent needs. These latter skills include how to say 'no', when to say 'yes', how to get what you want while letting the other person think they've won, how to do small talk at parties, how to massage someone's ego while tapping one-handed on a calculator, and that sort of thing. Sometimes an agent starts as an editor or another sort of publisher and then decides that agents have more fun/earn more money/work better hours. They're right . . . agents with good judgement, at least.

Checking Out Agencies

Someone who wants to be a literary agent has no exams to pass, serves no obligatory apprenticeship, and isn't required to seek membership of a professional association, so assessing the experience and ability of a potential agent is sometimes difficult. Recent years have seen a proliferation in the number of businesses purporting to be agencies and offering various services to writers. The following sections offer advice on separating the legitimate agents from the fly-by-nights, and point you towards finding information on agencies.

Looking into the Association of Authors' Agents

Although agents aren't required to belong to a professional body in order to practise (as is the case, for example, with financial advisers), agencies in the UK can apply to become voluntary members of the Association of Authors' Agents (AAA). At the time of writing, in order to qualify for membership, agencies must have been established for a minimum of two years and must be earning at least £25,000 worth of commission a year.

Most young start-up literary agencies join the AAA as soon as they're eligible, so if you're not sure of a literary agency's legitimacy, log on to the AAA website (www.agentsassoc.co.uk) and check the list of members.

Once a member of the AAA, an agency signs up to a self-governing code of practice, details of which are on the AAA website. This code of practice offers you, as a writer, a good insight into some of the working practices you can expect from your agent. For example, the AAA asks that its agents take no less than 21 days to pass a writer's money on to the writer, and that authors' money be held in separate client accounts. (This arrangement is so that an agency can't accidentally spend your money on its gas bill.)

If an agency's unwilling to discuss how it banks your money or any other aspects of the code of practice – whether or not it's a member of the AAA – you're right to be suspicious.

The best way to judge an agency is by its client list. If an agency represents a number of sought-after authors (people who in theory can take their pick of a lot of agencies), you can assume that the agency is a good one.

Working out which agents to approach

As well as the list of agencies on the AAA website, another popular source for lists of agents is *The Writers' and Artists' Yearbook*, published annually by Bloomsbury and widely available in bookshops and libraries. This book is also an invaluable source of information on many other aspects of the publishing industry.

Most agencies have websites that offer varying degrees of information about the agency, its clients, agents, and interests. Take full advantage of all the information that an agency's website offers you. Read all the agent profiles, check and follow the submission guidelines thoroughly, note the client lists, and then look up the clients' books to see what kind of books they write.

You can also find many agents on Twitter, on writing community websites and blogging for various publications. Search by name for particular agents online, and references to them will proliferate because most authors mention their agents. Agents work in the public eye to some extent, so if you do your research you can develop a useful impression of them.

If you have any burning questions about an agency, just ring and talk to the receptionist. If receptionists don't like your questions, they can choose not to answer them. Don't feel the need to give them your name, though; if your questions are really annoying, you're better off remaining anonymous. And don't suddenly start giving them a full plot outline over the phone.

Approaching Agents

Study the agency profiles in *The Writers' and Artists' Yearbook* (see the preceding section) to get an idea about the agencies that may suit you best. But don't worry if you end up making fairly random decisions about which agency to send your novel to. Knowing who will be the best agent for you at this stage is very difficult, so just go for it. Use your common sense where it seems applicable, write a few letters or emails, and see how you get on.

Making use of contacts and recommendations

You can choose from a lot of agents. The best way by far to find an agent is to ask for recommendations. If you have any contacts within the publishing industry, or if you or your Aunt Bea knows any authors, ask them for some suggested names. Don't feel guilty about exploiting personal contacts. And if the connection is strong, don't hesitate to mention the mutual friend in your approach letter, in the hope that it may make the agent feel obliged to have a proper look at your novel. A shortage of contacts isn't going to do you any harm, and some contacts help more than others, but if you've got them, use them.

Other sources of recommendations are panellists on talks about publishing, authors at author events, authors' websites (which always name-check the agent), writers' circles, and writers' magazines. Reading some book-trade publications is also worthwhile, such as *The Bookseller* magazine (available weekly, either online to subscribers (www.thebookseller.com) or through your library or newsagent), which reveals much about the publishing industry. In terms of information about agents, the magazine lists details of a few recent new book deals and the agents responsible. Also, any group of aspiring authors getting together for writing workshops can probably give you the names of a couple of agents who offered helpful feedback in the past.

In other words, if you're serious about wanting to be a published writer, get out there, start networking and researching, and you'll soon pick up some tips.

One of the most popular ways of choosing which agents to approach is by making a note of the agent's name on the acknowledgements page of a novel you think is rather like yours. You know the sort of thing: 'My heartfelt thanks to Jonty, my loyal agent, who was there for me even when I thought the novel would *never* be good enough.' If the agent enjoyed this novel, they may well appreciate yours.

One particular type of agent is gold dust – the agent who has a bit of experience as an agent, agent's assistant, or editor, but who has yet to build up a full list of clients. Such agents are particularly hungry for new projects and authors. They're more likely to offer feedback and encouragement, and more able to invest time in you. Try calling the bigger agencies, which are more likely to have agents in this position, and ask them whether anyone's looking for new authors at the moment. One out of ten phone calls may prove fruitful. (One in 14 million lottery tickets wins the jackpot, so these odds are good!)

Crafting your approach

The first step in approaching an agent is to check whether the agency accepts *unsolicited submissions*, submissions from people they don't know. If you can establish this without phoning – by checking the agency's website or one of the guidebooks mentioned in the 'Working out which agents to approach' section earlier in this chapter – so much the better. Some agencies give callers inquiring about this policy pretty short shrift, and they resent answering the same question a hundred times a week.

On the other hand, some agents recommend, off the record, that you call before posting your letter, to check whether any agents are particularly open to submissions, to verify the submission guidelines, and so on. Certainly call if you have an important question – which may mean asking to whom you should send your novel. If you're dissatisfied with the answer you're given, never mind; just thank the person politely and hang up the phone.

One thing you absolutely mustn't do as a first-time author is to call a particular agent and alert them to the fact that you're about to send them a wonderful new novel. Agents are not available on the phone for pitching.

You've probably heard that some agents prefer to be approached on an *exclusive basis*, which means they prefer you not to approach anyone else at the same time. However, most agents accept that a high level of competition exists in the industry, and that writers are understandably keen to meet more than one agent before deciding on the best representative for their work. So don't feel bullied. Whether you fix on one particular agency at a time, or approach several simultaneously, is entirely up to you.

If you approach just one agent, make sure that, in your letter, you alert the agent to the exclusive nature of your submission. But don't think it gives you the right to chase an answer from them more quickly. If you don't hear back from the agent within about six weeks, just write to someone else and keep going. You don't need to withdraw your submission from consideration; that would be a waste of time.

We recommend approaching about four (meaning maybe three, maybe five or six) agencies at one time. If nothing comes of those submissions, choose another four or so agencies and start again.

Remember, agencies can choose whether to read your work, and they aren't obliged to respond to your submission at all. They don't charge fees, remember? But you can assume that an agency's open to submissions if it claims to be open to them – on its website, in the *Writers' and Artists' Yearbook* or on the phone.

Some writers obviously feel they have a lot of rights: the right to speak to an agent on the phone, to receive a prompt response from an agent to their submission, lengthy and detailed editorial feedback, and a comprehensive list of reasons for a rejection with suggestions for alternative people to approach. Their attitude seems to be: here I am, I've written a wonderful novel, now it's your job to acknowledge my talent and drop everything else to make sure that my work receives its proper audience. Of course this is arrogant nonsense, and agencies don't respond well if you exhibit this attitude.

The only circumstances that warrant chasing an agency for a response are:

✔ Another agent is pressing you to commit to them.

✔ You have an offer on the table from a publisher.

In fact, should you fail to inform an agent who's actively considering your work of an offer of representation from another agent before accepting that offer, the agent ignorantly still considering your work would have every reason to feel annoyed!

Submitting Your Manuscript

The first step to finding an agent is to send them your manuscript. Find out an agency's submission guidelines, and follow them. You must have confidence in your novel's ability to succeed or fail on its own merits. Fussing too much over what to write in your submission letter is pointless – just make sure that it doesn't put anyone off! Taking the time to produce a good synopsis, however, is worthwhile. (See the tips we offer in both these areas in the sections 'Writing a submission letter' and 'Composing your synopsis' elsewhere in this chapter.)

If an agency states that it doesn't accept unsolicited manuscripts, and yet you really want to send your novel to them, do it anyway. Some agencies have a policy of non-encouragement because they don't want to open the floodgates to an unmanageable level of submissions, but they'll probably pay the same attention to your manuscript as the next agent. If the agency returns your manuscript unread, you've only lost the cost of the postage.

However, if an agency states that it doesn't accept a certain type of book – no science fiction, no children's books, and so on – accept this at face value. No matter how good your novel, it's probably not even going to get read if it falls within a genre that the agency isn't interested in.

You can help yourself by using common sense. If, for example, you ignore the agency's guidelines, you can't really be surprised if the agency assumes that you're an amateur who's unlikely to have written something worth looking at. Try to put yourself in the agent's place; it will save you time and heartache.

Following agency submission policies

Agencies receive hundreds of manuscripts and letters from aspiring authors every month. (A middle-sized agency typically receives about 20 a day.) In order to give all authors a fair and equal chance to attract the agents' attention, agencies have devised *submission guidelines* that request the same type of material from all authors. Considering submissions is a difficult and time-consuming task, so submission guidelines are geared towards making that job as easy and quick as possible for the agents. You can find an agency's submission guidelines in the *Writers' and Artists' Yearbook* and on agency websites.

This point is essential: if an agency accepts unsolicited manuscripts, follow the agency's submission guidelines to the letter. Don't quibble with the guidelines: it's annoying to an agent, doesn't get you anywhere, and the guidelines exist for good reasons.

The following list is a good guide to how to approach an agency if you can't locate the agency's exact submissions policy, and also offers an insight into the thinking behind the usual policies:

- **Send your submission by post, *not* by email.** Agents don't want to be cornered in their inbox or asked to prioritise your letter over someone else's. They want to put your submission aside and read it when they have a moment.

  Now that agents read manuscripts on ereaders, some agencies *do* invite submissions on email. However, if you email an agent against an agency's specific advice, or instead of attempting to contact the agency by post first, you're not in very good company, because 99.9 per cent of *unsolicited* email submissions are of low quality. Often writers send the email without addressing it personally, simply emailing a whole group of agents blind. Many unsolicited email submissions are sent from North America.

- **Enclose the first three chapters.** Don't bother trying to explain why you think it's best to enclose the middle three chapters rather than the first three. If the first three chapters of your novel are 'a bit slow' or 'atypical', you need to fix the problem and not try to compensate for it. If the first three chapters don't work, the book doesn't work. Anyway, have *you* ever tried to read a book intelligently from the middle onwards?

  If the guidelines recommend sending some chapters, don't fail to enclose them. Judging whether a novel is of interest from the synopsis alone is very difficult, and many agents simply reject work they're unsure about, as opposed to requesting more material.

- **Use double-spaced, single-sided, numbered pages.** If agents find themselves squinting over the pages or losing their place, they're likely to want to move on to the next manuscript. You're more likely to get feedback or editorial notes from an agent who can direct you to a page by number or fit comments between the lines of text on the page.

  Don't print the novel out as if it were a book, on side-by-side pages. Agents know what books look like, thanks. And don't get books printed especially for your submissions.

- **Send a full plot synopsis.** When read first, a synopsis can help an agent to decide quickly whether a novel's of interest. If you render your novel inscrutable by not accompanying the sample chapters with a synopsis, impatient agents aren't going to feel bound to battle on regardless to explore the novel in depth – they'll just be irritated by the lack of information. (The 'Composing your synopsis' section later in this chapter talks about writing a synopsis.)

  Even if the synopsis means that your book's quickly rejected, that's a good thing. A former boss (an agent) used to say that a quick no is the second-best answer; much preferable to a no following an agonising wait.

> Another agent says: 'Not sending a synopsis is like inviting me to your party and forgetting to give me directions to your house. I may find your house without directions, but I may not bother to try or may get lost on the way.'

✔ **Enclose a self-addressed envelope (SAE).** Not offering an SAE is like charging an agent for the privilege of rejecting your work.

✔ **Don't expect acknowledgement of receipt.** It's very time-consuming for an agency to acknowledge receipt of every manuscript. An insistence that your potential agent do so is generally perceived as a desperate excuse to keep phoning. An agent may not see your request for acknowledgement until they're ready to read the submission. Then it's going to irritate them, which isn't good when they're about to read your manuscript.

Agencies don't commit to getting back to you at all, and even if they plan to, they can only guess as to when. If you ring an agent and hassle them, you're certainly going to get rejected more quickly – which may be your aim. For example, if you ring to tell them that someone else is interested in you, they'll undoubtedly have a look at your book. No one likes to feel they've missed a gem. But if they don't like your novel, they still aren't going to be interested in you just because someone else is. They know that other agents are wrong all the time, just as they are.

Ringing up an agent and telling them that another agent is interested in your book when it isn't true is a very bad idea. Agents talk to each other, and no one likes to find out they've been lied to, especially when mutual trust's at the heart of the relationship between agent and author. Don't do it.

Don't approach publishers directly while also approaching agents. Every publisher who rejects your book constitutes one less reason for an agent to take a chance on you. Agents like to have a fresh start when working with an author.

Writing a submission letter

All your letter needs to do is more or less to list what you're enclosing, offer a few lines about what kind of book you've written, and convey a polite expression of hope that the agent enjoys what you're sending. Sounds easy, eh?

The best advice on how to write a letter to an agent is common sense for most people. But the truth is that many writers fall at the first hurdle.

The reality is that if you write a bad letter, your manuscript probably won't get more than a glance. If this sounds harsh, don't forget that agents aren't interested in how pretty you are (whatever the papers say), whether you make a great apple pie, or whether you caught a really big fish last weekend. They only care whether you can *write*. And so if you write a bad letter, you're at a pretty obvious disadvantage immediately.

Your submission letter isn't the main attraction, it's the warm-up act. As long as it doesn't do anything to put the agent off reading your novel, it's done its job. It doesn't have to be as interesting, funny, or moving as your book.

The following issues are the most important to consider when drafting an effective submission letter:

- **Length of letter:** Most submission letters need to be fairly short: letters that ramble on are obviously a bore. However, your letter shouldn't be so short that it seems impolite, clever-dicky, or careless. Your letter should be roughly a couple of paragraphs long unless you have a very unusual reason for needing to write at greater length.

- **Addressing the letter accurately:** The key in addressing your submission letter is to make each agent feel that you put some thought into *choosing* to write to them.

The following mistakes are easily avoidable with a little common sense, and yet any agent sees these errors made over and over again:

- **Misspelling the name of the agent or agency:** This gives a terrible first impression. Think about it: if someone wrote to you in an attempt to impress you and misspelt your name, how impressed would you be?

- **Using 'Dear Sir/Madam' or 'Dear agent' as the salutation:** Sir/Madam is an appropriate address only if your letter is addressed to the submissions department, which is some agencies' preference. 'Dear agent' is too informal and impersonal. Most agents expect you to have researched the name of the correct correspondent at the agency, as described in the section 'Crafting your approach' elsewhere in this chapter. You should then address the agent by their full name – 'Dear Lizzy Kremer', for example. Alternatively, use the polite address, as in 'Dear Ms Kremer'.

- **Making it obvious that the letter is mass-produced:** If everything is typewritten aside from the biro-scrawled name of the addressee and your signature, you invite the agent to make a shortcut – and reject your manuscript unread.

- **Addressing the letter to an agent who's at a different agency entirely:** This is the risk of making multiple submissions in the early hours of the morning, so always get a good night's sleep before you attempt a complicated submission.

- **Careful presentation:** Use good, clean, white, unlined writing paper, and word-process your letter. Spell check. Read it through. Don't smoke all over it (the smell of smoke sticks to the pages), or drop jam on it. These things matter because they determine the agent's first impressions of you.

✔ **Showing your sunny side:** Agents like working with happy and easy-going people who don't have a chip on their shoulder about the media, publishing, agents, being made redundant, or not having any money. They don't necessarily want to work with lucky, beautiful people – just people who don't want to unload their problems on the page. And people who enjoy writing! A good line to include in a submission letter is: 'I hope you enjoy reading my novel as much as I have enjoyed writing it.'

Surprisingly, quite a few submission letters to agents are rude. Would you be rude when applying for a job? Your letter should give the impression that you'd be pleased to hear back from the agent.

✔ **Foregoing the flattery:** Use flattery with caution. Spelling the name of the agent and agency correctly and being respectful enough to buy nice writing paper is probably enough. Quoting from articles the agent has written, or listing the agency clients you most admire, is too common a trick to do you much good, and can seem obsequious. For example, if after reading this book you decide to send your novel to Lizzy's agency, don't mention how much you enjoyed our book. If you're telling the truth, thanks! But save the compliment for another day.

✔ **Describing your book:** Don't try too hard to sell your novel within the letter. Even if you're a good novelist, you may be an appalling copy-writer. You're as likely to put an agent off with multiple comparisons to other novels, or by misusing words like dystopian. If you come up with a good, catchy, enticing, Hollywood-worthy, one-line pitch for your book, use it. Otherwise, let the novel stand or fall on its own merits.

You may like to describe the theme or plot of your novel in a couple of lines. Obviously, try to make it sound interesting. A full plot synopsis isn't necessary within the letter.

Don't teach your grandmother to suck eggs – in other words, don't tell the agent how the book should be marketed and to whom.

✔ **Leaving the humour at home:** Please don't try to make your letter funny unless you're so funny you don't even notice when you're being funny.

One example of misplaced humour is to send us your novel after reading this book and to pull out something we've said within these pages that has since been proved – possibly by you, or possibly by us – to be completely incorrect, and then to make a joke out of it. And don't try any other ways of setting yourself apart from the crowd either. Just fit in. Trust your writing to lift you from the crowd.

✔ **Curtailing your self-rejecting impulses:** Don't anticipate rejection in any way in your letter by:

- Pointing out your novel's faults

- Reminding the agent that they reject most of the books they read

- Telling the agent that your novel is 'only' 195,000 words long

- Mentioning all the encouraging advice you've received from other agents (inadvertently saying that other agents have rejected you and this agent wasn't first on your list)

Hundreds of types of self-rejecting letter are possible, but the type we really mean here are the ones that literally anticipate the rejection. 'I know you're probably thinking this isn't for you, but . . .'

✔ **Burying your background:** If an author has an unusual background, this can help to promote a novel. For example, if you're unusually young or old for a first-time novelist, this can be interesting to the press. If you're in prison or hospital, by all means tip off the agent. If you suffered some horrendous indignity in your past, then unfortunately newspapers are likely to be interested in you (your novel still has to be good, obviously).

However, your marital status, the names and ages of your children, your past career in teaching, and the fact that your father in law lives with you isn't relevant. Even if your novel is about a mum who works as a teacher and lives with her father in law, agents don't care about your direct experience; they just care whether the novel works.

An exception to the rule about not giving your background is if you're a journalist or broadcaster. In this case, you have more professional writing experience than the next person, and you have contacts that may prove useful when your book's published. So you're allowed to write a little about your career. Similarly if you're hugely successful in another field, this is worth knowing. That means CEO of Tesco – not CEO of your local shower-screen supplier. Your status doesn't turn a bad novel into a good one, but it may tip the balance in your favour if your novel's moderately interesting to an agent.

✔ **Knowing how much of your writing experience to reveal:** Many, many, many, many, many authors mention that they've wanted for a long time to write a novel, and after a long career in the City/bringing up their children/finally kicking their father in law out, they're now free to write, write, write! This doesn't particularly recommend you to an agent. An agent only cares how good your writing is now. If you've been doing something else entirely for decades, that's completely understandable and normal, but not always very promising. What is promising is if you're a member of a writers' circle, have completed a creative writing course, have been on a writer's retreat, have had short stories or poems published, have won writing competitions (outside school), or have had other narrative writing published, such as a memoir.

Don't bother mentioning your experience in writing articles for technical journals, press releases, or shopping lists. Novel writing is a different type of writing altogether.

✔ **Asking for feedback:** A happy author who's passionate about their writing is very keen to receive feedback or advice from agents, even in the form of a rejection. But surprisingly few authors ask agents for feedback in their letters. Agents tend not to offer feedback unless requested, because some authors are more offended than pleased to receive it. If you want feedback, ask for it politely in your submission letter. Let the agent decide what and how much.

Other random don'ts include:

✔ Don't pretend this novel is your third just because you have two under your bed. Until you're published, you get to call every novel your first novel.

✔ Don't mention that another agent recommended you to the agent. It's not always a compliment. Sometimes recommendations can be a subtle form of revenge on one agent by another. (You can mention recommendations by editors, which are always flattering to the agent.)

✔ Don't mention that all your friends and family love your novel. Of course they do! You thinking that this counts just makes an agent think that you're a few pages short of a novel yourself.

✔ Don't enclose local newspaper articles about your campaign against the new pedestrian crossing. Not relevant.

✔ Don't mock up a book jacket and enclose it with the submission. Publishers have highly paid people who do that.

✔ Don't, please, we beg you, send a photo. You open yourself to the judgement that you're really vain if you're good-looking, and if you're ugly it doesn't help. Agents absolutely don't care what you look like if your book's good. Have you seen any authors recently?

That's a lot of things not to do, isn't it? That's how simple and short your letter can be.

Composing your synopsis

The main thing to remember is that a synopsis needs to offer a complete exposition of the plot of your novel. *So you have to reveal the ending.* Don't worry, you aren't going to spoil it for the agent. Even with a whodunnit, agents are experienced enough readers to know how to read the synopsis most intelligently. Cliffhangers have no place at the end of a synopsis; agents aren't shop browsers but professionals who need a complete picture of your novel.

Write your synopsis in more or less the same tone as the novel itself. A synopsis should also be organised along the same principles as the novel itself. So if the reader doesn't find out until two-thirds of the way through the novel that the narrator's a man, don't reveal this until two-thirds of the way into the synopsis.

The job of a synopsis isn't to sell your novel, although hopefully it reflects the novel's interesting qualities. A synopsis isn't a book blurb of the sort you find on the back of a book jacket, so don't write it in sales-speak.

Equally as important as detailing the full plot, the synopsis needs to reveal the emotional development of the novel.

Showing emotional development may entail saying something like: 'By this stage, Fenella has grown deeply suspicious of Jake's motives in leaving his toothbrush at her flat. She remains unaware that it isn't even his toothbrush.' And later saying: 'Fenella is starting to learn to give people a chance. She understands, since the confusion about Jake's toothbrush, that she can't always jump to conclusions.'

Agents disagree about the ideal length for a synopsis. Don't feel you have to put everything you know about the book into it. Two pages is probably ideal as a maximum synopsis length. If necessary, the agent may ask you for something more detailed in the future. If you don't know yet what happens at the end of the novel, just say so at the end of the synopsis and explain your options.

Handling Submissions the Agency Way

When agencies receive submissions, they may or may not have a system for logging them. You can't complain if they don't. The submissions are inevitably piled up until someone at the agency finds time to go through them. Who this is varies from agency to agency, but often your work will be read by a junior member of the agency team or perhaps by a freelance reader. Those readers then pick out anything of promise from the heap of submissions (often termed with derogatory humour as the *slush pile*, a reference to the quantity and quality of what agencies are sent) and pass it on to an agent or several agents to read. At some agencies, agents may take it in turns to read submissions themselves. It doesn't matter that sometimes your first reader isn't an agent of decades' experience. No agency allows a junior member of staff to read submissions unless their judgement is trusted absolutely. Young people working in publishing very quickly pick up on what good writing is and what sort of books their agents are interested in representing.

Never be rude to a receptionist, agent's assistant, or reader on the phone (or anywhere else). They run the place.

The truth is that most agents aren't reading unsolicited submissions and thinking, 'What's good about this? Am I going to like this?' When they sit down with a big pile of manuscripts, they're more likely thinking, 'My, what a lot of reading. With any luck I won't have to spend long on this little lot. Right, what's wrong with this first one?' Agents have big reading piles already, are heavily committed to their existing clients, and consequently are very cautious about taking on new clients. They're certainly open to finding a great new talent. But they're waiting to be grabbed, thrilled, or impressed.

Avoid sending submissions to agents at the busiest times of the year. Two weeks before or after Christmas is bad timing. September is busy – probably because writers find time over the summer to finish their writing. The week after a bank holiday or seasonal break such as Easter is similarly busy with submissions, so wait a few weeks and avoid the crowd.

If an agent is interested in your novel, they may ask to read more of it. At some point, they may call or email you. Agents tend not to call or email unless their interest is very serious. They know that it's harder for them to reject you as a potential client once you've started communicating. For similar reasons, you may receive anonymous compliment slips or anonymous rejection letters; some authors, once they have a name at an agency, start haranguing an individual reader with calls and emails.

Submitting unfinished novels

You don't need to have finished your novel before submitting it to agents, but it's far preferable if you do. Generally speaking, the more you write, the better your novel becomes, so view it as a whole project rather than something you're 'starting and seeing'.

Agents are sometimes able to sell commercial plot-driven novels such as thrillers and women's fiction on the basis of a chunk of the book, such as the first 30,000 words. In these circumstances, they usually submit to publishers a very detailed outline of 'what happens next' alongside the partial manuscript. These novels are sold on the basis of brilliant characters, a cracking plot, a fantastic title or concept, and often a confidence or exuberance in the writing.

It's obviously tempting to test your novel-in-progress on agents at the halfway mark (they only ask for the first three chapters, after all), but if they ask to see the rest of your novel, you don't want to rush the rest of the writing or to discover weaknesses in the novel set-up too late. Also, if an agent shows interest in seeing more of your work, don't leave them waiting, but pounce on their interest while it's fresh.

Understanding Rejection Letters (or 'My Opinion Is Just One in a Business Full of Them')

Agents aren't interested in people whose writing is just okay, vaguely amusing, quite nice, averagely good, as good as the next thing on the pile, better than the last thing on the pile, or readable. They want clients who are Brilliant! Supremely Talented! Amazing! Surprising! Unique! Hilarious! The best thing they've seen in months! The reason is that agents realise – through bitter experience, usually – that if they offer representation to authors whose work they find to be pleasant but not awe-inspiringly good, it's going to be much harder for the agent to maintain their own optimism and motivation in the face of rejection by publishers. Your ideal agent should be able to call you after every rejection and say, 'It's okay, they just don't see it, but we know they're wrong – so let's try someone else.' If an agent doesn't completely fall in love with your writing, it's going to be hard for them to stick with you all the way, when so many other authors are competing for their attention.

So if an agent writes that they admired your work a lot, but just didn't *love* it, don't be cross. Look at it this way: you deserve an agent who loves your writing, and this one's actually doing you a favour in rejecting you.

Sometimes agents write very complimentary letters, only to reject the author at the end of the letter. You should be encouraged by their comments and trust their judgement if they know that they aren't the best agent for you. They may feel that they don't have time to help you develop your writing, for example, in which case you're better off finding someone else.

A lot of agents write in rejection letters that their opinion is only one, and that others may disagree with them. They use this line partly to reassure, because countless bestselling novels were rejected by many agents and publishers before being 'discovered' by a passionate advocate. Agents are subjective readers and often disagree with each other. But agents also use this line defensively. Every agent has received abusive correspondence from rejected authors, and so most opinions are offered tentatively.

Some authors are offended when they receive standard rejection letters or pre-printed compliment slips. But surely it's far preferable that agents spend their time reading submissions rather than composing letters of rejection? At Lizzy's agency, they spend probably ten times as much time reading work as rejecting it, but it didn't used to be that way until standard rejection slips were introduced. Is it more important that your book is read or that an agent pretends to care deeply about your individual submission by adding your name and address to the top of the letter? Some authors crave approval and respect more than anything, but it's worth putting those emotional needs aside or they start to interfere with what is a professional, not personal, endeavour. Remember, you're not looking for love, you're looking for an agent.

Agents have very little time to spend on letters to prospective clients, so their feedback may sometimes be expressed in a brief and direct manner. Sometimes it's very difficult to accept criticism like this of a book in which you've invested so much time and energy. But you can benefit from *everything* a reader says, even if you think the reader is mistaken. For example, if an agent doesn't like your novel's key protagonist – a character you love – perhaps you haven't written about her in the right way. Is she more alive in your head than on the page?

Sometimes agents know they can't hope to explain to an author why their novel won't succeed. Just as every mother thinks her child is beautiful, some novelists refuse to see that their writing isn't as good as that of the published authors they admire. In these circumstances, it's a relief to hide behind a standard response.

Meeting Agents and Finding Your Perfect Match

If an agent's interested in your work, eventually they'll suggest that you meet. (If the agent doesn't suggest it, you should.) The more agents you meet, the more perspective you gain on the industry, and the better you understand your own needs. Try to get a feel for what kind of agent you want to work with. A man? A woman? Someone your own age, or older or younger?

Spend some time choosing the best possible agent for you and your novel; the decision is every bit as important as finding the right publisher. A good agent can sell your novel and get you great deals. The *right* agent can make you great deals *and* help you enjoy the publication process rather than dread it.

Agents are all very different, and it may take persistence to find your perfect match. When you go to meet an agent, be someone they want to work with – a professional person who takes their writing seriously and is pleasant to spend time with. Try not to be too eager or too offhand. Just relax and be yourself – on a good day.

Some issues to consider as you meet potential agents include:

> ✔ **Communication:** It's important that you and your agent communicate effectively and like each other, or else working together won't be very enjoyable.

Pay attention to how the agent likes to correspond with clients. If you love emailing and the agent never answers emails, this may be a problem. If you live on the phone, would you feel happy calling the agent, and do you think they'd call you back?

✔ **Size of the agency:** Consider how the agency handles sales of US rights, translation rights, and film rights. Find out who looks after your agent's work while they're on holiday. The greater the number of important clients an agency has, the more power it wields in the industry. One of the reasons to have an agent is to benefit from the contractual terms they have already negotiated with publishers for their other clients. And if they know what publishers have agreed to for other similar authors, they're in a superior negotiating position.

✔ **Experience:** Look at the experience and success the agent has enjoyed. The more experience an agent has, the more contacts they have at publishing houses, and the easier they find it to get your book read. Does your agent have a special interest in your type of fiction? If they do, they know all the editors who buy such fiction and only have to pick up the phone to secure a reading of your book.

On the other hand, a less experienced agent at a respected agency also has the connections to make the right submissions, and may have more time to offer your feedback, talk you through the process, and search out those more elusive deals.

✔ **Editorial feedback:** Some agents offer lots of feedback, and some don't. When you meet an agent for the first time, see how much constructive feedback they offer you on your work. You may feel that they're more critical than other agents, but it may just be that they've read your work more carefully or have higher aspirations than you have for yourself. Some agents were editors in a former life, and this experience can be a huge asset to a writer. However, former editors aren't always the most experienced agents, and every successful agent must have good editorial skills or they won't succeed.

✔ **Agency agreements:** When an agent offers to represent you, they should give you a client agreement for your signature. This agreement sets out the agent's obligations to you and yours to them. Don't feel pressured to sign it immediately. Take it away and read it through carefully.

Like all contracts, your agency agreement is there for the worst-case scenario: if you fall out about something. Signing up with an agency is all very jolly and exciting, but if you have a disagreement, you're going to hope that you read your client agreement thoroughly.

Most agency client agreements are extremely simple documents and more or less reflect the AAA's code of practice (refer to the earlier section 'Looking into the Association of Authors' Agents'). Relationships with agents are open-ended. In other words, your relationship with your agent ends only when one of you fires the other one. Any contracts made by your agent while you're a client of the agency stay with that agency for as long as the contract is valid (which may mean for as long as the book is in print). In other words, your earnings from that contract continue to come through that agency, and that agency always takes full commission on sales of your book, even if you've left the agency. If the agency makes you a deal – or starts to – and you leave the agency before the contract is signed, this deal is still counted as one of theirs, and they are due commission on it.

Every serious aspiring author should join the Society of Authors. Membership confers many benefits, chief among them the society's willingness to advise authors on contractual matters.

Because giving an agent notice is easy – particularly before they start submitting your work – signing an agency agreement doesn't really bind you or them to working together. For this reason, some agents are quite slow to suggest signing up formally. They don't realise just how important it is to you that you've found an agent, and that you're one big step closer to being published.

Moving ahead without an agent

What if you can't find an agent, despite countless submissions, a fortune spent on postage, and many hours crafting the perfect submission letter and synopsis? Of course you need a night off and several drinks with some good friends, but you also need a plan B. Your dream of publishing your novel doesn't have to end here. You need to pick yourself up, dust yourself and your novel down, and start again.

In Chapter 19 we go into detail about how to self-publish your book, and this might be a good time to consider that option. Chapter 19 also includes information about sharing your work free of charge online with readers and reviewers who offer feedback.

Most big publishers don't accept or read submissions from un-agented authors – check their websites for specific guidance – but for every few thousand submissions they receive, publishers offer a positive response to just such a direct approach.

Smaller independent publishers – usually those focusing on literary fiction – are often more open to submissions from un-agented authors. Some small publishers are highly skilled teams who – although they can't command the same level of attention from the big retailers as large publishers do – still do a great job of editing and publishing good fiction. You may get reviewed, or shortlisted for a literary award, through a specialist publisher, and you may well become successful in ebook format. Once your book has been published by such a respected house, you often find that agents and bigger publishers take you more seriously, allowing you to translate your success into a relationship with a more mainstream publisher or agent – if you still want one. *The Writers' and Artists' Yearbook* includes a list of all publishers, and you can also take a look at the list of members on the Independent Publishers Guild website at www. ipg.uk.com.

Taking a Fresh Look

If you submitted your novel to many agencies without any luck or feedback, you might decide to put that novel aside and start something new. On the other hand, you may want to try submitting your novel again in a different way, perhaps in a revised form.

Your novel may well have one of the following obstacles to success:

✔ You sound like a pain in the neck in your submission letter.

✔ Your novel has a dreadful title or is far too long to tempt a reader (this can be anything over 120,000 words).

✔ Your pitch doesn't sound attractive.

✔ Your synopsis is impenetrable or too long to battle through.

✔ Your novel feels too familiar or too old-fashioned.

✔ Your writing is just not of a high enough quality.

Take a step back and consider whether any of these factors apply to you. You can try to address the first five problems yourself. As for the sixth, well, you're not in a good position to judge.

If you want some independent literary advice before resubmitting your novel, you can try using a literary consultancy. These consultancies, which vary in quality, offer you a reader's report for a fee. We know several authors who've appreciated their objective feedback. However, we sometimes think that literary consultancies have a tendency to be too kind – you're paying them, after all.

Maximising Your Chances

Aside from self-publishing, you can try other ways to bring your novel to wider attention and to maximise your chances of interesting an agent in your writing. One author told us: 'Winning a writing competition in a national magazine really kick-started my writing career very quickly. Suddenly agents and publishers were interested in me, and it opened a great many doors.' The trick is to make sure that you have material ready for that opportunity when it comes. Consider these options:

✔ Many national magazines, newspapers, and even TV shows and websites sponsor or organise writing competitions. If you have a piece of writing already or can write something suitable for submission, enter. There may not be as many entrants as you imagine, because many people think about writing for so long that they run out of time to actually do it. And even if you don't win, you gain experience from having prepared a piece for submission, and you may pick up some extra publicity.

✔ One reason for subscribing to a writing magazine is because such publications usually mention prizes and competitions. They can also offer unpublished writers advice and information about how other writers make money and find their way into print.

✔ If any writing communities focus on your particular genre, try to join them to gain specialist knowledge and to meet fellow authors who share your interests. You may be able to do this by signing up to an association. For example, the Romantic Novelists' Association supports unpublished authors of romance in multiple ways, through 'new writer' schemes, an annual conference, and local meetings. Alternatively, work out where authors of your kind of book hang out, either virtually or physically, and join them.

✔ If you like writing short stories, submit them for publication to all magazines and websites that accept them. Although it's unlikely that a publisher will want to publish a collection of your stories, because such collections are notoriously difficult to sell in large quantities, writing the stories offers you valuable experience and the gratification and prestige of seeing your work in print.

✔ Sometimes, sending your novel to influential people for a positive review is worthwhile, because you can quote the review in your approach to agents or publishers. Writers sometimes approach published authors, local personalities, literary consultants, publishers, local booksellers, local reading groups, or librarians for such quotes.

Our broad advice is that most published authors don't offer reviews to unpublished writers unless they know them already. And unless the quotes are from a recognised name, they're not worth very much.

If you're making submissions to agencies for the second time, don't mention your earlier unsuccessful submissions. The agency probably isn't going to realise that they have seen your novel before, particularly if you change the title and other crucial details. Do *not* resubmit identical work to agents repeatedly. Accept that your work isn't perceived as being suitable for publication in its current form.

Remember that you don't have to be a published author in order to be a writer. Allow yourself to feel proud of what you've achieved in finishing your novel. The next few chapters of this book will make you aware of the unpredictable and sometimes stressful nature of the life of the published author. Are you still sure that you want to write professionally? Perhaps you can enjoy writing without the anxieties associated with being under contract to a publisher or exposed to the critiques of others.

Chapter 17

Preparing for Publication

This chapter takes you through the process of finding a publisher with your agent, from submitting your novel to editors, to signing a contract with a publishing house.

If your agent sends your work to publishers without you really understanding how the acquisitions process works, you might find dealing with publishers disillusioning or disorientating. This chapter explains the decision-making process in publishers' commissioning meetings. We aim to demystify the way that books are auctioned and sold, and to explain the advance and royalty system so that you have an idea of how much you can expect to earn.

Preparing Your Manuscript for Submission

Finally, you're about to hear what actual publishers think of your novel. You may be excited about this; you may be terrified. Either way, now is not the time for impatience. Have lots of people read your novel, and take on board all the criticism available to you.

Resubmitting a novel to publishers who've already turned your book down isn't easy, so you usually get only one chance to impress. Before you take it, make sure that your manuscript is as good as it can possibly be.

Working with your agent

Most authors agree that the best thing about having an agent is feeling that it isn't just them pushing the rock up the hill. Perhaps more than in any other relationship in your life, your and your agent's interests are completely mutual. Consider the following aims that you and your agent share:

- ✔ You both want to earn some money (your agent doesn't earn money unless you do).

- ✔ You both want to enjoy success in the long term as well as earning in the short term.

- ✔ You both want to find an editorial relationship that satisfies you (otherwise you're unhappy and a heavy burden falls on your agent), and for that relationship to make the very most of your talents.

- ✔ You both want to hook a publisher who effectively markets and publicises your books, so that you can all develop a career together, not just celebrate one book deal.

- ✔ You want to succeed, so that you were both right about your potential.

So you're very much a team, working together on building your writing career. It shouldn't feel like you're working for your agent – but don't treat your agent as an employee, either. You're partners and reliant on each other's success and ideas, although at times you may have to defer to your agent's professional expertise.

Every partnership relies on open and honest communication in order to prosper. Your agent is the expert, but they owe you an explanation for everything they do on your behalf.

Getting the book right

Work on your manuscript until you're confident that it's in the best possible shape for submission to publishers.

Writing is a solitary job, and you can easily get too close to your own work and fail to maintain any sort of perspective on what you're doing. If you're lucky enough to find a good agent, they should be happy to read and comment on a draft of your novel – or successive drafts – before sharing it with others. A good agent pushes you hard to write to the very best of your abilities. You don't need an agent who's going to take a punt on your work or take risks on your behalf.

If you don't have an agent, ask your readers (whether they're friends, acquaintances, or paid editorial consultants) to be as honest and constructive as possible.

Chapter 14 has tips on doing your final edits.

Getting the title right

As well as undertaking general editing of your novel's text, your agent may also suggest changing the title or the length of the novel, or other fundamental details, such as the age of the protagonists, to better suit the market.

Giving your novel the right title is more important than you may realise. A great title helps bring debut novels to readers' attention. A fantastic title can successfully fire readers' imaginations, make them laugh, or help them remember to look for your book when they enter a shop. Publishers are aware that if shop browsers don't know your name, readers need another reason to pick up your book.

Together with the right jacket, your book's title often does most of the sales work for you. The right title makes a publisher covet your book for their list, even if they think you need some help in making the best of your material.

Generalising about what makes one title right and another one wrong is almost impossible. But if your readers and friends think that your title is just okay rather than great, you may need to change it before submitting your novel to publishers.

Most bad titles are bad because they tell readers nothing about what sort of book they are describing (modern? frightening? romantic?), or because they try to express something more amorphous than what the book is *about*, such as how the author feels the reader should feel about how the main protagonist feels about his girlfriend. But most titles aren't bad – they're just not good enough.

Although publishers expect to have to make some editorial changes to your manuscript before publication, and may change the title in consultation with you, only the strongest and most confident novels are bought in the first place. So don't imagine that you can postpone improving your novel or changing its title until you're collaborating with your editor. (See Chapter 15 for more details on the role of publishing editors.)

Submitting to Publishers

At some point, you start to realise that there just aren't that many publishers. At least, not many who publish debut novelists while also commanding the sort of marketing budget that gets your face onto the side of buses. Maybe ten large publishers exist who publish your sort of novel. (There are only approximately ten big publishers for each sort of novel). Your agent may feel that one of the many excellent smaller publishers can do a good job of bringing your book to the attention of reviewers and readers. But, still, your fate lies in the hands of relatively few people, and the publishing community can start to feel very small.

Developing a plan of attack

Your agent is probably pitching your novel to publishers while you're still finishing it, because publishing editors and agents meet and talk every day. Editors remember interesting-sounding books and sometimes follow up with agents, asking them to make a note of their interest for future reference. Editors are aware that they're competing with each other to acquire the most promising books.

When your novel is ready for submission, your agent draws up a list of possible publishers. Don't hesitate to ask your agent to talk you through the submission list so that you understand why particular editors or publishing imprints have been chosen. (Chapter 15 explains imprints.) You're not questioning your agent's judgement, you just want to go through the decision-making process. Ask your agent to let you know as and when they start to hear back from publishers.

Keep your own record of where your book has been submitted, in case your relationship with your agent breaks down in the future.

Discovering whether you're commercial or literary

Before working out which publishers to send your novel to, an agent has to draw conclusions about the sort of novel you've written. Fiction has long been notionally divided into two types: commercial and literary. Most publishing imprints focus on one part of the market over the other. Although the terms are meaningless to most readers and seem irrelevant to most authors, publishers and agents still use them tirelessly as a sort of shorthand:

✔ **Commercial fiction** encompasses genre fiction, including crime and thrillers, romance, blockbusters, and science fiction. Much commercial fiction is written to conform to certain understood rules about story-telling. For example, most commercial love stories have a happy ending. The writer's challenge is to make the journey to that inevitable ending appear surprising and entertaining. Most commercial fiction relies on plotting and pacing for its success. Characters in commercial novels usually have to be sympathetic, even when they're behaving badly.

✔ **Literary fiction** refers to all novels deemed to be even vaguely challenging to read because of their style or content. They may present more layering of themes or ideas, or be structured or written in a more complicated (but perhaps ultimately more satisfying) way. Literary fiction includes novels not easily categorised by genre and those that don't follow conventional story-telling rules. Literary fiction can be more character- or voice-driven than action- or plot-driven and focus as much on internalised thoughts as on dialogue and action.

Most literary novels aspire to be commercial, in that most literary novelists want to enjoy commercial success, and every year several such novels of perceived intellectual worth sell in far bigger quantities than most crime stories ever could. By the same token, many commercial novels are absolutely what you'd term clever – because of the success of the characterisation or plotting, or because of the author's mastery of their subject and ability to please their readership.

Putting such quibbles with the terminology aside, the majority of novels clearly fall into the vast grey area that lies between obviously commercial and obviously literary fiction. A book may be intricately plotted and frightening without being a conventional thriller, for example *The Wasp Factory* by Iain Banks (Abacus). A sweeping romance can be told through multiple viewpoints and include long rhapsodies on themes such as war and mythology, as in *The English Patient* by Michael Ondaatje (Bloomsbury). The lines are blurred all the time, and your novel's likely to be both commercial and literary too.

Publishers are losing interest (at long last) in these definitions and are forming imprints that are organised by different principles, such as the age or gender of the target reader. Now that book clubs are such a popular leisure activity, a vogue exists among readers for books that advertise the reader's intelligence, and so some quite commercial books are being packaged in a quite literary style.

Certainly most readers are unaware of these restrictive terms. Readers tend to prefer books that are surprising and challenging in some aspects while also being reassuringly accessible in their style or content. If you ask most readers what sort of books they enjoy, they usually answer, 'I like a good story.'

It's important to access an agent's knowledge of different editors and types of imprint. Publishers have contrasting approaches to publicity and marketing, jacket design, and sales. The marketing budgets at commercial imprints are sometimes higher and the sales targets more ambitious than those at literary imprints, although even this generalisation is pretty unsafe. Literary publishers are more likely than commercial publishers to publish your novel in hardback first, partly to signal to newspaper reviewers that yours is a novel to take seriously. Some publishers stagger publication in different formats, for example publishing in ebook first. Sometimes retailers are offered an exclusive retail window. An agent can weigh up each imprint's reputation and publishing strategies before deciding which to submit your novel to.

If you feel strongly that your book belongs in one imprint rather than another, you need to establish that your agent agrees with you right from the start.

Drawing up a submission list

Sometimes agents make submissions widely, sending your novel to as many as eight or ten publishers at once. The advantage of this approach is that if several publishers are interested in your novel, they compete more fiercely to secure the right to publish it. On the other hand, sometimes an agent cherry-picks a couple of editors (or even just one) that they think are the best possible publishers for your book.

Setting up an auction

If your agent decides to auction your book, this means that they want to send it to several publishers at once in the hope that they'll compete for the right to publish it. In an auction, your agent sends your novel out to all editors on the same day and sets a deadline for initial responses. The deadline can be anything between a few days and three weeks. The agent then plays the interested parties off against each other, like an auctioneer at an auction house, inviting ever-higher bids.

Sometimes publishers try to swoop in and buy books before the stated deadline. This approach is called *pre-empting* or *making a pre-emptive offer*. These pre-emptive offers tend to be quite high, in order to tempt the agent to call off the planned auction. If the agent holds out for the auction, they hope to receive several offers from publishers by the stated deadline.

Auctions can be exciting, but not all novels are suitable for submission in this manner. If your novel is very unusual, your agent may feel it's better to let a few editors take their time considering it.

If editors have an exclusive window in which to consider your novel, they're forced to read it more quickly and, if interested, to pay a good advance in order to avoid having to compete with other publishers for the right to publish it.

From your point of view, as long as you end up at the right publishing house with a good deal, there's no right or wrong way for your agent to approach this process.

Peeking into the Commissioning Process

If an editor reads your novel and knows that they don't want to publish it, they usually reject it quite quickly. And even if they do enjoy it, they need to win some support for the novel among their colleagues before being in a position to offer to publish it.

Securing the deal

Publishers or agents may refer to the good old days (usually holding their second glass of port in one hand) when editors ran publishing houses with more autonomy than they do now. Apparently – this is all long before our time, you understand – an editor used to buy a novel they admired, just because they admired it and thought it would sell. Then they went to their colleagues in the sales department and decreed, 'I bought this novel and want you to sell the hell out of it.'

That rarely happens these days, especially at big corporate publishing houses. Nowadays, editors get together with their colleagues in sales and marketing (and sometimes the rights and publicity departments too) and present the titles they want to buy, before making an offer to the author or agent. If sales say that they can't sell the novel, it doesn't matter how much the editor admires it, they probably aren't able to buy it.

Publishers hold weekly or sometimes fortnightly meetings at which they discuss books under active and positive consideration. These meetings are called, variously, commissioning, editorial, acquisitions, or publishing meetings. The editor who was sent the novel in question usually distributes some pages from the novel in advance of the meeting, so that everyone is in a position to contribute to the discussion. Sometimes the editorial department meet first to agree which projects to discuss with their colleagues in other departments.

The exact process varies significantly from publisher to publisher. Sometimes editors bring novels to the meeting only if they already have support from key colleagues and know that they want to offer for the book. In these circumstances, they may simply want their sales colleagues to give them some guidance as to how high an advance to offer the author – for example, how many copies do they hope to sell? But at other publishing houses, editors bring lots of projects to the meeting for wide discussion.

At the meeting, publication schedules may be discussed. Publishers don't want to commission too many books of one type, in case they compete with themselves for the top promotional spots in the shops. Therefore, some good books are rejected at this stage simply because publishers can't afford to have too much of a good thing. For example, they may feel that they can't launch two new crime novel series about forensic scientists in one summer.

Corporate publishers usually need a consensus before they offer to buy your novel. That can mean that publishers shy away from adventurous, brave, or riskier propositions. On the positive side, if the whole publishing team are behind the decision to publish a novel, they enjoy a shared sense of responsibility and excitement, which can propel your novel to the top of a salesperson's or publicist's list of things to do.

Before making an offer, an editor is probably obliged to *run costings* on the book, which means using in-house spreadsheet software to calculate how much they can afford to pay the author based on how much the book will cost to produce, how much the publisher will charge the customer for it, what overall income the publisher anticipates, and how many books they plan to print.

Meeting a publisher

If a publishing house is seriously interested in your novel, they often suggest that you go in to meet them. This might happen after they make an offer for your book (but before you've agreed a deal), or before they put any money on the table.

If the publisher doesn't suggest a meeting, often your agent does. Agents realise that only once you meet an editor face to face can you form a considered opinion as to whether you're going to enjoy working with that individual. And if several publishers are interested in publishing your novel, you need to base your eventual choice of publisher on more than money alone.

Meetings with publishers at this stage take one of two forms.

✔ **At a small table or desk (coffee in plastic cup, possibly biscuits).** You may meet the editor alone, to try to establish whether you can work together. The editor may have developed various ideas as to how to improve your novel, which they want to run by you.

Some good issues to consider at such a meeting:

- Do you and the editor see your book in the same way? If they see it as a dark contemporary love story for female readers, and you see it as an international thriller, you might start to pull against each other at the editing stage or when it comes to briefing the book jacket.

- How important an author are you going to be to this editor and this publishing house? How ambitious do they seem to be for your book?

- Have any of the editor's colleagues read the book? If they haven't, you know that you're not very far along the commissioning process.

- At what time of year does the editor want to publish your novel, in what format (hardback or paperback), and why?

✔ **Around a big table (coffee, tea, or water; definitely biscuits with chocolate; probably grapes).** The other type of meeting involves prospective authors meeting several personnel at once – usually someone from publicity, someone from marketing, possibly someone from sales or rights, and at least one editorial representative. These meetings perform two functions:

- They give the publisher the opportunity to show off and convince you that they're the right people to publish your novel. If a good team spirit surrounds the boardroom table, or if the marketing department has put together a fantastic presentation, this is going to inspire you to want to work with them.

  As well as thinking about whether you like these people, use this opportunity to try to get a feel for the sort of publishing company it is. How hierarchical? How big? How does it characterise itself? Publishers like to differentiate what they do from what other publishers do. (In truth there aren't very many differences, except in the way the companies are structured internally.)

- They offer the publisher a chance to get to know you better, and this goes for the smaller kind of meeting described previously as well. They want to see whether you're the kind of person they like working with.

The kind of person a publisher wants you to be

A publisher hopes that you're a paragon in every way, obviously, but they don't worry too much if you aren't. However, some of the qualities they hope you have include that you are:

- **Articulate:** Can you talk about your novel, and are you able to publicise it?
- **Friendly:** Do you laugh at their little jokes?
- **Relatively modest:** Are you going to allow yourself to be edited?
- **Confident in your work:** Can you inspire them to love it even more?
- **Attractive:** Are they able to smell you after you've left the room?
- **Someone like them:** Can both sides be straightforward with each other?

The kind of publisher you're looking for

You want to make a good deal with a publisher, and you have to do everything you and your agent can to get the publisher to invest in you, so that you can afford to write full-time. Often, the publisher who offers the highest advance is the most enthusiastic about your work, and that rightly has an influence on whether you make a deal with them. But the publisher with the deepest pockets isn't always the right one for you or your novel.

The most important things to consider when choosing a publisher are:

- Does the publisher have a good track record in this area? Have they proved that they can make a success of novels like yours?
- Do you think you'd be an important novelist on their list? Would your book be a lead title for the publisher in the month when it's published?
- Do you like your prospective editor, and do you think you can work together?
- Does the publisher have a convincing vision for how to publish your novel and any other books you may write?

All publishers, bookshops, and agents have instant access to authors' book sales figures courtesy of a company that logs sales through most bookshops using computer software. These sales figures show how each book performed in the market, and bookshops refer to them constantly when working out how many copies to order of an author's new novel.

A novelist used to be able to build a career over several books, but nowadays that isn't always the case. For this reason, you need to make sure that your first book has the best possible chance of success, which means choosing the right publisher in the first place.

If one of your books performs less than impressively, the figures can come to feel like a stone around your neck. Publishers find it hard to improve an author's sales once a decline has set in, and they're less likely to be able to stick loyally to an author whose books aren't selling. If this seems unfair, it is. It isn't your responsibility to sell lots of copies of your book, but you suffer if it doesn't sell. Quite a few authors have been known to have revived their careers by changing their names and changing tack.

Making the Deal

When you have serious interest from a publisher, and they indicate that they want to make you an offer, the process starts to get technical.

Negotiating

Once a publisher has made an offer to publish your novel, you or your agent can start to negotiate the terms. If you have an agent, allow them to handle the negotiations in their own way. However, your agent shouldn't agree to a deal without your authorisation.

Publishers very rarely make their best offer immediately, because they expect to be persuaded to pay more. When a publisher's initial offer is their very best, they usually states this clearly.

Publishing contracts contain many variables, so there's quite a lot to play for. Some of the key issues that have to be established early on in every contract negotiation include:

- ✔ **Territory of rights:** Are you selling UK publishing rights or the right to publish your book worldwide?
- ✔ **Grant of rights:** Are you selling rights other than publishing rights, such as audio book, film, or serialisation rights?
- ✔ **Advance:** What level of advance is being offered and what payment structure is being proposed?
- ✔ **Royalties:** What royalty rates are being offered?

Chapter 18 offers a more detailed analysis of a typical publishing contract and how you should be paid. But as you can see from this list, as an author you need to understand two fundamentals: what are you selling, and how will you be paid?

A word about territory

UK publishers like to have the right to sell their English-language edition of your book in places further afield. Australia and New Zealand are collectively a big market for British publishers, of course, and Canada is important too. But all around the world from Algeria to Austria, English-language books are sold in specialist bookshops. An author's British and American publishers hotly contest exclusive distribution rights in some of these countries. These sales abroad are called *export sales*.

The standard territories included in most UK publishing contracts are referred to as the *UK and Commonwealth*, even though many of the countries listed in the schedule of territories left the Commonwealth long ago.

Understanding what you're selling

You've created something completely original in your novel, and you're always going to own the copyright unless you formally assign it to someone else. In other words, just by being the exclusive creator of your novel, you own the copyright under English law.

You don't want to sell ownership of your work to anyone; that's like selling the right to earn money from your work.

What you can do is to issue *licences* that permit others to exploit your work in particular ways. For example, you can license to a publisher the exclusive right to print, distribute, and sell your novel within the UK. You can issue a licence for the right to print a large-print edition of your novel, or the right to translate it into German and distribute the book in Germany, and so on.

All the potential licences that you can grant are known collectively as the *rights* in your novel.

Think of the rights in your novel as a big apple pie. You can divide the pie between as many people as you like. If you sell the whole pie to one party – your British publisher, for example – that party pays you more than if you only sell them a couple of slices, which can be tempting.

However, it's unlikely that one person will want to eat the whole pie, even if they buy the whole thing. The buyer is likely to sell pieces on to third parties, licensing the large-print rights to a large-print publisher, and the German rights to a German publisher, for example. The big-pie buyer gives you some of the money earned from these deals and keeps a proportion of it (you don't get your share until they earn back what they pay you for the pie – that's called *earning out your advance*).

If you don't want to give up a share of your rights income to your publisher, selling your rights individually is best (slice by slice!).

Sometimes publishers rely on the income from the sale of other rights to help fund their publication of your novel, and therefore they refuse to make a deal at all unless you agree to sell them most of the rights. Sometimes, when you sell a publisher a whole pie of rights, they get very excited, and their inevitable extra involvement and investment in you and your novel can be very valuable in building a positive long-term relationship with them.

If you don't have an agent, you have more reason to sell all rights in your book to your publisher.

However, publishers call all rights other than the right to publish your novel in their home territory *subsidiary rights* or *subrights*. This is because selling them is literally subsidiary to their core business. Some agents think that this is reason enough not to license those rights to your publisher. Agents also query whether a publisher can always act wholly in the author's interest when making subsidiary rights deals, given that they're bound to prioritise their own interests as publisher.

One set of rights we recommend you never consider surrendering are film and TV rights in your book. Few publishers have any expertise in licensing these rights, and if your novel has dramatic potential you can hire a specialist film agent to make such a deal for you at a later date. You certainly don't want to give your publisher a share of the potential income from these rights.

Other rights you may decide to retain include:

- ✔ **Translation rights:** All reputable literary agencies have specialist agents to sell these rights on their clients' behalf.
- ✔ **US rights:** Agencies work in collaboration with US agents or directly to sell these rights.
- ✔ **Audio book rights.**
- ✔ **Serialisation, anthology, and quotation rights:** These are the rights to use some of your work in another form.

Not making the deal

If your novel has been submitted to publishers and you've yet to find one who sees its commercial potential, it may be time to think again. If your agent is loyal and remains committed, despite enduring rejection with you, arrange to see them to devise a strategy together. Your agent may ask you to revise your novel in order to take on board some of the advice you received from publishers, or they may tell you to put this novel aside and start work on a new one. Resubmitting work that's already been rejected isn't often successful, and most agents recommend that you start something new instead. A really good agent with time enough to give will offer you guidance throughout the process.

Alternatively, you might consider self-publishing your novel with or without the help and support of your agent. Turn to Chapter 19 for our guide to self-publishing.

Ideally you and your agent will continue to work together. Most agents are very cautious about taking on new clients, and only offer you representation if they think they want to work with you beyond the novel you've already written.

However, some agent–client relationships break down irrevocably when an author's novel is rejected by a lot of publishers. Sometimes the agent loses heart and starts to withdraw from the author. You deserve an agent who returns your phone calls and emails promptly and who reads your work in a timely manner.

In truth, the agent is usually not at fault as long as they submitted your novel widely to the right editors, but every situation is different. A large chunk of your second novel might re-inspire your agent and heal a rift between you.

But if you still feel dissatisfied with your agent, you should probably start quietly seeking new representation for your next novel. The fact that you've been represented before doesn't put other agents off; actually it puts you at a slight advantage compared with authors who've never received interest from an agent. Never indicate that you've fallen out with your current/former agent – your new agent would be sure to wonder whether you're 'difficult'. Just say that you want to work with someone who is able to come to your writing with a fresh perspective.

Chapter 18

Coping with the Business Side of Being an Author

Congratulations if you've made a deal with a publisher. You no longer have to strive to prove your credentials as a writer of promise, because somebody has staked money and their reputation on your ability to write a book that others are going to share and enjoy. From this point on, your private writing life exists side by side with a more public life as an author.

This chapter offers you insight into the business aspects of your life as an author – showing you how to read a contract and acquainting you with how advances and royalties work. The better you understand the life of a published author, the easier you're going to find it to be one.

Reviewing Publishing Contracts

The first step in your professional relationship with a publisher is to sign a contract that encapsulates your obligations to one another. In this section, we explain your obligations to your publisher and their obligations to you.

We can't offer detailed contracts advice here, but we can help you to understand the broad strokes of what your contract requires of you and of your publisher.

Contracts are vital to ensure that you're protected in the very worst-case scenario. But even if things are progressing well with your publisher, you often need to refer to your contract in order to be reminded of exactly what you've agreed. This can include anything from how much time you have to review your typeset pages, or *proofs*, before your book is sent to print (usually 14 to 21 days), through who has responsibility to clear permission for use of quotations in your novel (probably you, although your publisher may help pay some of the fees), to how long your publisher's allowed to hold onto your novel for without actually publishing it (usually 12 to 18 months).

The Society of Authors (www.societyofauthors.net) offers excellent contracts advice to all authors, and so even if you don't have an agent, you can always make sure that you're well-informed before signing anything.

Publishers are usually very happy to make changes to the standard contract that they send to new authors. In fact, your agent may already have some significantly improved template contracts in place with publishing houses, the terms of which have been hammered out between the agency and the publisher over a period of time. These pre-agreed contracts between agencies and publishers are known as *boilerplate* contracts, and boilerplate terms are not usually negotiable by either side, which is usually to the advantage of the first-time author. Advance and royalty, territory, and grant of rights terms are never boilerplate and vary from deal to deal, but all the important clauses about legal liabilities, reasons for termination, and so on should all be on any boilerplate contract.

What you promise

Most contracts outline the following responsibilities on the part of the author:

- ✔ To deliver a novel of an agreed length, genre, and subject matter. If your novel is only partially written, the contract may also state that the novel should be of a standard deemed suitable for publication.

- ✔ To deliver the novel by an agreed date. The contract should allow for delivery dates to be changed by mutual agreement, and as long as publishers are warned well in advance of an expected delay, it's not usually a bar to publication. However, publishers aren't obliged to accept late books.

- ✔ To warrant that the novel is original (not plagiarised) and that you aren't libelling anyone within it. You also agree to pay the cost of your publisher's defence in the event that the publisher is the subject of legal action if you did plagiarise or libel someone.

- ✔ To license the granted rights exclusively to the publisher. (Chapter 17 explains what types of rights you may be granting.)

If you meet these expectations, you still can't compel your publisher to publish your novel. However, you can demand compensation if they fail to do so.

What your publisher promises

Your publisher's main contractual obligations to you should include:

- ✔ To publish your novel in print and electronic editions within a fixed period, usually 12 or 18 months from the point at which you deliver it to them. Without a time limit, you can't determine at what point your publisher fails to fulfil their promise to publish your book.

- ✔ To keep the book in print or at least available in digital formats and to revert the rights to you (which means cancel the contract) should the book go out of print, be unavailable, or sell fewer than a pre-agreed number of copies per year.

- ✔ To allow you the opportunity to review and correct proofs of your work.

- ✔ To consult you regarding the book jacket, blurb, and your author biography and photo.

- ✔ To pay your advances in a prompt manner and your royalties twice a year. (See the later section 'Earning Advances and Royalties' for more on money issues.)

- ✔ To pay you certain stated percentages of subsidiary rights income, and to set those earnings against your royalty account. (Chapter 17 explains subsidiary rights such as translation rights.)

- ✔ To allow you to terminate the contract if the publisher is in breach and fails to correct that breach within 30 days of you writing to inform them of the breach.

What your publisher doesn't promise

Contracts usually do *not* promise:

- ✔ A marketing budget or lead title status.
- ✔ Final say over your book's jacket design.
- ✔ That your editor is certain to stay with the company until your book is published.
- ✔ A certain print run or level of sales.
- ✔ Maternity leave or sick pay.

Much has to be taken on trust, so maintaining a spirit of goodwill and mutual endeavour between you and your publisher is essential.

Contractual clauses to watch out for

Contracts aren't the easiest of documents to fathom. Apart from the key obligations set out in the previous section, here are some other clauses to look for:

- ✔ What happens if the publisher isn't happy with the finished book you deliver? You have the right to proper editorial feedback, and should be given enough time to revise your work.

- ✔ In what circumstances will the rights under licence revert to you? It used to be the case that publishers held onto publication rights for as long as they kept a book in print. Now that it costs nothing for them to keep an ebook on sale in perpetuity, publishers are keen to keep hold of publication rights even after they deem that the life of a book in print is over. Make sure that, even if they have no obligation to keep a book in print, they have an obligation to keep ebook sales above a minimum level and perhaps to update the book jacket every decade.

- ✔ Once you've earned out your advance, make sure that your share of sub-rights income is paid to you within 30 days of its arrival in your publisher's accounts rather than you having to wait for the next royalty period.

- ✔ Who pays for use of illustrations or quotes from other authors' works? What other costs may fall to you – for example, in the case of a non-fiction book, who pays for an index?

- ✔ Make sure that your contract caters for the very best- and worst- case scenarios. Ask yourself, what's the worst that could happen, and am I protected in that event? (Illness, failure to deliver, the publisher's failure to publish, and so on.) What's the best that could happen? Will you be properly rewarded if your book is a huge bestseller and film rights are sold?

Earning Advances and Royalties

Publishers usually pay authors by way of an *advance* – quite literally money advanced as a sign of good faith that the author is going to earn royalties. Both advances and royalties are explained in this section.

Your advance may be as low as £500 or as high as £500,000. The size of the advance a publisher is willing to pay for your novel completely depends on how fiercely they've had to compete with other publishers for the right to publish your novel, and how many copies they think they can sell.

Even when you have your contract in your hand, you can't predict accurately what you can expect to earn in royalties. (The section 'Accepting the Unpredictability of the Business' explains why this is the case. Also take a look at 'How to calculate your royalty earnings roughly' for how to predict your income – *in*accurately.)

Authors earn royalties

A *royalty* is a percentage of a publisher's income from the sale of each copy of your book. Most royalties are calculated on the recommended retail price (RRP) of a book. A standard paperback royalty is 7.5 per cent rising to 10 per cent after a certain number of copies have been sold. (On a £7.99 paperback, this works out at 60p to the author rising to 80p per copy sold.) Some royalties are calculated on a publisher's net receipts rather than the book's RRP (for example, a royalty of 15 per cent net receipts). So if a publisher sells a £7.99 paperback at 50 per cent discount to a bookseller, net receipts are £4.00, and 15 per cent of the receipts is worth 60p to the author.

Every six months – usually at the end of December and the end of June – publishers check their accounts and produce author royalty statements declaring how many copies of an author's book they sold in the previous six months. They allow themselves three months for this process, so authors tend to receive royalty statements in September and March. Any royalties owing to the author at this time are paid by cheque or bank transfer with the statement.

Publishers hold a certain percentage of an author's royalties (often 20 to 25 per cent) for a fixed period – usually three royalty periods or 18 months – to allow for the fact that some of the copies sold may be returned by shops unsold. This is known as the *reserve against returns*.

So you're paid 75 per cent of what you've earned, twice a year, up to nine months in arrears. Not ideal is it? That's why authors are paid advances.

Authors need advances

Realising that you can't write books without money to pay for coffee, ink, and candlelight, publishers advance money on account of your future royalty earnings.

Publishers calculate how high an advance they can afford to pay by working out how many copies of your book they hope to sell. But advances don't always simply reflect your potential future royalty earnings. Sometimes publishers are happy to pay advances they know are never going to be earned out, because the market dictates that a particular book or author is so in demand among publishers that their value is much higher than their royalty earnings alone. The reality is that publishers often go into profit before an author earns out their advance.

You only start to see royalties when you've earned enough from them to pay back the advance you've received. Paying off your advance is known as *earning your advance*. Advances are non-returnable as long as you don't breach the terms of your publishing contract.

Advances are often paid in thirds or quarters. The first instalment is paid on signature of your publishing contract and the second on delivery of the finished manuscript. You may then receive the final third on first publication of your book, or if your advance is being paid in quarters, you may receive the third quarter on first publication, and the final quarter on paperback publication.

Accepting the Unpredictability of the Business

Publishers try to predict which books are going to be bestsellers, and then throw heavy marketing support behind those titles to try to realise their expectations. But for every predictable bestseller (for example, the movie tie-in, a bestselling author's latest, or the debut author hyped and marketed into the stratosphere by a publisher), there's a surprise hit or unpredicted (and expensive) flop. The unpredictability of the business can be miserable for all concerned, but every publisher relishes the challenge and tries to overcome the odds through canny and opportunistic publishing.

For this reason alone, saying whether you're going to earn out your advance is impossible. Even if you make a guess as to how well your book's going to do, it's nearly impossible to answer the question of how many books you have to sell to earn out your advance. You may wonder why; after all, your contract states your royalties and the book's RRP.

Some of the reasons why you can't accurately calculate your royalty earnings are due to the following factors:

✔ **Subsidiary rights sales:** If your publisher sells translation rights, US rights, or any of the other rights you may have granted them, from audio to large-print rights, your share of that income is offset against your advance. A great US deal alone can write off your advance before the UK edition is even published! On the other hand, the absence of any sub-rights deals may mean that you have to sell an awful lot of books in the home territories before you earn out your advance and start receiving royalties.

✔ **High discount sales:** Many books sold to shops by publishers are sold at a high discount or at an export royalty rate, which means that you receive a diminished royalty on those copies. You don't know how many copies will sell at what discount, so it's difficult to be sure of your royalty amounts.

✔ **Reserve against returns:** Publishers withhold a percentage of your royalty income for an agreed time (usually three royalty periods, or 18 months) as an insurance against large numbers of your book being returned unsold by bookshops. Even if your publisher ships 50,000 copies of your book to the shops, unless customers pick up and pay for those books at the tills, they eventually wend their way back to the warehouse.

The following sections clarify why royalties are even more complicated than they seem. We also show you how to calculate roughly what you might earn.

Why one royalty is not like another

We describe a standard paperback royalty structure in the earlier section 'Authors earn royalties'. Hardback royalties tend to start at 10 per cent of RRP, rising to 12.5 per cent when 2,500 or 3,000 copies have been sold, and 15 per cent after 5,000 or 6,000 copies have been sold. But most author print book royalties aren't paid at this level.

Here are the two main reasons why your standard paperback or hardback royalty may be diminished:

✔ **Export:** Copies of your book sold in export territories attract a lower royalty to take account of higher shipping costs.

✔ **High discounts:** Copies of your book sold to booksellers at a higher than average discount attract a lower royalty in order to allow the publisher to make such deals without carrying the full burden of their cost.

Increasing numbers of books are sold at a high discount, so it's more common than ever for an author's royalties to be much lower than they originally expected. For this reason, being represented by a literary agency that has pre-agreed royalty terms on such high-discount sales with publishers (as part of their boilerplate contracts, explained in the earlier 'Reviewing Publishing Contracts' section) is invaluable, because these terms are bound to be more favourable than a publisher's usual terms.

How ebook royalties are accounted

Ebooks are currently sold to retailers using the same 'discount off the RRP' business model, but the royalty paid to the author isn't calculated as a percentage of the RRP (as described in Chapter 15). At the time of writing, in 2014, the standard ebook royalty is 25 per cent of the publisher's net receipts from the retailer. The Society of Authors continues to campaign for a higher royalty, and agents push publishers as often as they can to improve these standard terms. Some authors are now paid an escalating royalty, which means that it increases as the author sells more books. Sometimes it's possible to negotiate a higher ebook royalty for backlist books and for digital-only editions, or when no advance has been paid.

Unfortunately, publishers' accounting systems haven't kept pace with the rate of change in the industry, and authors' royalty statements offer very little information on how much customers have paid for their ebooks. Agents argue that ebook accounting needs to become more detailed and transparent to enable these sales to be better audited.

Digital printing has had a great impact on the publishing industry. The technology, known as *print on demand* (POD) allows publishers to print just one or two copies of a book at a time for a relatively low cost. This means that some out-of-print books can still be ordered in print editions, to be printed in single copies. The quality of the POD editions isn't as good as that of a normally printed paperback, and the books tend to be expensive to the customer (about £10 to £15), so agents don't often favour books being put into POD programmes if paperback buyers have an ongoing demand for the book.

How to calculate your royalty earnings roughly

When your publisher informs you how many books they've sold or expect to sell into the bookshops on publication, you can start to do a very rough calculation to determine whether you may earn royalties. Before showing you the calculation, here are some points to remember when estimating your royalties:

✔ **Subsidiary rights sales:** As a first-time and therefore untested author, err on the side of caution and ignore this potential income – just assume in your calculation that your publisher sells no subsidiary rights at all. This would be very disappointing, particularly if you sold world rights to your publisher. However, if they do go on to make subrights deals, you can quickly recalculate, and for now you can rest assured that this is the worst-case scenario.

✔ **High discount sales:** How many copies of your book are sold at high discount very much depends on what kind of novel you've written. If it's the type of fiction that sells in supermarkets, you're more likely to receive diminished royalties than an author whose novel is being published by a small independent publisher that sells most print books through independent specialist booksellers. The very safest thing to do is to average out your royalties at a slightly diminished rate – 75 to 80 per cent of the standard royalty rate. This allows for the fact that some books earn a full royalty (hopefully) and some a much lower one.

✔ **Reserve against returns:** If your publisher withholds 25 per cent of your royalties as a reserve against returns, it makes sense to take 25 per cent off the initial sales figures they give you.

As an example, say you received a £20,000 advance, your paperback book is selling for £7.99, and you have a standard royalty agreement in which you earn 7.5 per cent royalty on the first 20,000 copies of any paperback edition of your book sold and 10 per cent thereafter.

Your publisher informs you that your book has sold 20,000 copies in paperback, so you grab your calculator and do the maths: £7.99 × 7.5 per cent = 60p per book × 20,000 books = £12,000. Figuring that you may see 80 per cent of this due to high discount sales, you get to a rough figure of £9,600 (£12,000 × 80 per cent). So, you have £10,400 left to earn from your initial £20,000 advance.

To figure out how many more books you have to sell to earn out that advance, start with your new 10 per cent royalty (having now notionally sold 20,000 copies), which is 80p. If you figure 80 per cent of that (for the high discounts), you may earn 64p per book from this point on (£7.99 × 10 per cent = 80p × 80 per cent = 64p).

Dividing your remaining advance, £10,400, by 64p tells you that you probably need to sell another 16,250 books to earn out your £20,000 advance and start to receive royalty payments – so, that's 36,250 books in total. But bear in mind that you may have to sell many more than this – or many fewer.

The main reason why this back-of-the-envelope calculation doesn't work is that it doesn't take account of any ebook sales. To factor in your income from ebook royalties, you first need to see roughly what royalty you're being paid per ebook sale. You could guess that you're being paid 25 per cent (the standard ebook royalty) of 50 per cent of the book's RRP – if the discount being offered to the online retailer is 50 per cent (in reality it could be higher, and your publisher will never disclose it to you).

However, it isn't wholly likely that you'll know what the RRP of your ebook is; at the moment, the first you know of it is when it appears on your royalty statement, because the only price visible on Amazon is its discounted selling price. Ask your publisher or, alternatively, wait until you've received a royalty statement. Take a look at what your income was for ebook sales and across how many copies sold. If you received £5,000 in ebook royalties and sold 10,000 ebooks, then you know that you're likely to receive approximately 50p in royalties per ebook sold. You can then factor some ebook sales into your back-of-the-envelope calculations.

Thinking about a two-book deal

Two-book deals are one way of overcoming some of the unpredictability of the publishing business.

If a publisher wants to publish your novel, they may feel that it's advantageous for them to contract your first two novels at once, offering you a *two-book deal*. The advantage to the publisher in making such a deal is that they can put a lot of effort and money behind launching your first novel in the sure knowledge that they're going to potentially reap the benefits themselves when your second novel is published. And if they *jointly account* the two books, set the contract up so that all royalties and income from one book are set against not only the advance paid for that book but also the other book, they're also able to spread their risk across two books and two advances. (Agents

often request that books contracted together are 'separately accounted' but publishers don't always agree to this.)

The advantage to you in making a two-book deal is that your financial future is secure for the next couple of years at least. And it's also good to be able to plan a career with a publisher, rather than just one book. If you all feel as though you're working together as a team in the long term, that usually has a positive effect on how you communicate and strategise.

The key disadvantage to such a contract is that you have to fix the value of your second novel before your first has been published. If your publisher is underestimating the value of your books, you or your agent may feel that you're better placed to make a one-book deal now and negotiate the second contract later.

Facing the Realities of Being Published

Your first book deal feels fantastic. When you find a publisher who passionately loves what you do, it can feel as if you're truly understood and appreciated for the first time. Planning your book's publication is hugely exciting, as is suddenly finding yourself in such stimulating company after months or years of relatively isolated work. It can all seem to happen very quickly, after a long period of writing and preparation.

In fact, making a book deal is *so* exciting and enjoyable that logic dictates that being an author can only get less exciting as time goes on.

Being published can also be stressful for the following reasons:

- ✔ Significant aspects of the publishing process are completely out of your control. The marketing, the sales, and the pitching to supermarkets all impact hugely on your career, yet you have very little, if any, influence on how these activities are conducted.

- ✔ Circumstances and your publishing plan are liable to change. Publishing houses are constantly reshaping their lists and their budgets, and the plan at one meeting can be revised at the next. Your editor is hopefully perfectly sincere and honest with you, but what they tell you is almost certain to change in the months before you're published: a huge print run may dwindle; a vast marketing campaign may be scaled down; your publicity director may be replaced by an assistant at the last minute.

   Of course, the absolute opposite may also happen. Sometimes a book for which a publisher has paid only a modest advance, and of which they have only limited expectations, can grow through word of mouth into a massive success.

- ✔ Marketing and doing publicity is physically and mentally taxing. Publicity is usually crammed into a fairly short space of time, around the launch of a book, and so it can be exhausting as well as nerve-wracking. One author says: 'I go from the solitary business of writing to being surrounded by publicists, interviewers, technicians, an agent, and so on. It's a bit of a shift, and then there's the shifting back – from loads of attention to solitary confinement with the keyboard once again. It's odd for me and not comfortable like my daily writing routine.'

- ✔ Developing a public profile as an author on social media is daunting, as is promoting your books to readers on Facebook or Twitter. You may also find that this kind of promotional activity distracts you from your writing.

✔ The publishing business isn't predictable or particularly loyal. Many authors feel quite vulnerable because their long-term future isn't guaranteed. Authors are often led to believe that they're only as successful as their last book.

When their books are finally published, a lot of authors realise that publication isn't as important to them as they thought it would be. Actually, writing is what they love, and being published is just a way of allowing them to do that for a living.

Chapter 19

Taking Control: Self-Publishing

*N*owadays if you're an author who has yet to find an agent or a publisher for your work, you have another route to readers that circumvents the need for approval from the publishing establishment. You've probably read stories in the press about authors who found acclaim and financial success through self-publishing. Authors no longer have to accept that they will never share their work with others. Publishing your work yourself as an ebook is easy.

One conclusion you may draw from those media reports about self-published authors who go on to sign huge publishing deals is that for some, self-publishing is another route into traditional publishing. Many self-published authors are tempted to switch to traditional publishing to help them build their careers and because, at the time of writing, print books still sell in greater volumes than ebooks do. Running a small business alongside writing novels is an inevitable part of self-publishing, and the strain can also start to take its toll. So for many, self-publishing may become a path to something else.

However, for others, self-publishing is simply a great way to publish their work and earn money from writing. For those who enjoy the freedom and control of self-publishing, the benefits outweigh the downsides, and they may decide that a deal with a corporate publisher isn't the right option for them. In this chapter we focus almost exclusively on self-publishing ebooks rather than physical books. Ebook publishing has become the most favoured route for self-publishers, due to the low start-up costs and easy routes into online bookstores, versus the challenges of publishing and selling print books.

Determining Whether Self-Publishing is Right for You

Publishing your work, yourself, on your own terms, can be a great fit for some writers. Do you have what it takes to successfully self-publish? We frame this section around a series of questions you can ask yourself to help make your decision.

How do you define success?

Although certain self-publishing platforms – for example Amazon's Kindle Direct Publishing (KDP) programme – make publishing your writing as an ebook very easy, you still need to put in a certain amount of work if you care about the way your novel looks on the page, what sort of cover it has, and so on. Are you prepared to take on the tasks we outline in 'Can you wear a lot of hats?' later in this chapter?

In order to establish whether self-publishing will be a successful route for you, revisit the questions we pose in Chapter 15. First off, what does *successful* really mean to you in the context of your writing? Is finishing your novel achievement enough, or can you only consider yourself a success after you're published? And, if you want to be published, do you want to see your book in print or would an ebook publication be enough? Are you hoping for, or in need of, financial success? Or do you just want to share your work with others, get some feedback or start a conversation? Lastly, if you're seeking financial or critical rewards, what level of reward is likely to satisfy you? Do you need to earn a living?

If you develop self-awareness about your personal aims and ambitions now, you're much more likely to make the right choices at every stage of the process, saving yourself time and probably working more effectively towards personal goals. You can also avoid disappointment and disillusionment later if, after reading this chapter, you find that self-publishing probably doesn't fulfil your ambitions.

Are you the kind of author who makes a good self-publisher?

Everyone can self-publish, as long as he or she has access to the Internet and a modicum of technical confidence. Good self-publishers aren't necessarily the most technically savvy of authors. Plenty of guides are available – such as *Publishing E-Books For Dummies* by Ali Luke (Wiley) – that take you through every stage of the process.

Authors who enjoy the greatest self-publishing success are those who have more than a little marketing know-how. These days the challenge is no longer working out how to be published: it's working out how to be *discovered* by book buyers. If you can't face thinking about your book blurb, growing a Twitter following, opening a Facebook account, or asking people to review your book, then successful self-publishing is going to be a huge chore for you.

Discoverability is a buzz word not only among ebook authors swimming in huge shoals online, but also among the big fish and sharks at corporate publishers. With the closing of most independent booksellers, bookseller chains, and even libraries, introducing new authors to book buyers is growing ever more difficult.

Self-publishing is nothing like writing. In no way does your journey as a self-publisher somehow heighten your skills as a writer or deliver an identical enjoyment to the one you reap when you sit down with a blank page and a burning idea. Self-publishing may be enjoyable to some, but it doesn't automatically follow that because you enjoy writing you also enjoy self-publishing.

However, self-publishing does develop your market awareness and offer other rewards that may enhance your writing experience. Self-publishing is very like publishing. As well as having marketing skills, a good self-publisher is able to do a passable impression of all the personnel in a typical publishing house. (See 'Can you wear a lot of hats?' for details.) If publishing in general doesn't interest you, don't read on; skip to Part VI – it's good!

One view in self-publishing is to forget the marketing – just spend your time writing more and more books. Sooner or later someone will notice you. You can try that approach. The better your books, the more likely you are to find a positive response.

Can you wear a lot of hats?

To be a successful self-publisher, you have to fulfil the following roles in your little publishing company – or find (and probably pay) someone else to fulfil each role for you:

- ✔ **Editor:** You must look at your own manuscript with fresh eyes and try to ensure that it delivers a high-quality reading experience, both imaginatively and grammatically. Turn to Chapter 14 for more editorial insights.

- ✔ **Production manager:** You need to format your text so it looks good on the page after it's converted into one of the software file formats (such as EPUB and MOBI) used by online ebook retailers.

- ✔ **Commercial director:** You have to choose the right price and publication date for your novel, and create online data, or *metadata*, that makes your work easier for buyers to discover.

- ✔ **Marketing director:** Your must create a public profile for yourself as an author, write a blurb for your book, and consider how to bring your book to public attention.

- ✔ **Publicity director:** You have to use social media to find your readers and reviewers. You have to write press releases and distribute them.

- ✔ **Sales rep:** You have to engage with various retail platforms and maximise your profile on each one. You also have to promote yourself without embarrassment.

- ✔ **Head of finance:** As soon as you earn money from your writing, you have to keep adequate records of your income and expenditure and fill in a tax return. If you're earning money from abroad, you have to take steps to ensure that tax isn't withheld from your earnings.

- ✔ **Intern:** You also get all the boring admin tasks, as well as a chance to learn on the job.

Publishing houses include other roles, several of which you may struggle to fill yourself. You likely lack the expertise required to license your work to translation publishers across the world, for example. And, as things stand, you aren't able to sell your book in print through a supermarket. So the roles of head of translation rights and key accounts executive go unfilled.

Do novels like yours sell well online?

You can publish any novel online (as long as it doesn't break the law, for example by breaching someone's privacy or copyright). But novels in certain genres seem to find success online more often than those in other genres do. These genres include (in no particular order):

- ✔ Crime and thrillers of all kinds (study the many subcategories on Amazon to work out what kind you are before you title and jacket yours)

- ✔ Fantasy and sci-fi (all shades; some more popular than others, of course)

- ✔ Romance (very successful this one)

- ✔ Chick-lit (favourite old genres live on online)

- ✔ Nostalgia and historical saga (the average age of the most acquisitive Kindle owner is older than you think)

- ✔ Human drama (stories of grief, abuse, loss of child)

- ✔ Erotica (*Fifty Shades of Grey* was a hit online first)

- ✔ Horror and other categories of genre fiction we don't name individually

For the love of self-publishing

In addition to its democratic nature, self-publishing has other merits:

- ✔ **Speed.** You can finish your novel tonight, finesse and upload it tomorrow, and then read reviews a day later. Traditional publishing works on a different timescale: most novels are written about a year before they're published. The comparatively quick turnaround in self-publishing allows you to be as prolific as you care to be.

- ✔ **Control.** You can choose your own title, jacket, price, and so on. You can also change any of those, whenever you want.

- ✔ **Nearly instant sales figures.** Easy and frequent access to your sales figures allows you to gauge the effectiveness of each element of your marketing, so you can run a stellar campaign and refine your approach quickly.

- ✔ **Another route to agents and publishers.** For some, self-publishing opens up a new route to traditional publishing deals, as agents and publishers note how popular certain books become among the reading public.

- ✔ **The business model.** For every ebook you sell via Amazon's KDP (priced between £1.49 and £7.81), you receive 70 per cent of the price paid by the customer, as opposed to the usual publisher's ebook royalty of 25 per cent of the price received by the publisher from Amazon. So, if you're a successful KDP author, you could earn a lot more from each ebook sale than you would via a publisher. For many self-published authors, this difference compensates for the lack of advances and the obstacles to successful print publication. See 'Amazon KDP: Royalties, rates, and rights' for more details.

Although the most successful categories of fiction online are the most popular and accessible, the paradox is that the next most logical book to self-publish is a niche book with a very targeted readership. Whether it's gay cowboy erotica, or novels about military wives, or a book about a specific kind of ceramics, if you can market directly to gay rodeo fans, military wives, or ceramicists through a society, blog, or club, you may enjoy a great hit rate.

Does your work appeal to established ebook buyers?

If you self-publish in ebook format exclusively, then your only customers are people buying books online. Online book buyers behave in certain ways and – as we acknowledge in the preceding section – they buy far more self-published genre fiction than self-published literary fiction. We speculate that this is the case because:

✔ The environment of most online bookstores encourages buyers to purchase certain types of book more than others. Customers shop impulsively, buying books that offer very clear messages about what they are and what they can deliver in terms of reading experiences.

✔ Typical online buyers love quick fixes. Make me laugh! Make me cry! Turn me on! Genre fiction delivers great quick fixes. We love it for that. Yes, we're typical.

✔ Because contemporary online bookstores aren't easy to browse aimlessly, customers tend to browse by category, which points them towards genre fiction categories.

✔ Genre books benefit more from online recommendation systems. Think about your own experiences. If you bought a certain sort of romance before, you've surely been offered one like it again. General fiction recommendations are more diffuse. Just because you read one literary novel set in Afghanistan doesn't mean you want to read another.

✔ Readers of genre fiction tend to be voracious (one quick fix can only lead to another), so genre readers tend to buy more titles, more frequently.

✔ Genre fiction fans often become experts in the field, so customers are keen to consult other readers' reviews rather than wait to read reviews in the press.

✔ Some genres lend themselves readily to marketing online, for example if they have big online communities that self-published authors can access.

✔ Some genres do well for self-published authors because they've been all but abandoned by traditional publishers. Recent examples of this include humorous fiction (there's no consensus on what's funny), fiction with older protagonists (considered too risky), and relationship novels for men (unpopular with supermarkets).

Some guides to self-publishing start out with the assumption that although the readers of the guide have decided to self-publish, they may not yet have worked out what they're publishing, much less written anything. Those self-publishers have the opportunity to be quite cynical about the market and to create novels that are more likely than others to please casual ebook browsers online.

We don't recommend choosing to write a particular type of novel just to tap into a market. As we mention above, a lot of your target readers are experts in your chosen field and more than capable of picking up on an inexperienced, derivative approach. And you're trying to start something good for yourself here, not to waste time on a type of novel you don't much enjoy. Why write 95 per cent of a romance novel only to remember you don't believe in happy endings?

We assume you've read Parts I to IV of this book first and are prioritising writing over publishing.

The politics of publishing

Self-publishing has become a (relatively) political and tribal activity. Some successful self-publishers are as vocal about the failings of traditional publishers as they are about the attractions of self-publishing. Many dub publishing houses 'legacy publishers', which is a bit like smiling while saying they're totally out of date and irrelevant.

Not helping their cause much, some traditional publishers and traditionally published authors are derogatory about the quality of self-published works. The context is that a lot of self-published authors used to be published by traditional publishers and felt let down by the experience, or have been rejected by traditional publishers and consider publishers and agents to be gatekeepers rather than enablers.

Add to that the fact that publishers are operating in a retail environment dominated by one monster success – Amazon – and that Amazon is the greatest facilitator of self-publishing, and it's easy to see why self-publishing is a sensitive area for publishers. Amazon is most publishers'

biggest single customer – and also the biggest single threat to their profitability and viability. Amazon isn't just a great place to find books you love, it's now also the manufacturer of the world's most popular ereading device, controls 95 per cent of the ebook retail market in the UK, operates a self-publishing platform, and is a publisher in its own right.

You don't have to belong to one camp or the other. You can love traditional publishing and bookselling and still be a self-publisher. We predict that in the future we may see more 'hybrid' authors. These writers may self-publish sometimes, and sell rights to a publisher sometimes; publish some books exclusively in print, and publish others in digital-only format. But predictions are dangerous in a market changing as rapidly as this one is.

The other thing to bear in mind as a self-published author is that, given its dominance in ebook retail, Amazon can switch from enabler to gatekeeper at any time. Are you really in control?

The other books that sell really well as (self-published) ebooks are series of novels about the same characters or that collectively form a larger story. The main reasons for the success of ebook series come down to marketing and discoverability – the twin key challenges facing any self-published author. In keeping with our earlier speculation about online buying habits, trilogies of novels eliminate the need to browse: readers can get a quick fix of a known quantity. Also, the author benefits from retailer recommendations: there's no better advert for your second book than your first book.

Are you still tempted to try self-publishing?

If the answer's 'yes', then great! Self-publishing is accessible to all and a wonderful way to share your work with others for very little cost and practical trouble. It may be a route to great success; every bestselling novel had a moment when only one person had bought it, and seeing your book take off via reader reviews and word of mouth is really exciting.

Amazon KDP: Royalties, rates, and rights

Many people claim that Amazon's Kindle Direct Publishing (KDP) pays 'better royalties' than traditional publishers. We've been careful not to use that terminology in this chapter, because it's a false comparison.

KDP is not a publisher and collaborator in the way that a traditional publisher is. In fact, the 70 per cent you receive from KDP isn't a royalty at all; it's the price paid for your product by the customer, minus a 30 per cent sales commission taken by Amazon.

KDP doesn't license rights in your novel or share control in the way that a publisher does when you sign a publishing deal. The rights all rest with you, the self-publisher. The percentage received from a traditional publisher, on the other hand, is actually a royalty based on the publisher's earnings from its role as exploiter of your work, which it has under licence from you. The publisher collaborates with you in the manufacture of your book – in its editing, formatting, design, and marketing. In taking on more responsibility and underwriting the costs, it earns a greater share of the profits.

When you earn 70 per cent from Amazon, you may receive a greater share of the list price of every copy sold, but this arrangement makes sense. You're entitled to the money because you're the sole owner of your book's rights and you did all the work.

Seek out a successful self-published author if you want to hear a rave review of self-publishing. Luckily, many of them are as drawn to blogging about self-publishing as they are to self-publishing, so you can easily find lots of success stories and encouragement online.

Travelling the Road to Self-Publication

Make some aspects of preparing your novel for self-publishing much easier with a detailed how-to guide at your side, such as the excellent *Publishing E-Books For Dummies*, or an experienced self-publisher's blog. A lot of people have been through the process already and can help you avoid pitfalls.

We don't have space here to offer you a detailed technical guide, so we mention the critical issues that warrant your careful consideration and offer you our perspective on ways to think about each one. After you've read this chapter, you'll hopefully be in a good position to broaden your research and knowledge from a position of greater insight.

Sharing your work online

First remind yourself of your self-publishing goals (see 'How do you define success?' earlier). Are you seeking to sell copies or – at least initially – are you mostly interested in publishing your novel in order to gain readers, feedback, and reviews rather than to earn money?

Some authors start their self-publishing careers by posting some chapters or whole novels on *community writing platforms* – online spaces where others can read their work at no charge. These authors then move on to selling copies on a retail site after they've build up a bit of a following.

We think that sharing your book with other readers and writers can be a useful editorial step. Most authors are surprised by the amount of critical feedback they get when they post chapters online.

If your main aim is to attract the attention of publishers or agents, you may consider sharing your work online to be an end in itself, because some authors have been so successful in sharing their novels for free that they've transitioned directly from that model to contracts with traditional print publishers.

Before you post any work online, spend quite a bit of time on the writing platform that interests you. Lurk on the site for hours until you fully understand not only its rules and structures but also its unspoken preferences and behaviours.

Here are some suggestions for things you can do online before you share your own work:

- ✔ Read lots of authors' material to see what sort of standard yours should meet before you share it.

- ✔ Check out which genres are most popular and how active those niche communities are.

- ✔ Read reviews on books you have dipped into, to gauge what tone to use in your own reviews.

- ✔ Look at what other members are reading and recommending, to see whether a particular type of book seems to do well.

- ✔ Investigate members' profiles to gather some ideas for how to present yourself online.

- ✔ Look at the visual content, noting which author photos, book jackets, and other images draw you in.

Wattpad

At the time of writing, Wattpad is probably the most successful 'story-sharing website' (their term). In 2013, Wattpad users spent 41 billion minutes on the site. Several authors have launched hugely successful writing careers on Wattpad.

By the time you read this book, another similar but different story-sharing site may have superseded Wattpad. But such sites' key functions are likely to remain more or less the same.

Wattpad favours certain kinds of genre fiction and particular demographics. (Right now we see a lot of fanfiction about a particular huge British boy-band.) So have a good look around and see where your novel may fit in.

Wattpad members are readers, writers, and reviewers. These three activities are regarded by the site as related and overlapping. However, you can come to the site as just a reader or a reviewer. The one activity we don't recommend practising in isolation on Wattpad is writing. When you launch your book on Wattpad, the way to attract attention to it and to yourself is to raise your profile as a reader and reviewer of other people's work.

Authonomy

Authonomy shares plenty of characteristics with Wattpad but operates in a slightly different way and has a unique atmosphere as a place to hang out and talk about reading. 'We're much more than a community of book lovers,' they say, and that's true. Most of this community also write, but it's well worth browsing for inspiration if you're a reader who's still at the 'thinking about writing' stage. HarperCollins own Authonomy, and one of their digital publishers runs day-to-day activities.

As on Wattpad, the way to raise your profile as a writer is through offering thoughtful and honest critiques of other authors' work. Authonomy users generally offer high-quality, constructive feedback, even if the criticisms are sweeping. These are experienced readers who have a genuine interest in writing technique.

When visitors come to the site looking for something to read, hopefully about to chance on your novel, they can search by genre, but they're also encouraged to look first at the users who've reviewed the most books. They're also drawn to look at what the 'top talent-spotters' on the site recommend and have written themselves. The site promotes an implicit association between good reviewing and good writing; between good reading and good writing. That seems fairly sensible to us. Not everyone who writes a useful review has a great novel under their belt, but they're clearly engaged with the right literary issues and have a strong enough voice to articulate views on character, technique, and story.

After you've raised your profile on the site and drawn other members to review your novel, the way your novel rises to the top of the pile is via its reader ratings. Members can place only five books on their virtual bookshelves, so readers are forced to make a proper quality call and not just trade multiple good reviews with other writers. Every week, the top five most highly rated books land on the virtual editor's desk, where real live HarperCollins editors review the work.

Several authors have been acquired by Harper's regular imprints as a result of success on Authonomy, and even more have been offered the opportunity to earn royalties by seeing their books published by the Authonomy digital imprint. But the best reason to share your book on Authonomy has to be as a soft launch prior to selling your novels – either to garner critical feedback or to draw readers to buy your novels on another site after enjoying a chunk of your writing for free.

Selling your work online

When you're ready to see your novel in an online bookstore, familiarise yourself with such shops so you can work out how to present your product to its best advantage. You also need to consider whether you want to start by publishing your book on one online bookstore exclusively, or whether it's important to you for your book to be available everywhere immediately.

If you don't own an ereader, buy one! Try each ereader in store (all are available to purchase in physical stores). Familiarise yourself with how customers use each type of ereader to shop, as well as how each feels while reading.

After you buy an ereader, experience it as a customer for a while. Observe your own behaviour:

- ✔ Why do you choose to browse particular parts of the store?
- ✔ Why do you buy the books you buy?
- ✔ How many sample chapters have you downloaded?
- ✔ How much notice do you take of reviews? How many stars does a book need to have in order to draw your attention?
- ✔ How much of each book blurb do you read?

✔ How important is the book jacket to you, and which ones appeal to you and why?

✔ How does the experience of accessing the store directly from your device differ from visiting its corresponding website?

Sharing your novel-in-progress on a community writing platform such as Wattpad differs from publishing your book free of charge on a bookselling platform. In both scenarios, you can easily update your file, creating a revised or improved version. However, community writing platforms expect that your novel may change and improve as time goes on, and your author profile can reflect that track. On a retail site, on the other hand, your reviews are customer reviews, whether these people paid for the book or not. You can't delete those reviews. So if you don't think your book is quite ready to sell, don't give it away for free in a bookshop.

One reason some self-published books have enjoyed such spectacular success on Amazon and other online bookstores is because many readers shop from bestseller lists. Success breeds success, and some titles stay in the top 100 for a considerable length of time. Getting into a bestseller list within an ebooks category or subcategory is one of your key challenges.

Kindle Direct Publishing

Kindle Direct Publishing (KDP) is Amazon's self-publishing platform. If you publish your book using KDP, it appears on as many Amazon websites internationally as you like. A simple structure guides you through steps such as pricing your book and uploading a product description.

Take care to format your Word document carefully before Amazon converts it into Amazon's version of a MOBI file. See 'Tackling the technical bits' for more information on how to do this.

At the time of writing, Amazon takes a 30 per cent commission on all copies sold for you within certain price boundaries, and a 65 per cent commission if you charge above or below that price range. (Check the website for up-to-date commission rates.)

The wonderful thing about KDP is that after you've published your ebook on Amazon, nothing signals to the casual book browser whether you're a self-published author or an author on a curated publishing list. Your book has equal status with every other book on the site. So if your novel reads and looks like a professionally edited and published piece of fiction, well, then, it is.

Currently, if you choose to enrol in Amazon's Kindle Select programme, which necessitates selling your work exclusively through Amazon, you can access extra features such as being able to offer your book free of charge for several days for promotional purposes. Amazon Prime customers can borrow your book from a virtual library for free, and Amazon pays you for those borrows.

(How much is not wholly clear, but the amount is respectable in our experience.) Self-published authors are heatedly debating the merits of Kindle Select; take a look at the different points of view by searching for 'Kindle Select' online.

One important point to remember is that KDP always matches the price that your book sells for on other platforms, even if your book is being given away for free on other platforms. So if another store discounts your novel, your selling price on Amazon goes down – and your profits with it.

Amazon uses different types of rankings and lists across its site. As far as we can tell, the bestseller list is a sales ranking list based on sales over a relatively short period of time, with weighting given to the most current sales. The popularity list is based on a number of factors over the last 30 days, including price (the lower the price, the harder it is to climb this list).

Kobo Writing Life

Kobo offers a self-publishing programme very similar to Amazon's KDP. At the time of writing, just over 10 per cent of Kobo's global sales are for books by self-published authors. Kobo – like Sony, Apple's iBooks Store, and Barnes and Noble's Nook – requires your Word file to be converted into an EPUB file before it can be published. Kobo Writing Life converts your Word file (or MOBI file) to an EPUB file for free. As on KDP, Kobo pays you 70 per cent of your book income if you price your novel between certain price boundaries, and less (45 per cent) if your novel is cheaper or more expensive.

Amazon and literary agents

After the success of KDP, Amazon quickly launched a special version of its self-publishing platform available exclusively to literary agents and their clients. Amazon is keen to see as much content as possible on the site, so this platform is partly designed to encourage agencies to publish some of their authors' catalogue of out-of-print books as ebooks.

Speculation among self-published authors about this service is rampant online. You find lots of chat about whether it's worth it and why you'd give up a percentage of your hard-earned self-publishing income to your agent when you're doing all the work.

We're not in a position to go into the opportunities offered by this service, but suffice to say

it offers significant marketing benefits. As we discuss in Chapter 16, good agents offer a lot of editorial support, publishing strategy, and other services such as translation rights representation to their clients, and we say that self-publishing without your agent (if you have one) is not a logical option for authors seeking strong, long-term, collaborative relationships with their agents. On the other hand, we don't recommend giving agents more than a standard commission for any services; an agent should never own your rights and receive anything like the kind of profit share a publisher does. They should always be an agent for your rights, taking a usual commission, or they risk facing a conflict of interest.

Apple iBooks store

Owners of iPads and iPhones can buy books from Apple's iBooks store. Because Apple device owners can also buy books from Amazon using the Kindle app, you don't have to publish onto iBooks to be read on an iPad. However, the Apple iBooks store is a growing retail space. Because not all self-published authors are in store yet, you benefit from a bit of exposure. (The same is true of Waterstones' own ebookstore, which isn't highly populated at the time of writing, and whose charts are easier to scale.)

If you use the app iBooks Author to publish your book (and if it isn't illustrated or full of graphics, there isn't much reason to), you can only sell your book through iBooks.

Generally speaking, iBooks doesn't accept files from individuals – only from aggregators – which leads us to . . .

Smashwords and other ebook distributors/aggregators

Smashwords is currently the best known of several ebook *aggregators* – service providers that, for a slice of the pie, will publish your book on all the different digital publishing platforms around the world. Smashwords says that it made £12.1 million worth of sales in 2013. Recently, Smashwords came to an agreement with file-sharing website Scribd, whereby all Scribd subscribers can access Smashwords books.

Smashwords offers to format your book using its legendary 'Meatgrinder' conversion process, but authors claim that it throws up as many problems as it solves, and that they often end up creating different file formats for the various platforms themselves.

The real advantage of using Smashwords is that your book is published across many more platforms (including some in Australia and Canada). Readers can also buy directly from Smashwords, because it's a retailer in its own right.

Self-published authors point to some disadvantages of using Smashwords, too, such as complications involved in working out when they'll be paid and addressing international needs on a US-focused site.

Your income from Smashwords differs depending on which platforms your novel is sold on. Although you earn 85 per cent of book income from sales on the Smashwords site, sales on other 'affiliate' platforms are subject to transaction fees, discounts, and payment processing fees.

You can choose only one aggregator to represent your work. You can't sell your books to Apple via Smashwords *and* another distributor. So make that choice wisely. Not all the aggregators offer their own retail outlets, but some offer other services:

- ✔ Lulu can also publish your book in paperback for you.

- ✔ The (UK-based) eBookPartnership offers ebook conversion, cover design, and international distribution on a wide range of platforms. Its online statistics are easy to understand, and you're paid monthly. You can choose which formats you manage yourself and which the aggregator manages for you.

Self-publishing services

Because the self-publishing industry is growing quickly and enjoying success, lots of businesses have sprung up that offer to take on some or all of the work involved in publishing your novel.

Some companies are reputable and useful, and if you can't face worrying about formatting your text or writing a product description, then using one of these companies may be the answer. However, your sales may not earn back the fees you outlay, so set a budget and choose wisely which tasks you spend money on. Perhaps you know that with a bit of effort you can figure out how to format your text, but you don't have a clue how to design a jacket.

Always bear in mind that ultimately you have to make choices about how much to charge for your book, as well as to keep tabs on reviews, packaging, and merchandising. You can't delegate the role of publisher entirely. You're the only one with an overview of how things are going and with a long-term vision of your novel's potential.

Crowdfunding: The future of publishing?

Of the notable alternative business models in the self-publishing market, crowdfunding (when money is raised, usually online, from many different people, to fund a project) is one of the most interesting. On Unbound, for example, readers commit funding to your book in exchange for (as a minimum) an acknowledgement in the finished book and a free copy. When you reach your funding target, Unbound publishes your book. Unbound launches a relatively limited number of projects, so authors have to go through a selection process. Unbound's projects tend to be non-fiction, but we can envisage crowdfunding being extended to commercial fiction by a publishing platform in the not-too-distant future.

Packaging Your Book

Some books become bestsellers because – in addition to being really good reads – the publisher or author has somehow struck upon an alchemical mix of great title, great jacket, great subject, and great timing. Many bestselling authors profess surprise when they enjoy success, and say things like, 'It just took off' or 'I got lucky.' Alchemy is magic, but trying to be lucky in the four areas of title, jacket, subject, and timing when you're self-publishing is a sensible strategy.

Generating a great title

Look back at Chapter 17 to remind yourself of some basic tips about titles. The right title is even more critical when you're publishing an ebook, because the title is visible and prominent at all times. It's also a frequent search term in shops or search engines.

Titles are as subject to fashion and trends as anything else. Sometimes a long, quirky, narrative feel strikes a chord. Then a style becomes over-used, and the next bestseller has a single-word title. You have to walk the line between standing out from the crowd and building on publishing techniques that are already working for others.

Most importantly, remember that although you're picking it alone, your book title isn't there *for you*. Its role is not to confirm your vision of your novel, or your or your loved ones' image of you as a novelist. The title's job is to attract readers to your amazing novel, and to entice them to buy and then read it. For example, a title may work if it reflects back something of who the reader is or desires to be. F Scott Fitzgerald's original title for *The Great Gatsby* was *Trimalchio in West Egg*. Although he wasn't able to read this book, his editor thankfully stepped in. No one wants to be Trimalchio – but everyone wants to be the Great Gatsby.

Getting a great jacket

Our biggest tip regarding your book jacket is to make sure your book doesn't look like a self-published novel! If you want your novel to enjoy the same status as any other ebook online, it needs a jacket that is either professionally designed or so well designed by you that it seems professionally designed. If you only have a limited budget for publication of your novel, prioritise the jacket over everything else. You can find jacket designers online, so review their portfolios and seek recommendations. Some websites help connect you with multiple designers who each pitch for your job.

The jacket of your self-published novel most often appears as a thumbnail online, so your most important words and graphic elements should still read clearly even when very small. Also, your jacket must be effective in black and white, so that it stands out on the black and white screens of ereaders.

As with titles, jackets are subject to fashion. Spend time browsing online and working out which seem to be attracting sales, as well as looking great to you. (For example, in 2013, blue jackets seemed very popular.) Of course you don't want your, say, serial killer thriller, to look like every other serial killer thriller out there – that's a signal to book buyers that your book isn't very special or unique. But you do need yours to look like a serial killer thriller, or you'll never find serial killer thriller fans.

Promoting a great subject (or writing a great blurb)

We encourage you in numerous places in this book to think about how marketable your book is, so we assume you've made all the big decisions about subject matter. But now you must convey to readers that your novel has a great subject, one that the market is hungry for.

The *blurb* is the text on the back of a print book. The book's editor, in collaboration with colleagues in sales, traditionally writes this copy with the chief function of encouraging readers to sample the first few pages of the novel itself. Online, this blurb performs the extra function of using words, phrases, and reviews that can contribute to the discoverability of your book (see 'Minding your metadata' later in this chapter for more on metadata).

Writing your book blurb yourself forces you to pinpoint what your book is about – not what it's about to you as its writer, but to the readers you wrote it for. What situation or dilemma can you describe that creates immediate intrigue or recognisability? Lead with that. Don't try to mention every character or more than one or two turns of the plot. Take the story to another point of intrigue and leave readers wanting to know more.

A useful exercise here is to read blurbs for the same classic novel – one with which you're familiar – from different publishers. Which blurbs grab your attention even though you already know the story, characters, and themes? If a great blurb can make a hundred-year-old novel seem compelling, think what it can do for your new novel.

Going for great timing

Timing is the fourth corner in the 'make your own luck' square we're drawing. Getting the timing right for your publication is partly about catching a wave.

Perhaps your novel focuses on a subject that somehow addresses interesting issues of the moment. Or maybe your work heightens a current popular obsession or theme.

However hot your topic, ensure that you publish only after you have certain marketing building blocks in place, such as a website. Release your book on the right side of significant seasonal events such as Christmas. Although holiday sales are important, remember that launching the next bestseller at Christmas is extremely challenging. One self-published author told us she had to sell three times as many books to get into the Amazon top 100 in the week after Christmas 2013 as she did the week before, as new Kindle owners stocked their bookshelves.

Tackling the technical bits

Nearly there! The following are some final few issues you need to research and consider as you wrap up your self-published novel.

Converting files

For many first-time self-publishers, a big challenge in the run-up to publication is formatting their books so they look good when customers download them to their ereaders. Formatting is more than just prettying up your word-processed document: it's about cleanly converting your file into EPUB, MOBI, and any other formats.

All writers have their little habits and automatically add all sorts of features to Word documents without realising it. An extra space at the end of every line, a tab at the beginning of every paragraph, or a series of returns to reach a new page may seem like minor quirks – but each can result in text that flows improperly, or yawning gaps in surprising places.

Lots of tricks are available when creating a new Word document or cleaning up an old one – such as how to insert a page break to start a new page. Become familiar with using styles in Word to create fixed formats for chapter headers and text, so you don't have to apply these on a line-by-line basis.

Preparing your file for conversion into EPUB and MOBI is an art. Use one of the many step-by-step guides available to help you fully understand what to do. After you've converted the file, make sure you upload it onto your ereader to verify that everything reads the way you mean it to.

Minding your metadata

Metadata is 'data about data' – but to you and us, metadata is a series of unseen tags and prompts that you can add into your book file to make your book easier for readers to find. Seek out good advice online on how to create effective, accurate metadata for your novel. The process is a bit like learning about Search Engine Optimisation when you build a website. You want people to be able to see and find your book as often and as easily as possible.

One way to add good metadata to your novel is to include good review quotes in your Product Description, and to specify the right genre subcategories for your novel's retail listing.

Specify subcategories

You want the online bookstore to recommend your novel to your kind of fiction reader, so figure out in which online categories your novel belongs. For example, Amazon features many different subcategories of crime novels; some are busier and more competitive than others. Choosing the right category definition for your book can therefore massively improve your chances of rising to the top of a category or subcategory bestseller list.

Picking your price

Many authors choose to launch their ebooks at 75p (or 99c), which is the minimum list price permitted by KDP. These authors don't want readers to question for too long whether to invest in buying their novels. They also realise the importance of quickly building up as many reader reviews as possible, so they prioritise reach over price.

In income terms, you currently must sell *four times* – not two times – as many books at 99p as you do at £1.99 to make the same amount in earnings. This is due to the fact that Amazon's sales commission (the company's share of your book's selling price) doubles if your book is priced under a certain level. If you have a confident marketing plan, building attention for your novel at a higher price point may be a better strategy. You can reduce the price at any time, and doing so may be more effective after you've created some demand for your product.

Some authors think that Amazon's algorithm (see the next section) tends to group books by price point (so that buyers of 99p books are recommended to buy more 99p books). If this is the case, you may want to consider that an early association with other low-price books can mark you out as expensive later if you start low and then increase your price. Also, lower priced books seem to thrive less well on the popularity list.

If you do reduce the price, make sure you do it for an advertised limited period. Encourage readers to buy now rather than later, and stick to your decision – or people feel cheated.

Analysing algorithms

You find lots of discussion online about online bookstores' *algorithms* – particularly Amazon's. We think these complex pieces of computer programming are a bit like the KFC recipe: no one knows what's in it exactly, but lots of people think they've got a pretty good idea. Amazon's algorithm determines what appears in ranked search results, including where books sit in the 'most popular' bestseller list rankings and the 'sales rankings' list. Some seasoned self-publishers believe they're extremely good at spotting when Amazon develops or changes the algorithm, because the site suddenly starts throwing up different behaviours and results when authors implement their tried-and-tested marketing strategies.

You only need to think about the algorithm if you want to. Some authors spend an awful lot of time working out how to get the best out of Amazon. You may prefer to write your next book instead, because the best way to double your exposure in a bookshop is to double the number of books you have for sale in it.

Pondering print editions

You can make your book available in print, either through Amazon's digital print service, CreateSpace (which registered 131,340 ISBNs in 2012), or by using a printer such as Lightning Source. If you want a print edition to be available at the same time as your ebook, you need to organise it while you're finalising your ebook. Your margins on print sales aren't great, but if you enter the Amazon bestseller lists, demand is likely.

Bringing Your Book to the Attention of Readers: Marketing

Marketing is the one subject that most successful self-published authors know quite a bit about – either from their previous professional lives or because they taught themselves as much as possible online.

In fact, many of the issues we discuss throughout Part V relate to marketing. Decisions about title, price, book subject matter, genre category, and so on are all marketing decisions in the broad sense in that they come down to how you target consumers.

As in all matters relating to self-publishing, you can find a massive amount of information online and in published guides to help you plan a marketing strategy. You can also buy help from marketing professionals. However, the most important thing is that you actually have a strategy – whatever it may be. If you have no idea how to write a press release, have zero interest in Twitter, and break out in a cold sweat at the thought of using Facebook, these tools are never going to work as ways to market your novel yourself.

Nowadays, even authors published by traditional publishers learn how to help market their works through social media and innovative thinking, so much of this section is applicable to all authors, however their books are published. Although publishing houses employ marketing experts, no one is as ambitious for your novel as you are, and a little expertise helps you to oversee your publisher's activities.

Creating your marketing plan

Many self-published authors fail in their marketing because they dabble at hundreds of different things and don't take the time to sit down and plan exactly how they're going to draw attention to their books.

Don't be drawn into mimicking a strategy that worked for one author, assuming it will also work for you. Trust your instincts about how you need to present your novel to the public. Think about where your readers gather – either online or physically. Use what you know about your readers and your genre to devise a plan that works for you.

We recommend drafting your marketing plan early, ideally several months in advance of publication. At the very least, taking time to design your plan focuses your research and fine-tunes how you use the various marketing tools at your disposal. A plan also encourages you to schedule activities and differentiate between things to have in place before you publish and strategies to implement later.

Bursting out of the gate: The first 90 days

If you take a look at Amazon, you see that one way to search for books is by titles published in the past 30 or 90 days. Regular customers use this option as a way to discover new books. As a result, the first 90 days after self-publication are the most important in marketing terms; during this period you have your best opportunity to find readers and win those all-important reviews. See 'Gathering reviews for your book' for much more advice on this.

Your place in the self-publishing community

A spirit of generous collaboration unites many self-published authors. Many feel that they're 'all in it together' and can cheer each other on and learn from one another's mistakes. (After you become a bestseller, things may get a bit more competitive.) Taking your place in that community – by blogging about the issues, contributing to forums, following fellow authors on Twitter, reviewing other self-published books, and so on – builds a ready-made audience for your books.

However, your most important relationship is always with your readers. If you want to build a career as opposed to publish one book, you must always be thinking of ways to start a conversation with your readers, which means giving them opportunities to reply, and keeping the conversation open.

Think about how you can find and influence buyers in your genre in this crucial early period for your book. Perhaps you want to generate interest through social media. If so, the time to start building your following on Facebook or Twitter is way before your book is published. You may like the idea of engaging with people via forums at Goodreads, Amazon, or Kindleboards. You need to begin engaging with people in advance, so that when the time comes for you to notify people that your book is launched, you have a voice – and people are listening.

Scheduling your social media

Evidence suggests that customers tend to buy certain kinds of fiction at different times of day. For example, romance readers tend to be online in the later afternoon. Crime and thriller sales go up after dark. Plan your social media announcements to coincide with the times that make strategic sense for your title and readership.

Gathering reviews for your book

Reviews are crucial to building your novel's profile, because a popular tool on Amazon is the option for customers to sort books by average customer review rather than by popularity when browsing categories.

'Free day' finesse

If you register with Kindle Select, spend time planning whether and when to use your 'free days'. Currently, you can give away your novel for free on five in every 90 days when your book is on sale. You can either cluster the days together or spread them out. Free days are a good way to draw new people to your product, and several websites are available to help you alert subscribers to free ebooks.

Those who study algorithms (see 'Analysing algorithms') believe that free book downloads can impact on the rankings in the popularity charts – but only to a relatively minor degree. (Some believe that ten free book downloads equate to one book sale.) However, more readers can mean more reviews, which alone can make your book more visible. Authors disagree about whether free days work in a book's long-term interest.

As soon as you start to accumulate good reviews, your book's ranking rises, increasing the likelihood of more reviews. When you first publish your novel, encourage friends and relatives to read it and to post good reviews if they enjoyed it. You don't want any huge favours from your friends and family. Amazon browsers are very canny and are easily able to tell if all your reviews are by aunties who've never reviewed anything else and didn't get past the first few pages of your book. You just want to ask the readers in your circle to spend some time with your book.

Avoid asking for reviews from anybody who can gain financially from your writing, such as your spouse. Amazon removes these reviews.

After family and friends, approach other people you trust – maybe people you meet in an online forum – to be early readers of your book. If they have an opportunity to read your book before it's released, their reviews can be ready to go live as soon as the book's published. However, any copy you give people to read for free doesn't show as an Amazon-verified purchase, so earlier readers need to state in their reviews that they were given a copy of the book in exchange for an honest review. After that, if you feel comfortable doing so, you can ask anybody who drops a line of praise on Twitter, Facebook, or in any writing community whether they're willing to post a review.

Amazon itself is a good place to find people who may read and review your book for you. You can go about doing this a few different ways:

- Check out competitors' reviews and click on the positive and useful ones. (You only want people who are generous with their reviews.) See whether these reviewers provide email or blog addresses in their profiles. If so, you can then contact them directly.

✔ Amazon features lists of top reviewers on the site. Some write reviews of everything from cat litter to bottle openers, so be careful about who you approach. Look for those who've written a lot of book reviews, and drop them a line to see whether they're interested.

✔ Find a software programs that sorts Amazon reviewers by a range of criteria. You could search for all the reviewers of a specific type of book or a specific author, or ask to see only a list of those who provide email addresses.

You can take a similar approach on Goodreads (www.goodreads.com), an online community of passionate readers who post reviews of books they're reading. Why not offer some free copies in a competition? Spend time identifying who enjoys your kind of book and who posts reviews (good ones, mostly). Approach them and offer reading copies in exchange for fair reviews.

Goodreads is an increasingly popular place for readers to hang out. In the middle of 2013, it boasted 20 million members internationally, double the number of members registered 12 months earlier. Members create libraries of books they enjoyed and rate them, and in return receive recommendations of other books to try. You can create a profile on the site as both a writer and a reader. In early 2013, Amazon bought Goodreads, which is a sign of how influential the site is.

In terms of reviews elsewhere, newspapers and magazines are unlikely to notice your book, and even some bloggers are still a bit reluctant to review self-published novels. Study as many book blogs and review sites as you can, find the ones that are particularly pertinent to your genre, and note which bloggers are most likely to offer you reviews. Personal, professional approaches are most persuasive, so write to each person individually, providing a clear information sheet about your novel and offering a review copy. Be sure to include links to any previous reviews, Twitter feeds, and websites, and offer to write a guest blog or to be interviewed.

As you establish yourself in the writing and reading community, you may start to review other authors' books. Try to be positive and helpful while at the same time cultivating a reputation for honesty. In other words, don't give a good review to a bad book, but try not to make an enemy of your fellow author either. Sometimes, making an excuse for your silence is easier than posting a potentially damaging review. We hear quite a few stories of authors who act very unprofessionally and publish low-star reviews in revenge for bad reviews. Also, you may see calls on forums asking for 'review swaps' with other authors. Avoid this type of commitment, even if other authors insist they can be unbiased; neither review is likely to be wholly honest if it's been traded for one in return.

Whatever approach to collecting reviews you choose, be professional. Never expect reviewers to buy your book in order to review it, and always provide them with the blurb and details of the length. If you have some extracts from previous reviews (good ones), share them. Don't send the book initially. Send potential reviewers an email with the details, and ask whether they're interested in reviewing the book. If they are interested, ask which format they prefer. Taking these extra steps establishes that reviewers are genuine, and makes it easier to follow up with them after a couple of weeks to ask whether they've had an opportunity to read your novel yet.

Building your website and blog

As social media was initially proliferating, having a professional website seemed less and less important as a marketing tool. But actually the way that Twitter and Instagram feeds flow like rivers in an always-moving conversation creates a transitory and somehow incomplete picture. Bottom line: you still need to establish a hub for information about you and your books – somewhere to log your reviews, your press cuttings, and sample chapters from your work.

The idea of building a website or blog may feel daunting, but lots of tools and packages are available to make building a site or a blog easier. Every small business owner needs to have a presence online, and self-published authors are no exception.

Don't confuse a website, which generally has fixed, though up-to-date, information, with a blog, which serves as a platform from which to speak at greater length than you can with 140 characters. Your website may be accessible from the blog, and vice versa. Indeed, using certain blogging platforms – you can have fixed pages of information that can act as your website – but you need to consider the purpose of your blog versus your website, and therefore how to make both of them most effective.

Your website must have an attractive *home page* – the landing page that draws people into the site when they come to find out about your books. This page provides information about you as a writer and a person, as well as insights into your books that aren't available anywhere else. Look at some writers' sites and see what types of pages they incorporate. In general, though, your website contains relatively static information, with updates when you write a new book, have some very significant news to share, or want to update the reviews that you list.

Your blog is a place where you can talk, share your opinions, start conversations, and invite others to speak. The home page of a blog features your most recent post, so the page is fresh and different each time people visit.

People visit your blog because they like your writing. So write! Blog about everything from your publishing and writing experiences to the impact your new writing life is having on your dog. But do think about your audience here. Many authors blog about their self-publishing experiences, and so their blogs are generally read by other writers. That's great, because they're readers too. But if you want to attract readers to your blog, think about what interests them. Perhaps something related to the topic of your book, or more about you as a person – what you get up to each day – as opposed to how to format an ebook.

After you've written a blog post, be sure to promote it through Twitter and Facebook. Remember that each post has a permalink, so if the post isn't too topical, you can add tweets to your Twitter queues to remind people of this post in the future too. If you write about subjects that interest the writing or reading community at large, others retweet your blog links.

If you feature your Twitter and Facebook feed on your static web home page, the site's no longer static and enjoys improved Search Engine Optimisation. See the following sections for more on both social media tools.

A contact form is essential on both your website and blog. Invite visitors to leave their names and email addresses, and promise never to pass them on. Readers can tell you how much they enjoyed your book – and you can ask them to sign up to a newsletter that you, perhaps, distribute monthly with your latest updates or musings. Some readers may feel reluctant to sign up to a newsletter (and keeping one going is difficult and time-consuming when you're writing), but may be interested in hearing when your next book is published.

Make sure you have a system to record visitors' addresses. Some website and blog tools include tools for automatically gathering and organising this information. But be careful: over a certain number of addresses often attract additional management charges, which can be quite expensive.

You can develop your public profile beyond your personal website. Join various reading and writing communities, always linking back to your website. And don't forget to create a profile on Author Central on Amazon. It's worth carefully considering what parts of your biography will be the most interesting to readers, and which parts you might like to hold back. You should also think about how you 'sound' – what kind of person you seem to be – in a virtual world. Unless readers feel comfortable around you, they won't want to enter your fictional world.

Stepping into social media

Social media undoubtedly offers all authors a powerful marketing tool. More and more readers are discovering the pleasures of connecting with their favourite writers online. Authors also enjoy the benefits of chatting to colleagues on Twitter and other media in a profession that can be lonely and isolated.

The number of books you can sell via social media is unclear. A recent Verso survey estimated that 12 per cent of books are discovered from social networks, whereas 50 per cent are passed on via personal recommendations. We say that one thing feeds the other. Keep talking.

We focus on just two social media tools: Twitter and Facebook. Apply our insights to whatever social media platforms make the most sense for you as a self-published author. Different social media platforms appeal to different demographics. As a social media tool, Facebook, many contend, is now dead and buried to under 18s and has become the forum of their parents. However, Facebook's popularity among users above 30 continues to grow, which may be a great fit for your novel.

Some authors stay online all day, offering updates alongside their writing. But most prefer separating the two activities and leaving proper space for creative thinking. An author told Lizzy that she uses one device for writing and another for email and social media, which allows her to literally switch off her social media duties during work time.

Trending on Twitter

By the time you read this book, another social media tool may have overtaken Twitter, in the way that Facebook had its glory day a few years before Twitter. Right now, young people are signing up to WhatsApp and Snapchat in droves – closed communities in which they can communicate in confidence. Still, Twitter is a *public* forum, and its open qualities may prove key to its longevity, because people want to broadcast all sorts of things about themselves – and this is more true of self-published authors than for most!

Subscribing to Twitter is easy. Here are some basic pointers for self-published authors:

- Choose your name or *handle* wisely. If your name is already taken, try adding 'author', 'writer', or 'books' to it. But bear in mind that if your handle is too long, people won't want write to you or about you, because your handle uses up too many of their 140 characters.

- Put together a little biography for your Twitter home page, including the name of your novel, and set it against your cover art as an extra piece of marketing.

✔ Follow some other authors and *tastemakers* (bloggers, journalists, publishers, agents). Watch what they tweet and start to think about what you want to say.

✔ When you follow others, they receive notifications and may decide to follow you back.

✔ Have a look at who's following your favourite authors, and when you find ardent fans of your kind of fiction, follow them. Ordinary readers are more likely to follow you than are big-shot journalists or authors – and they are indeed your desired audience.

✔ Read up on the best approach to pitching your book to your followers without over-selling.

Pretending to be anything other than who you are on Twitter is pretty difficult. Faking your identity just doesn't seem sustainable for very long. Just be the best version of yourself when you're on Twitter.

Some authors worry about not having enough to say on Twitter, but lots of different types of tweeter exist. The most popular aren't always tweeting original information; some act as gatekeepers to other information, sifting through the web for things that interest their followers. These nuggets often become the most retweeted tweets, and being retweeted is the best way to build followers.

Twitter isn't just for broadcasting your thoughts and information about your book. Its great potential is in giving you a place to start a conversation with readers and to establish relationships. Make sure you reply to tweets and also write open-ended tweets that propose interaction.

Finding friends of fiction on Facebook

Facebook, the social networking site through which you can grow a web of friends and share news and photos, also offers a really good platform for authors to share news about their books and set up a community of fans.

You may already have a personal Facebook profile to keep in contact with friends and family. Consider carefully whether you want to use the same page for your messages about yourself, the author, or whether you want to keep the two sides of your life separate. Not everything you say to your friends is worth saying to the world at large, and you may not want your family's updates to get lost in a newsfeed full of your readers' shenanigans.

You can choose whether to make your author page a normal personal Facebook space or to create a *Facebook Page*. (Facebook replaced its earlier fan pages with Facebook Pages that others can 'like'.). An author's Facebook Page is similar to the kind of page that commercial brands favour.

Alternatively, authors may choose to brand a normal profile page. The benefits and disadvantages to both choices are balanced; some successful authors run both. For example, one key advantage to using a normal personal page is that you can see your fans interacting in your newsfeed, and can comment and join in with their conversations. On the other hand, the number of friends you can have personally is limited, while 'likes' on Facebook Pages appear to be limitless.

If you run an author Facebook Page, your posts are normally delivered to only 16 per cent of the people who like your page. To ensure that your post appears in the newsfeeds of everybody who likes your page, you have to pay to promote your post. The costs vary. You also have an option to promote an update to friends of people who liked your page or to target specific user groups – by location, age, interest, and so on. Again, various fees apply.

Your next chapter

Good luck as you continue your writing and research. Whether you're at the beginning of your novel or about to sign your first deal, you're now part of the conversation. We look forward to reading what you have to say. Welcome!

If you self-publish without much success, don't give up. Write another book and continue to reach out to readers. Remember that some of the successful self-published authors you see on the bestseller lists have been writing for a long time. They may have had long careers with publishers before turning to self-publishing. They bring their experience as writers and marketers to bear; you're just gaining yours.

If your self-publishing endeavour goes really well, agents or publishers may approach you, unlocking translation rights income for your book and perhaps making your book available widely in print.

Some self-published authors are reluctant to forego their ebook income, but for understandable commercial reasons publishers are not at present willing to make print-only deals, and expect you to let them take over your ebook rights if they commit to publishing you in print. You have to weigh up the financial pros and cons. Amazon itself has publishing imprints and may approach you with the offer of an advance. Talk to some of Amazon's authors about their experiences of transitioning from KDP to Amazon Publishing.

Take a look at Chapter 16 for some advice about agents, and at Chapter 18 for some information about publishing contracts.

Part VI
The Part of Tens

the part of tens

In this part . . .

- ✔ Find ten tips to help you *start* writing and *keep* writing.
- ✔ Read tips from published authors to inspire you.
- ✔ Beware of the common pitfalls to avoid.
- ✔ Benefit from the insights of agents.

Chapter 20

Ten Top Tips for Writers

In This Chapter

▶ Keeping track of your ideas

▶ Writing what you know and like in your own way

▶ Saving your sense of humour

▶ Catching and respecting your reader

▶ Sticking with it

*W*riting is complicated. You need to get many different things right in order to write a novel that really works. That's the bad news. The good news is that most of these things are tiny; they do matter, but not much. Writing a novel is a bit like building a house. You need to get a fairly small number of things right, and if you do that then the house won't fall down and you can live in it comfortably. Everything else is decoration. A novel's the same. Get the main things right, and a few ragged edges don't matter. (Of course, you need to try and get them right too, but you see what we mean.) Here are ten of the most important tips to keep in mind.

Keep a Writer's Journal

It doesn't matter what you call it or what form it takes, but you need to keep a writer's journal in which you write down anything that happens, anything that occurs to you, one-liners, jokes, overheard remarks, anything at all. Your journal is where you write your ideas, make notes, try out scenes, stuff photographs and articles, and keep whatever you need. We like a hard-back notebook and a pencil, but the details are up to you.

If you can, get a journal with an elastic band attached, like a policeman's notebook, especially if you plan on stuffing it with scraps of paper. This design saves you a lot of picking things up every time you drop the journal, and if you do drop it in (say) long wet grass, it probably won't come to harm.

Show, Don't Tell

Many inexperienced writers make the mistake of telling their readers everything instead of simply showing them. If you tell readers something, they can only agree. If you show them something, you let them come to their own conclusions.

Showing rather than telling helps readers to get involved in a story. The popularity of detective novels points to the fact that readers like to work; they want the satisfaction of participating in the story.

Table 20-1 gives a couple of examples of telling versus showing.

Table 20-1	Telling Versus Showing
Telling	*Showing*
Joanne and Jeremy were dancing together. Simon watched them with a jealous expression on his face.	Simon was standing in a dark corner, watching them. His fists were clenched tight by his sides and the muscles of his jaw moved as if grinding hard corn. Someone walked past and spoke to him, but he ignored them. His eyes never left the dancing couple.
Joanne was beautiful.	Joanne walked into the room, and the atmosphere changed. An animated conversation taking place next to the door stopped in mid sentence. Simon realised that, along with the rest of the room, he was staring. He realised this at the same moment that he noticed that his glass was overflowing and whisky was pouring onto his shoes.

Through showing, you allow readers to use their own interpretation and standards. Beauty, for example, is always in the eye – or imagination – of the beholder. Showing the effects that a character or an object has on the surroundings also allows you to surprise the reader: if a character brings the room to a halt just by walking into it, and you later reveal that she's decidedly plain, you say something about her without having to spell it out.

Showing rather than telling also brings characters and situations to life. 'Joanne was beautiful' is vague and unhelpful, as well as being lazy. You need to work to keep the reader's attention. Showing the reader things rather than telling them is one way to achieve this aim.

Put very simply, don't *tell* your readers something, *show* it to them.

Write about What You Know

'Write about what you know' is the oldest piece of creative writing advice around. It's also one of the most misunderstood, in that writers tend to get this piece of advice back to front – they assume that something they know about is interesting by definition because of the level of accurate detail they can bring to it. But what most people know most about is day-to-day life, and, face it, day-to-day life isn't a great story.

You need to think about what you know *after* you decide on your story.

'What you know' can take two main forms:

✔ **Background:** John le Carré's Smiley novels are about people involved in the secret services. Le Carré knows a great deal about espionage, spying, and deception, and about the effect that it has on those who are involved in it. However, the books aren't 'about spying', they're about people and how they deal with the unique pressures they're subjected to. Le Carré's readers find out about a world that's virtually unknown to them, and are shown how men and women adapt to it. Readers are forced to ask how they'd react in that situation, and asked to understand a different morality to their own. Thus le Carré's knowledge is a background for an examination of a particular form of human behaviour, not the point of the book itself. However, much of the interest of the book comes from the level of knowledge demonstrated about a strange world.

You can use your own experiences and knowledge in a similar way. Think about your life, the things that have happened to you, the things you've done, and the things that you know about. Two main areas are sure to come in useful for your writing:

• **Things you know about a subject that most people don't, and that may well surprise them.** In *The Day of the Jackal*, Frederick Forsyth describes in some detail how to obtain a fake passport. Most people don't know how to do this. The detail's unusual, startling, and adds to the authority of the writing. So, if you know about astronauts, deep-sea diving, nuclear physics, or brain surgery, consider using some of that information. Most people don't know much about those things, and are probably interested to find out (or no documentaries would ever get made). Sprinkle the information on; you're writing a novel, not a lesson, but people love to learn as long as it's wrapped up appealingly.

- **Things you know about familiar subjects that most people don't.** Many people think they know a lot about gardening. If you're writing about a garden and you happen to know that slugs and earwigs come out on midsummer's night and let off fireworks, well, readers probably don't know that, and so you've got their attention. Note that it isn't necessarily enough for your information to be true. It must also be interesting and/or odd. Your reader needs to think 'Gosh, I never knew that,' not just 'Oh.'

✔ **Realism:** Having personal experience of what you're writing about can help you paint a realistic picture (it also saves time on research!). For example, having driven the road from Bombay to Calcutta helps you a good deal in describing it in your novel. You can provide the telling detail that good stories need. If you've felt jealousy yourself, you can exaggerate, twist, and spin your real-life experience to imagine a character capable of killing a former lover in a jealous rage – you multiply some emotions, remove your self-control, and produce your own fictional killer. (This is, of course, an over-simplification, but you take the point.)

William Trevor's response to 'write what you know' is, 'For goodness' sake, don't! Use your imagination.' We agree with that.

Write What You Like to Read

Surprisingly, many writers make the mistake of working on stories without thinking about what they themselves like to read. The advice to 'write what you like' is a bit like 'write what you know'. If you spend most of your life reading historical novels, you know how a historical novel works – how it's constructed, how the characters act, and so on – so you have a leg up, so to speak, if you set out to write a historical novel.

Of course, we encourage people to write whatever they want to, but it makes sense to consider the sort of book you already know quite a lot about, and what you and people like you enjoy reading about. Then you need to make sure that you put these things into your own novel.

Joking: It's Only Funny if It's Funny

If what you're writing has comedy potential, and the humour works and doesn't feel forced or out of place, fine. Leave it in. But if you have to shoe-horn humour in and it feels forced and stands out, unbalancing everything around it, maybe it shouldn't be there.

We're certainly not saying don't try to do humour at all. We're saying be careful. Less can be more.

Use All the Senses

If you're like most people, your dominant sense is sight, which means you probably write good visual description. However, writing a book that's overwhelmingly visual is like constructing a house with only one strong wall. Including the full range of senses helps you communicate with all your readers, and takes the pressure off making your visual description do all the work.

Don't go too far the other way! Don't let every piece of description turn into a tick-list of the senses. Just remember to use more than one sense.

If It's Been Done (and It Has), You Have to Do It Better

You've heard the saying that 'there are no new stories'. It's true. There are no completely new stories, just versions of stories that have been written before.

And yet hundreds of thousands of stories are written every year. To take an analogy from cooking: each writer combines different ingredients, varies the quantities, adjusts the temperature, changes the cooking time, and finds a new way to present their story.

You have a long list of variables available for every story. In order to make a new story, you take the same variables that everyone else has used to make stories throughout time, and you combine them in a way that's unique to you.

Yes, it's all been done before. But it hasn't yet been done in the unusual and wholly original way in which you're going to do it. (Chapter 5 offers advice on the basic stories and how to work off them.)

Get Yourself a McGuffin and a Gotcha

Alfred Hitchcock invented the word *McGuffin* to describe the thing in a story that every character wants, or that everyone's trying to get rid of, or around which everyone's dancing in some way. Stephen King uses the term *Gotcha* to describe the thing that grabs readers' attention and makes them want to read a book. The Gotcha, or hook, can be a situation, a character, an unusual phrase, something slightly off-balance or wrong, something quirky, something interesting or unusual, something utterly outrageous, a piece of utterly compelling description, or just a word used in an unusual way. Face it, when it comes to telling stories, Hitchcock and King know what they're doing. So take a tip from these masters and make sure that your story has a McGuffin and a Gotcha. (Hooks are discussed in Chapter 7.)

Find Out What You Want Your Story to Do

Write down three adjectives or short phrases that you want to apply to your book. They may be three descriptions that you hope reviewers will use about your novel, or three words that you'd like to appear on the cover because someone famous used them to describe your book. These three phrases or words may be three ways of describing the same thing, or they may be three quite different things.

Keep those descriptions in mind as you write. Losing sight of what's actually happening in your book can be all too easy. Perhaps at the end of every page, probably at the end of every scene, and definitely at the end of every chapter, ask yourself whether you followed those descriptions. If you haven't, you need to do one of two things: rewrite the chapter, or change some (or even all) of the three descriptions. The novel you set out to write can turn into something else while you're writing it. Keeping your three words or descriptions in mind can help you determine whether that's happening with your book, or whether you just need to focus more closely.

Never Give Up

When your writing's going well, all you need to do is ride the wave. Unless you're near the end of the novel, don't edit – always do new stuff when you're really flying. Editing is for rainy days.

When you're having a middling, normal sort of day, don't get discouraged. Definitely don't let yourself be tempted to turn on the TV and not write for an hour or so. Instead, do a couple of pages, and you'll be pleased that you did it even though you didn't feel like it. It's like going to the gym when you feel lazy: the feeling of virtue's that much greater.

When you're having a bad writing day . . . ah. It's torture, isn't it? You sit there looking at the screen and can't imagine ever hitting a keystroke that doesn't drop off the screen with shame. Your mind's empty and you haven't an idea in your head. But you must still write. You write whatever it takes to cover two pages of the screen. Forget quality control – you've already decided it's going to be rubbish. Just write.

Put your trust in the process. When you haven't one solitary idea, you write anyway. Write anything at all. Rant about your neighbour's noisy dog. Describe a family Christmas day. Complain about your own lack of talent. Make a list of all the bad ideas you've ever had. Just write.

The odds are that you'll be able to use something, somewhere, on those pages. (Avoid starting to write a novel about how difficult writing a novel is. We've read a lot of these, and they're not very good.)

Whatever you do, don't ever stop. The one thing that every writer on your bookshelves has in common is that, no matter how much they felt like not writing, they didn't stop. So, if you want to be published like them, be like them, and don't ever stop.

No one ever wrote a novel by not writing.

Chapter 21

Ten Common Mistakes and How to Avoid Them

In This Chapter

▶ Including care and reason in your writing

▶ Focusing on writing well

▶ Immersing yourself in the writer's world

*T*his chapter contains a quick checklist of the ten most common mistakes (in no particular order) that beginner writers tend to make. Making these mistakes is all too easy, but fortunately they're also fairly simple to combat.

Promoting an Unfair Fight

You want your reader to be cheering for your protagonist and booing your antagonist, but you need to make sure that the fight's fair. (Chapter 8 contains more on fighting fair.)

Falling in love with your hero is all too easy, as is making them a paragon of the virtues – gorgeous, witty, and fun. And that's fine, except for the fact that everyone has flaws. If your hero has no flaws, your reader can't believe in them. By the same token, your antagonist must be worth the trouble. If the villain is pathetic in every way, your reader isn't concerned when the hero comes up against them. Remember, every Superman has his Kryptonite. Give your protagonist and antagonist the weapons to be worthy opponents to each other.

Forgetting to Focus on the Problem

Your *problem* is the root of your conflict. (See Chapter 11 for more on conflict.) The problem is a one-line summary of the reason for your conflict, which is the reason for telling the story – no conflict, no story. So, think hard about that. What's the problem in your story? Make sure that you have one. Write it on a piece of paper and stick it on the wall in front of you. 'John loves Jane, but Jane loves Roger,' or 'Smith will take over the world unless Jones can stop him, but Smith is the richest man in the world and Jones is a five-year-old boy.' If you can't write your problem down like that, think about it until you can.

Giving a Little Too Much

When you tell an anecdote, you don't tell it with every single possible detail. You choose when to start and when to finish, cut out unnecessary detail, and speed things up and slow them down. Writing a novel uses the same techniques. Tell readers what they need to know – no more and no less.

Neglecting the Reader

If you want to write stories for yourself, that's fine. Writing for yourself is quite easy because you can take a lot of things for granted. However, if you want other people to enjoy your novel, you have to put yourself in the reader's place.

Ask yourself whether a reader is likely to enjoy a prolonged recitation of your childhood problems. Consider whether the cute bits that amuse you are going to strike your reader as funny or just incomprehensible. Ask yourself whether you're providing enough information to allow the reader to understand the complicated story you're telling. And, even if you're interested in every minute detail of the workings of the steam train your characters are travelling in, pause to wonder whether your reader's going to feel overwhelmed with too much detail. Always think about your reader.

Using the Passive Voice

The passive voice makes a story slow and dull. Remember the golden rule of writing: 'The cat sat on the mat' not 'The mat was sat on by the cat.'

Tell the story in a way that keeps it active: things should be done, as far as possible, in the authorial present, which is simply writing as if you're telling a story in real time. Most novels are written using this construct. For example: 'Jones went to the sink, picked up one of the recently washed glasses and brought it back to the table.' This isn't exactly the present tense, because that would be 'Jones goes . . .' or 'Jones is going . . .' rather than 'Jones went . . .'. However, it's called the authorial present because the author's there telling it to you.

Holding Only One Note

A story is a symphony of words. Symphonies aren't all played on one note, at one speed, or at the same volume throughout, and your story shouldn't be either. Slow down and speed up; be serious by all means, but don't forget light relief. Think about light and shade, loud and quiet.

If you want people to scream when the ghost appears, you need to have a moment of calm just beforehand. Get readers to drop their guard and *then* shout at them.

Keep in mind that action scenes often have a pause in the middle to allow a short burst of dialogue, a joke, or a search for a weapon. That's deliberate. Frantic, constant action dulls the senses. You need to pause once in a while before returning to the action, in the same way that a spoonful of yoghurt makes the next mouthful of curry taste even spicier.

Re-inventing the Wheel

Sometimes you may feel like you're the only person who understands what writing a novel is like and how hard it is to tell the sort of story you're trying to tell. Well, it's certainly possible that you're writing the sort of book that's totally unlike anything that's ever been written before – possible, but unlikely.

Of course, you should try to be as original as possible, but other writers have already met and wrestled with many of the problems you're running into. So don't try and do it all yourself. Read everything that you can lay your hands on, and while doing so ask yourself, 'Does this have anything to teach me about what I'm trying to do?' Almost all books can help you a little, and some will help you a lot. Read reviews in newspapers to see what's around and what may help you. You aren't alone, and you probably aren't the only person to have had the problem.

Overlooking Mattering

Things have to matter. You don't want your reader to get to the end of your book (or worse, to the end of the first chapter) and ask, 'Why are you telling me this?' To avoid this response, you need to be telling a story that matters to you and matters to your characters as well. If the writer and the characters don't care, why should the reader?

Sort out why your story's worth telling and keep the reason in mind as you write. (Turn to Chapter 6 for advice on making your story matter.)

Running Out of Steam

Lots of stories run into trouble somewhere between a third of the way and halfway though. This problem is natural, so don't worry. Perhaps the story has nowhere to go, and sometimes a writer has to recognise that and put it to one side. (Remember to recycle so that material's never wasted.) However, it's more likely that you've just come to the end of what runners may call their first wind; you need to find your second wind.

The easy way is to do what Raymond Chandler called 'bringing in a guy with a gat (gun)'. In many novels, a message, arrival or departure, revelation, event, or discovery occurs somewhere before the halfway stage. In terms of the three-act structure (discussed in Chapter 7), this occurrence is the event at the end of the first act that allows the curtain to close on a cliffhanger.

Feeling Alone

Writing is, by definition, a solitary pursuit, but it needn't be lonely. We suggest that you read all the time, and books can be good company. Joining a writers' group is always a good idea, although you need to be aware that some people join such groups in order to make themselves feel better by criticising other writers. But so long as your fellow members are honest and helpful, joining is always a good idea. Remember that giving criticism as well as getting it makes you a better writer.

Chapter 22

(Answers to) Ten Questions Put to Agents

*I*n this chapter we share some of the common questions aspiring authors often ask agents.

How Much Do Authors Typically Get Paid?

Ninety-five per cent of Lizzy's clients earn a decent salary from their writing, but the statistics reveal that most people working as writers earn far less than the national average wage. No recent survey data is available to verify exactly what the median wage for a writer is today, but it probably hasn't risen much since 2005, when a survey found it to be just over £12,300 a year. Many writers earn a lot less. The mean, or average, author wage is higher because of the skewing effect of the massive sums earned by a few; the top 10 per cent of writers in the UK earn 50 per cent of writers' total income. You may think that self-published authors would have a more democratic spread of income, but according to the findings of a survey of 1,000 self-published authors conducted by website Taleist in 2012, 75 per cent of the income earned by those surveyed was earned by 10 per cent of the authors, and the median earnings were $500 a year.

Only 5 per cent of those authors surveyed by Taleist, however, consider themselves to be 'unsuccessful'. So although Lizzy has dedicated her career to maximising authors' income, we surmise that for some writers it's fortunately not all about the money . . . and for a few others, the financial rewards are immense.

Is an Agent More Likely to Offer Me Representation If I'm Self-Published?

Agents are always interested in unpublished work and open to loving your book, and the majority of submissions haven't been self-published.

If you decide to self-publish first, and you do so successfully – achieving lots of good reviews, plenty of sales, and recognition of all kinds – then you're very likely to attract the interest of agents. The more reviews and sales you achieve, the more interest you'll get. No hard-and-fast guidelines exist, of course, but if you appear in an ebook bestseller list, somewhere near-ish to the top, and have a three-figure number of four- or five-star reader reviews, then you've proved that there's strong interest in your work. The reality is, however, that most authors who self-publish don't achieve this level of success, so there's no huge advantage to self-publishing before you seek an agent.

If you're a very successful self-published author, make sure you choose an agent who really loves your work and is keen to collaborate with you on your future books. Some less scrupulous agents who offer you representation will be more drawn to the idea of quickly making a big publishing deal for you than in investing lots of time in your career over the long term.

How Can an Agent Reject My Book if They've Only Read an Outline/One Chapter?

Most people can tell from an outline whether a book is likely to hold their interest; that's the basis on which people make buying decisions in bookshops. Agents are choosier readers than most casual browsers, so this is even truer of them. They're usually happy to give authors the benefit of the doubt, though, and go on to read some pages of text. But if an agent reads a chapter and knows they don't want to read more . . . well, most agents decide to work with an author because of their voice and style, rather than because the author has come up with the most unique and brilliant plot. Plots can easily be sucked empty of any flash of inspiration by uninteresting writing. So unless an agent finds your writing really attractive and successful in the first couple of chapters of your book, there really is no need for them to read on, because they're unlikely to ever love your writing style quite enough. Hopefully, the next agent who reads your work will be 'the one'.

Should I Hire a Literary Consultant or an Editor?

If you think your work needs editing, or if you'd like to read a report on your manuscript by a third party, you can consult a friend, fellow author, cousin, or even a literary consultant. Some literary consultants are really experienced editors with a lot of useful advice for authors. Others aren't. Seek out author testimonials to establish which editors are the most useful, and only work with those whose advice chimes with your own instincts and seems really constructive and specific. You really need their criticism, not their praise, so don't be seduced too much by uncritical feedback.

Should I Study on a Creative Writing Course?

Sure, if you have the time and money. You're probably never going to regret focusing exclusively on your writing for an hour a week/a week of your summer/a year of your life (delete as applicable). What a treat! Coming together with good tutors and a room full of other writers can be fun, revelatory, and ground-breaking for an unpublished or unconfident writer.

Different courses seem to develop different 'house' characteristics and styles, depending on the taste and personality of the course leaders. Sometimes these are only discernible to agents, who read quite a bit of the material students on various courses produce. Be wary of being too heavily influenced (for example, reducing your massive cast lists to small ones, or your leggy saga of a novel to a novella, just because that's what everyone else is up to).

Most of all, be influenced, inspired, and taught, by all means. It won't make you a writer if you aren't one, and it won't guarantee you a book deal, but writing courses are usually very interesting and could make all the difference to your social life as well as your professional one.

What are an Agent's Top Writing Tips?

Every reader, not to mention every agent, has their little bugbears and obsessions – the characteristics they love or loathe to spot in a writer. Lizzy's rather keen on point of view. So her top tip is to be very careful to know in every line from whose point of view you're writing and to remain faithful and consistent to that viewpoint throughout (and to distinguish carefully one point of view from another if your novel is written in the third person across several characters). Good point of view is the trademark of excellent characterisation. Never let your own point of view as author intrude upon a novel.

Lizzy's other tip is to be unselfconscious in your emotional response to your material. In order to move the reader, you have to feel it first. It might hurt, a bit. If it doesn't hurt occasionally, you probably aren't doing it right.

No writer writes in just the same way as another. Some like to start blindly with just a voice or a scenario in mind; others plan meticulously. Some writers write in formal blocks of time, others scribble on notepads strewn around the house day and night. So one big tip is never to listen too hard to any one writer's or agent's advice. Find your own way.

I'm Not on Twitter: Does it Matter?

If you've written a wonderful novel which has a fantastically strong appeal then no publisher is going to turn you away because you aren't on Twitter or some other popular media platform. They might feel discomfited if you said you *never* wanted to be on Twitter, though, because publishers know how much readers love to connect with their favourite authors across social media. Publishers are very happy to support authors who aren't used to writing in the public spheres of traditional and digital media. They offer training days and advice sheets, and try to make it as painless as possible. Nevertheless, it's difficult to be an introverted author in the 21st century.

All that said, although being absent from social media won't stop you from finding a publisher, developing a more public profile in the run-up to submissions to agents and publishers certainly shortens your odds. Reach out to other fans of the genre in which you're writing, and to other authors (both published and unpublished). You'll make friends and win support for your own efforts – a lot of other aspiring authors are out there to cheer you on.

Should I Take a No-Advance Publishing Deal Offered by a Small Publisher?

How exciting! But if you haven't yet tried to find an agent, do that first. If your book has market potential, you ideally want it to be considered by the most influential houses before you commit to a tiny press without any funds for advances. You deserve to be paid for your work and to be marketed too. If you've been through that submissions process already or have another reason to really want to accept the deal (perhaps the offer is from a specialist list such as a digital romance list, and you wrote your book with just such a publisher in mind) then just make sure you scrutinise the terms on offer. No deal is worth taking if you have to sacrifice too many rights in the process. The Society of Authors can help you with any contractual queries and may know if you're ever likely to see any royalties. Make sure that the publisher has a good track record financially – scout around online for any of their other authors, and quiz them politely.

When you're not receiving an advance and the proposed publication is digital only, it's more important than ever to clarify what the publisher will bring to the table in terms of marketing and editorial support. Without a strong collaborative relationship, you could try self-publishing after all.

How Do I Know You Won't Steal My Idea?

Well, you don't. (We won't: no good agent has time to read and rip off ideas systematically. Oh, and it's unethical.) Ideas aren't subject to copyright, so it's a tricky area. If you're really afraid that your words may be plagiarised, send a copy of your manuscript to yourself in the post, and keep the unopened postmarked envelope on file – this way you can always prove the date when you created the story.

Consider sending your submissions to agents by registered post. If you later spot another novel very like your own, don't forget that very few ideas are new ones, and often books are like buses: several of the same sort come along at once. Many of Lizzy's authors have worried at one time or another about their book being similar to someone else's (not because their idea has been stolen, just because of the bus thing), but they're usually imagining it. There's only one you and only one version of your story.

Can You Recommend Any Other Agents?

Sometimes agents recommend competitors they like. Sometimes they don't want to help any agent outside their own agency! Any recommended agents are worth checking out, although they're more likely to be friends of the agent rather than the absolute best agents in town.

Ask after any agents who are hungry for new clients or building a list (that is, with capacity for new clients). If an agent declines to share any names, don't be disheartened. It may be a strong sign that they know that your book is great and they don't want any competitor to benefit, even if they've turned down the opportunity to do so themselves . . . after all, no one said agents were generous.

Chapter 23

Ten Tips from Published Authors

*W*e asked some published authors what they found most surprising about the publishing process. We include their advice here. All the authors were very keen to offer advice to first-time writers and wanted to emphasise that as long as you manage your expectations, being published is potentially hugely thrilling. Here are the authors' top tips.

Get an Agent

One author summed it up as follows:

> Writers are by nature usually quite sensitive souls, which is why we need agents to be tough for us and with us sometimes. If it hadn't been for strong and practical agenting, I would have given up after my last novel and done something else; feedback from my editor was poor, and sales of the novel I had written before were so uninspiring. The great thing about having an agent is the feeling that there's someone on your side, no matter what. There's also someone who has the guts to go and tell the publisher that you hate the jacket when you're too afraid to say anything in case it makes everyone loathe you. And there's someone who will tell it like it is, even when it's not necessarily nice to hear, and who will hopefully always return your call and read your script quickly. Editors can go AWOL for weeks on end when they're busy and stressed. If you're lucky enough to have an agent whose editorial judgement you trust, you're doubly blessed.

Listen to Your Editor

Listen to what your editor tells you about the text and be prepared to change it, although you must stand your ground over something you truly believe in. Trust your publisher's judgement as to the best time of year to publish your book, the best price and format to choose, and so on. Publishers are the experts.

Keep Your Feet on the Ground

Thousands of books are published every year, and not all of those authors are rich and famous. It doesn't mean you can't dream, but keep your feet on the ground as well. Remember that some careers grow more slowly than others; be prepared to be hard-headed and realistic.

Know that the Deal isn't Everything

With the benefit of hindsight, one author had quite a jaded view of the initial heady excitement of finding a publisher:

> Selling a book to a publisher is exactly like a relationship; it starts off in a flurry of attention-seeking present-giving, before slowly tailing off in a trickle of disappointment and petty squabbles about money, before one of you is lured away by a better, more enthusiastic partner.

Another author found her first book deal hugely exciting, but her second deal less so:

> For my second deal I had to wait several months for them to come back to me with a decision about whether to re-sign me. After the wooing, trumpeting, and fanfare of the first deal, I felt invisible and spent months not knowing what was going on. They did offer me a deal in the end, but it was a disheartening and difficult experience and I was so grateful to have an agent for professional and emotional support.

Ask Questions but be Flexible

Try to keep on top of what's happening at every stage of the process and don't be afraid to ask questions. Tread the fine line between being a truly irritating, pushy author and fighting your corner and reminding them that you're there. Always be charming and amenable, but don't be a wallflower. They don't want that anyway (even if they think they do).

You may well hear nothing from your publisher for weeks and then get a sudden demand for something to be done immediately. That's just the way they work. Be as professional as you can.

Publicise Your Book

Make yourself available for absolutely anything that can help sell your novel: offer to write for the publisher's website and so on.

Don't be a pest in your local bookshops or complain rudely when you can't find your book in WH Smith, but do work together with your publisher to ensure that you're both maximising all the opportunities available to you – and that may include 'local author' promotions in those local stores.

Be Prepared for Anticlimax

Once your book is in the shops, you can feel a sense of anticlimax if it isn't selling like hot cakes.

One author confessed:

> Sometimes you can watch the book you spent a year slaving over sink without trace because it was published in the 'wrong month'. The publishers then move on to the other 45 books they're publishing that week, but you're left nursing your wounds for a year until the next one comes out.

The reality is that after an intense period of writing and preparing, your publication often isn't the dramatic or ecstatic moment you thought it would be, even if everything goes perfectly well. When your book is published, you send it out into the world to sink or swim on its own merits, and you can experience a sense of loss mixed in with relief.

Pick Yourself Up and Start Again

If your book doesn't sell well, try not to take it personally. Instead, pick yourself up and start another book.

If your book does sell well, don't let it go to your head, because this only makes writing the next one more difficult as you try to recapture what worked so well in the first one.

Enjoy It!

Seeing someone buying and reading your book is a marvellous feeling, and you've every right to be proud of yourself. All the authors we spoke to had one thing in common: they all still love to write. In the final analysis, the process was worthwhile because none of them envisaged doing anything else for a living.

Remind Yourself that You're a Real, Live Author

If all else fails, remind yourself that lots of people want to write a novel, but few do, and even fewer are published. As Peter Cook used to say when people told him they were writing a novel: 'Neither am I.' But *you* actually did it. This novel may or may not be published one day, but either way, the next novel you write is going to be even better.

Index

• D •

• Q •

• W •

Notes

Notes

About the Authors

George Green works for the Department of English and Creative Writing at Lancaster University. He is the author of *Hound* and *Hawk,* both published by Transworld.

Lizzy Kremer is a literary agent and director of David Higham Associates in London, representing authors of both fiction and non-fiction. Before becoming an agent, Lizzy was a book publicist at a publishing house.

Dedication

To Linda Anderson, teacher and friend.

—George

To Ed, for trying to teach me everything he knows.

—Lizzy

Authors' Acknowledgements

With thanks to Mike and Rachael at Wiley and Georgia and Laura at DHA for their expertise and support. To Michael and Adrienne with love for suppers eaten at the keyboard and all the things that matter. Lizzy would like to thank her clients for their inspiring input (that includes you, George!) and Anthony for his wise words. George would like to thank Lizzy for a calm head, and the Department for its understanding.

Publisher's Acknowledgements

We're proud of this book; please send us your comments at http:// dummies. custhelp.com. For other comments, please contact our Customer Care Department within the U.S. at 877-762-2974, outside the U.S. at (001) 317-572-3993, or fax 317-572-4002. Some of the people who helped bring this book to market include the following:

Acquisitions, Editorial and Vertical Websites

Project Editor: Rachael Chilvers

Commissioning Editor: Mike Baker
    (*First Edition: Alison Yates*)

Development Editor: Brian Kramer
    (*First Edition: Kathleen Dobie*)

Proofreader: Mary White

Assistant Editor: Ben Kemble

Publisher: Miles Kendall

Cover Photos: © iStockphoto.com/lutavia

Project Coordinator: Sheree Montgomery

Take Dummies with you everywhere you go!

Whether you're excited about e-books, want more from the web, must have your mobile apps, or swept up in social media, Dummies makes everything easier .

FOR DUMMIES®

A Wiley Brand

BUSINESS

978-1-118-73077-5

978-1-118-44349-1

978-1-119-97527-4

MUSIC

978-1-119-94276-4

978-0-470-97799-6

978-0-470-49644-2

DIGITAL PHOTOGRAPHY

978-1-118-09203-3

978-0-470-76878-5

978-1-118-00472-2

Algebra I For Dummies
978-0-470-55964-2

Anatomy & Physiology For Dummies, 2nd Edition
978-0-470-92326-9

Asperger's Syndrome For Dummies
978-0-470-66087-4

Basic Maths For Dummies
978-1-119-97452-9

Body Language For Dummies, 2nd Edition
978-1-119-95351-7

Bookkeeping For Dummies, 3rd Edition
978-1-118-34689-1

British Sign Language For Dummies
978-0-470-69477-0

Cricket for Dummies, 2nd Edition
978-1-118-48032-8

Currency Trading For Dummies, 2nd Edition
978-1-118-01851-4

Cycling For Dummies
978-1-118-36435-2

Diabetes For Dummies, 3rd Edition
978-0-470-97711-8

eBay For Dummies, 3rd Edition
978-1-119-94122-4

Electronics For Dummies All-in-One For Dummies
978-1-118-58973-1

English Grammar For Dummies
978-0-470-05752-0

French For Dummies, 2nd Edition
978-1-118-00464-7

Guitar For Dummies, 3rd Edition
978-1-118-11554-1

IBS For Dummies
978-0-470-51737-6

Keeping Chickens For Dummies
978-1-119-99417-6

Knitting For Dummies, 3rd Edition
978-1-118-66151-2

FOR DUMMIES

A Wiley Brand

SELF-HELP

978-0-470-66541-1

978-1-119-99264-6

978-0-470-66086-7

LANGUAGES

978-0-470-68815-1

978-1-119-97959-3

978-0-470-69477-0

HISTORY

978-0-470-68792-5

978-0-470-74783-4

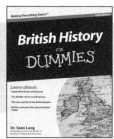

978-0-470-97819-1

Laptops For Dummies 5th Edition
978-1-118-11533-6

Management For Dummies, 2nd Edition
978-0-470-97769-9

Nutrition For Dummies, 2nd Edition
978-0-470-97276-2

Office 2013 For Dummies
978-1-118-49715-9

Organic Gardening For Dummies
978-1-119-97706-3

Origami Kit For Dummies
978-0-470-75857-1

Overcoming Depression For Dummies
978-0-470-69430-5

Physics I For Dummies
978-0-470-90324-7

Project Management For Dummies
978-0-470-71119-4

Psychology Statistics For Dummies
978-1-119-95287-9

Renting Out Your Property For Dummies, 3rd Edition
978-1-119-97640-0

Rugby Union For Dummies, 3rd Edition
978-1-119-99092-5

Stargazing For Dummies
978-1-118-41156-8

Teaching English as a Foreign Language For Dummies
978-0-470-74576-2

Time Management For Dummies
978-0-470-77765-7

Training Your Brain For Dummies
978-0-470-97449-0

Voice and Speaking Skills For Dummies
978-1-119-94512-3

Wedding Planning For Dummies
978-1-118-69951-5

WordPress For Dummies, 5th Edition
978-1-118-38318-6

Think you can't learn it in a day? Think again!

The In a Day e-book series from For Dummies gives you quick and easy access to learn a new skill, brush up on a hobby, or enhance your personal or professional life — all in a day. Easy!

Available as PDF, eMobi and Kindle